The Errors of Atheism

The Errors of Atheism

J. Angelo Corlett

continuum

2010

The Continuum International Publishing Group
80 Maiden Lane, New York, NY 10038
The Tower Building, 11 York Road, London SE1 7NX

www.continuumbooks.com

Library of Congress Cataloging-in-Publication Data
A catalog record for this book is available from the Library of Congress.

ISBN: 978-1-4411-5187-2 (hardback)
         978-1-4411-5893-2 (paperback)

Typeset by Newgen Imaging Systems Pvt Ltd, Chennai, India
Printed in the United States of America

To my mother, Diana Bellotto,
and my brothers, Frank S. and Waldo W.

Contents

PREFACE

It takes a brave voice indeed, it is said, to question the assumptions on which a common public discourse and its conception of a common reason and experience are said to depend.

—*D. Z. Phillips*[1]

Come now, let us reason together.

—*Isaiah* 1:18

The Errors of Atheism has grown out of three decades of study of numerous works in philosophy of religion and Christian theology as an orthodox Christian theist, then as a student of neo-orthodox, liberal, revisionist, and radical (including secular, process and liberation) Christian theologies,[2] then as an atheist, and currently as an agnostic. Having converted to Christian theism three decades ago while an undergraduate student, and having assiduously studied philosophy, philosophy of religion, Christian (and some non-Christian) theologies both as an undergraduate and throughout my seminary years, I found what I then thought were good reasons to believe in the unorthodox and radical Christian conceptions of God, reasons supplied by theologians such as Thomas Aquinas,[3] Anselm,[4] Walter Rauschenbusch,[5] Paul Tillich,[6] Rudolf Bultmann,[7] process thinkers

---

[1] D. Z. Phillips, "Religion, Philosophy, and the Academy," *International Journal for Philosophy of Religion*, 44 (1998), p. 130.

[2] For a helpful taxonomy and discussion of these "models" of Christian theology, see David Tracy, *Blessed Rage for Order* (New York: The Seabury Press, 1975), especially Chapters 1–2.

[3] Umberto Eco refers to him as "*doctor angelicus*" [Umberto Eco and Carlo Maria Martini, *Belief or Nonbelief?* Minna Proctor (trans.) (New York: Arcade Publishing, 1997), p. 61.]

[4] S. N. Deane, Translator, *St. Anselm: Basic Writings* (LaSalle: Open Court, 1962).

[5] Walter Rauschenbusch, *A Theory for the Social Gospel* (New York: Abingdon Press, 1917).

[6] Paul Tillich, *Systematic Theology*, Volumes 1–3 (Chicago: The University of Chicago Press, 1951).

[7] Rudolf Bultmann, *Jesus Christ and Mythology* (New York: Scribner's, 1958). It is said by David Ray Griffin that Bultmann was "the greatest New Testament scholar of the post-World War II generation" [David Ray Griffin, John Cobb, Jr., Richard Falk, and Catherine Keller, *The American Empire and the Commonwealth of God* (Louisville: John Knox Press, 2006), p. 146].

such as Alfred North Whitehead, Charles Hartshorne, John Cobb, Jr., and David Ray Griffin, and first wave Christian liberation theologies of James H. Cone and Gustavo Gutiérrez. But nearing the end of my seminary studies, I was assigned to study J. L. Mackie's "Evil and Omnipotence."[8] After several dedicated years of study and practice of Christian doctrine and polity, I lost my faith as powerfully as I gained it years earlier and converted from Christianity to atheism as I realized how Alvin Plantinga's "free will defense"[9] of orthodox Christian theism simply made insufficient sense of the problem of evil [not to mention his own Reformed (Calvinistic) theology], how inadequate Richard Swinburne's equally gallant traditional Christian theodicy seemed, and how unsatisfying Hans Küng's exploration was regarding the problem of God.[10] The Humean rendition of the problem of evil as Mackie had argued it reduced the orthodox Christian idea of God to conceptual rubble. To use Tillich's phrase, there was a profound "shaking of the foundations"[11] of my faith in God. After all, if divine omnipotence, omnibenevolence, and omniscience were in need of serious rethinking because of the problem of evil, then this poses difficulties for the traditional "proofs" of God's existence that are contingent on the plausibility of these and certain other divine attributes. What I thought God was, was unfounded. And it was unclear to me then that radical or secularist theologies were able to fill the void where my religious faith once stood.

Throughout this book, I refer often to orthodox Christian theism. By this I mean that conglomeration of beliefs not only in certain divine

---

[8] J. L. Mackie, *The Miracle of Theism* (Oxford: Oxford University Press, 1982), Chapter 9. Other works that influenced my change in thought at that time were Antony Flew, *God and Philosophy* (New York: Harcourt, Brace, and World, 1966); *The Presumption of Atheism* (London: Elek for Pemberton, 1976); and Kai Nielsen, *Philosophy & Atheism* (New York: Prometheus Books, 1985).

[9] Alvin Plantinga, *God and Other Minds* (Ithaca: Cornell University Press, 1967). Nor did my study of Anthony Kenny, *The Five Ways* (Notre Dame: University of Notre Dame Press, 1969); *The God of the Philosophers* (Oxford: Oxford University Press, 1979); Richard Swinburne, *The Coherence of Theism* (Oxford: Clarendon Press, 1977); *The Concept of Miracle* (London: London University Press, 1981); *The Existence of God* (Oxford: Clarendon Press, 1979); *Faith and Reason* (Oxford: Oxford University Press, 1981) convince me that the arguments for God's existence were plausible.

[10] Hans Küng, *Does God Exist?* E. Quinn (trans.) (New York: Doubleday & Company, Inc., 1980); *Why I am Still a Christian* (New York: Houghton Mifflin, 2006).

[11] Paul Tillich, *The Shaking of the Foundations* (New York: Charles Scribner's, Sons 1948).

attributes (that God is omnipotent, omnipresent, omniscient, omnibenevolent, etc., in the strict senses of these terms), but also that what Christians call "scriptures" are divinely inspired and authoritative. If one is a fundamentalist Christian, one also believes, among other things, that such writings are inerrant. Moreover, traditional Christians also believe in the particularly Christian doctrines of the virgin birth of Jesus of Nazareth, his divinity, his resurrection, as well as a host of other doctrines such as life after death. While I shall not discuss these ideas, I mention them because the divine attributes are relevant to the discussion of God's possible existence in ways that I make clear in the following chapters.

Socratically following the arguments wherever they led me, I became an atheist, though I hardly stopped thinking about questions of normative ethics and other matters of "ultimate concern," as Tillich and John A. T. Robinson[12] would put it. After I completed my seminary studies, I became a philosopher-ethicist, confident that I could make significant sense of the world without God. To be sure, I have, with the assistance of many philosophers such as Socrates, Immanuel Kant, Karl Marx, David Hume, John Rawls, G. A. Cohen, my mentor at the University of Arizona Joel Feinberg,[13] among some other philosophers, made a good deal of sense of the world absent the orthodox and neo-orthodox Christian ideas of God. While I am a committed moral and metaphysical realist, I am also a fallibilist, epistemically speaking. I do not argue for, but from, these positions largely, but not solely, because of what many philosophers have argued is the logical self-contradictory nature of standard antirealist views. The finer details of meta-ethics and metaphysics I shall leave to those whose concerns along those lines run deeper than even mine.[14] Given my more modest aims herein, they are beyond the purview of this project.

---

[12] John A. T. Robinson, *Honest to God* (Philadelphia: Westminster Press, 1963); *Exploration into God* (Stanford: Stanford University Press, 1967); *In the End God* (New York: Harper & Row Publishers, 1968); *The Human Face of God* (Philadelphia: The Westminster Press, 1973). Also see Harvey Cox, *The Secular City* (New York: The Macmillan Company, 1965). For a discussion of Robinson's Tillichian notion of God not as an actual personal being, but as the ground of being and yet at times describable in terms of divine personhood, see Ian Ramsey, *Christian Discourse: Some Logical Explorations* (Oxford: Oxford University Press, 1965), Chapter III.

[13] For a discussion of parts of Feinberg's corpus of philosophy, see *The Journal of Ethics*, 10:1–2 (2006), pp. 1–204.

[14] For some central contemporary studies in meta-ethics, see Simon Blackburn, *Ruling Passions* (Oxford: Oxford University Press, 1998); Michael Smith, *The Moral Problem* (Oxford: Oxford University Press, 1995).

The Errors of Atheism seeks to do what has not yet been done in the field of analytical philosophy of religion, where the field is for the most part divided in the West between mostly orthodox Christian theists, on the one hand, and a few atheists on the other. But the debate between these parties has rarely been interrupted by agnostics,[15] who are more often than not dismissed by the habitué of often presumptuous argumentation of atheists and theists alike. Meanwhile, several leading defenders of orthodox Christian theism, whether theologians or philosophers,[16] seem to rest content that their primary or only antagonists are atheists, and most atheists seem to be rather confident that their defeat of orthodox Christian theism justifies their often peculiar versions of atheism. According to these parties to the discussion, there appears to be no significant and meaningful room in the debate for a third way of seeing things. As they see it, agnosticism is only a theoretical option. No one really has the nerve to defend it in the midst of such hotly contested matters between what theists and atheists seem to understand, for practical purposes, to be their own private debate, which, by the contents of their own writings, seems to have little or no bearing on theology.[17] Indeed, just as some of the black Christian liberation theists would charge that when it comes to orthodox or neo-orthodox Christian theisms and discussions of the finer points of these theologies, it is implied that "no dogs, Jews, niggers or Mexicans allowed," when it concerns theists and atheists on the matter of God's existence it appears that "agnostics" ought to be added to the list of the unwelcome. For the unstated attitude appears to be one of disallowing agnostics into the domain of discourse, at least as serious interlocutors. As we shall see, this attitude implies the disallowing of Bertrand Russell into the discussion, an obvious embarrassment for those atheists who inattentively claim him as one of their own.[18]

---

[15] One notable exception is found in Anthony Kenny, *What I Believe* (London: Continuum, 2006).

[16] For a parochial discussion of the issues dividing Christian theologians and Christian philosophers, see James A. Keller, "On the Issues Dividing Contemporary Christian Philosophers and Theologians," *Faith and Philosophy*, 10 (1993), pp. 68–78; "Should Christian Theologians Become Christian Philosophers?" *Faith and Philosophy*, 12 (1995), pp. 260–268. It is a rather presumptuous and parochial discussion in that it is assumed all along that "Christian" is a category definable by orthodox or neo-orthodox proponents. This kind of discussion can take place only within orthodox limitations of "faith" in "God."

[17] A notable exception to this claim, of course, stands J. L. Mackie's Humean statement of the problem of evil for orthodox Christian theology.

[18] The common mistake of misconstruing Bertrand Russell as an atheist is found in Kai Nielsen, *Naturalism and Religion* (Buffalo: Prometheus Books, 2001), p. 31.

The difficulty is that, however effective this misplaced debate has served the interests of traditional Christian theism, on the one hand, and atheism, on the other, it is hardly acceptable as a form of legitimate philosophical dialogue between those genuinely devoted to the pursuit of truth about God's possible nature and function in the world. As D. Z. Phillips writes, "Unless we uncover the routes to conceptual confusion, there is no road back to clarity."[19] Thus we must expose the conceptual confusion and seek clarity with all our philosophical might, and this, with the Wittgensteinian recognition of a degree of indeterminacy.[20]

Indeed, something needs to change concerning the age-old debate about God's existence, something that disallows traditional Christian theists to so often hide behind fideistic pleas of "faith" or revelation in the midst of running for cover from the barrage of poignant atheistic objections to traditional Christian theistic "proofs" for God's existence, and something that, on the other hand, fails to permit atheists to get away with declaring victory over theism (which is what "atheism" implies) at too soon a juncture in the discussion. Indeed, an atheist's declaring victory over theism by boldly announcing her atheistic proclivities is a bit like U.S. president G. W. Bush standing on the deck of a U.S. aircraft carrier, in full pilot's garb, declaring victory over terrorism and in Iraq!

What is needed now more than ever before is for those who seek to take philosophy of religion sufficiently seriously to consider in some depth a theism that might well defeat atheism once and for all, one that entails a theology that is sensitive to and duly respectful of the best findings and methodologies of the sciences, and one that also seeks to address matters of justice and oppression. Thus what is needed is a development of a renewed theism that is simultaneously scientific (though not scientistic) and political in the justice-centered sense, one that refuses to deny the sciences their proper place in the demythologization of orthodox theologies, and one that also seeks justice for severe harmful wrongdoing. And while there exist theologies of science that are sensitive to ways in which theology can accommodate science in terms of creation and evolutionary matters,[21] and

---

19 Phillips, "Religion, Philosophy, and the Academy," p. 131.
20 Phillips, "Religion, Philosophy, and the Academy," p. 133.
21 Philip Clayton, *Mind and Emergence* (Oxford: Oxford University Press, 2004); Christopher Knight, *The God of Nature* (Minneapolis: Fortress Press, 2007); *Wrestling With the Divine* (Minneapolis: Fortress Press, 2001); Arthur Peacocke, *All That Is* (Minneapolis: Fortress Press, 2007); *God and the New Biology* (London: Dent & Sons, 1986); *Theology for a Scientific Age* (London: SCM, 1993). Among others, these theologians of science understand that "nothing in

whereas there exist liberation theologies that seek to articulate theistic notions of justice for the oppressed, neither of these approaches seems to devote adequate attention to both of these elements. In light of this fact, I shall develop a theism that explicitly blends each of these theistic models in search of a most plausible theism that sheds the albatross of doctrines (including vitalism) that haunt orthodox Christian theology in the hope of posing a much stronger, indeed naturalistic, challenge to atheism by recognizing the importance of a theism that takes science and justice seriously. Thus naturalistic theism need not lead to reductionistic atheism. While this latter claim is not a new one in the context of the history of Western Christian theology, it seems to go largely unrecognized in analytical philosophy of religion, where for the most part conservative or orthodox Christian doctrines are defended as if science and religion cannot be reconciled in terms of cosmogony and cosmology.

Furthermore, "atheism" is a misnomer given the current status of the debate about God. How can someone who is serious about truth declare herself an atheist without first addressing deeply various of the most plausible forms of theism, and then demonstrating how and why *they* fail? No self-proclaiming philosopher-atheist has done so, at least, not by my search of the philosophical literature during recent decades. The only atheist philosopher of whom I am aware who has even somewhat attempted this task is Mackie, who in his critique of orthodox Christian theism, devotes some energy to the examination of a particular brand of highly unorthodox theism set forth by John Leslie, one of Mackie's own contemporaries. But no effort is made by any philosopher-atheist to take seriously the varieties of more robust and plausible unorthodox theisms that can and do evade the atheistic objections to orthodox theism. Instead, what we find are various and sundry dismissive comments to the effect that supernaturalistic forms of theism are problematic and anthropomorphic renditions of theism are either implausible on their face, or simply not worthy of the name "theism" at all.

So for the most part what we have in the debate about God's possible existence in analytical philosophy of religion is two opposing sides each of

---

the scientists' description requires a denial that we live in a universe designed a sustained in being by God" (Knight, *The God of Nature*, p. 2), contrary to atheistic science. For an attempt to unite religion and science by way of a certain kind of "radical theology," see Richard Grigg, *Beyond the God Delusion* (Minneapolis: Fortress Press, 2008). However, Grigg's work does nothing to address concerns of liberation theism and matters of justice. Nor does his version of pantheism take seriously what panentheism brings to the problem of God.

which declares victory over the other, yet neither of which seems to grant the subject sufficient respect to take seriously the possibility that there are unorthodox theisms quite worthy of the name "theism" that fail to fall prey to the numerous objections facing orthodox Christian theism. There is a real sense in which atheists and orthodox Christian theists alike are akin to Black Mary in August Wilson's play, *Gem of the Ocean*, about whom Ceasar says: "You thinking wrong and don't even know it."[22] Something must change in this discussion if meaningful philosophical progress is to be made. Otherwise, the importance of what is at stake is lost in the valley of some despairingly bad arguments on both sides of the discursive table.

The Errors of Atheism seeks to change this unfortunate situation. It thrusts into the forefront of analytical philosophy of religion and orthodox Christian theology a piece of unfashionably theological philosophy of religion (or philosophical theology, if one prefers), one that will challenge orthodox Christian thinkers to take more seriously certain aspects of their own theological roots, and likewise one that will challenge atheists to take seriously the very same theological nuances that can bring new life to a discussion that has seemed to stall in a dialectical stalemate[23]—regardless of each side's proclamation of victory (or at least philosophical superiority) over the other. Often times in philosophy when a position for which one argues reaches a dead end vis-à-vis its dialogue with competing theories, the honest thinker can see and appreciate this, and must adapt to the conclusions of such arguments. Clinging desperately to a claim or set of claims no matter what objections it faces is a sign of a weak mind that fails to grasp the end of the run for a particular standpoint. And if one cares enough about the Christian church, one must also demonstrate that concern in terms of relinquishing the set of dogmas that have held back Christians (and in many cases, the world) for centuries, what Dorothee Soelle refers to as "the distortion of Christian faith by Christian history."[24] This is one part of what I refer to as the "double-duping" of others by orthodox Christian theism.

One of the main arguments for the implausibility of orthodox Christian theism is that it is excessively loaded with unnecessary and highly problematic doctrines, ones that can only be accepted on the basis of one's faith

---

[22] August Wilson, *Gem of the Ocean* (New York: Theatre Communications Group, 2006), p. 39.

[23] I borrow this phrase from John Martin Fischer, "Epicureanism about Death and Immortality," *The Journal of Ethics*, 10 (2006), pp. 355–381.

[24] Dorothee Soelle, *Political Theology*, John Shelley (trans.) (Philadelphia: Fortress Press, 1974), p. 16.

in the divine authority of the Christian scriptures:[25] the virgin birth of Jesus, the resurrection of Jesus, the trinity (implying the divinity of Jesus), the omniscience and omnipotence of God, the *parousia*, the rapture of believers, as well as some other controversial soteriological, ecclesiastical, and Christological beliefs. While the degree to which these and related doctrines are held tends to separate mainstream (orthodox) Christianity from fundamentalism, I take these and other related doctrines to constitute part of the core of Christian orthodoxy. But insofar as such doctrines originate, or are said to originate, from Christian scriptures, this itself confronts a problem of its own, one which John Locke refers to as the "wax nose problem"[26] wherein texts can be pushed and turned like soft wax to appear as they may. Thus the more the orthodox Christian theist seeks to ground her views of God in scriptures, the greater her philosophical challenges become.

As Soelle exclaims, ". . . whoever wants to proclaim the *solus Christus* cannot overlook the *Christus in ecclesia corruptus*" and the "'text-fetishism' of the exegetes"![27] What is needed is a fresh consideration of theism absent the trappings of religios;[28] what is needed now is a minimalist scientific and political conception of theism that is intellectually respectable—one that does not embarrass God Herself should She exist! This is precisely what *The Errors of Atheism* brings to the discussion. It seeks to re-introduce the problem of God absent the idolatry of ideologies that has plagued orthodox Christian theism from its inception. More specifically, scientific process theism and political liberation theism are brought to bear on the

---

[25] By "divine authority," I mean that such Christian theists hold fast to the idea that the informational content of the most plausible translations of the Dead Sea Scrolls [For an early study of these documents, see Millar Burrows, *The Dead Sea Scrolls* (New York: Viking, 1955)] and other documents from which the extant and officially accepted canonical texts are derived or on which they are based are inspired by God and that they contain directives of God for humans to follow. But even if it is true that the documents in question are historically accurate as some suggest [F. F. Bruce, *The New Testament Documents: Are They Reliable?* (Downers Grove: InterVarsity Press, 1975)], it hardly follows that they are inspired by God in the requisite or special sense. No amount of textual criticism can prove such a seemingly unfalsifiable claim. Nor can it prove that the claims found therein are true to fact.

[26] Michael P. Levine, "Contemporary Christian Analytic Philosophy of Religion: Biblical Fundamentalism, Terrible Solutions to a Horrible Problem, and Hearing God," *International Journal for Philosophy of Religion*, 48 (2000), p. 90.

[27] Soelle, *Political Theology*, pp. 16–17.

[28] I mostly have in mind here fundamentalist and evangelical Christians.

central problem of philosophy of religion in order to present a hybrid but minimalist conception of God that is significantly more plausible than any existing version of the theology of Christian orthodoxy. Only then will we hope to have a sufficiently clear understanding of theism in its more plausible form such that we can much better discern the respective plausibilities of theism, atheism, and agnosticism.

In concurring with atheism concerning some of the problematics of the orthodox Christian notion of the nature of God, *The Errors of Atheism* poses a novel challenge to atheism.[29] Unlike many orthodox and neo-orthodox Christian theists who spend much of their energies defending their views about God against the onslaught of explicit or implicit atheistic critiques of the traditional theistic "proofs," *The Errors of Atheism* goes on the offensive against atheism and exposes its ramified fallacious reasoning. But this is no help for the orthodox Christian theist, as the atheist's errors do not pertain to the challenges to the traditional Christian theistic proofs by Kant, Hume, Mackie, and various others.[30] Rather, the conceptual resources of radical "secularist" theologies, along with process and liberation theologies, are mined and synthesized in order to provide a new challenge to atheism and theism alike from the perspective of a less biased inquirer. In so doing, it is recognized that liberationists have had some serious reservations with the other radical, especially liberal, theologies, even if they were somewhat influenced by them. But this does nothing to discount my attempt to use what I take to be the least controversial components of these respective theologies in concert with one another to pose a new challenge to both orthodox Christian theistic and atheistic analytical philosophers of religion alike.

Thus my hybrid theism is minimalist in at least two senses. First, it is minimalist with respect to theologies as a whole, subscribing to only those theistic beliefs that are deemed necessary in order to establish a theism

---

[29] While Kenny, *What I Believe* seeks to render problematic atheism on the one hand and traditional Christian theistic belief on the other, it does so in more general terms than I do, and it does not set forth and defend a substitute theism that is meant to challenge each view, including agnostics, to consider a more viable theism as I do herein. Also see Anthony Kenny, *The Unknown God* (London: Continuum, 2004) for an agnosticism similar to mine in that it rejects both atheism and traditional Christian theism.

[30] John Hick, Editor, *The Existence of God* (New York: The Macmillan Company, 1964); *Philosophy of Religion*, Second Edition (Englewood Cliffs: Prentice-Hall, 1973), Chapters 2–3; Anthony Kenny, *The Five Ways* (Notre Dame: University of Notre Dame Press, 1969); Mackie, *The Miracle of Theism*.

worthy of the name. Second, it is minimalist with respect to process and liberation theologies, as it appropriates some but not all of the central features of these important perspectives. While some would refer to my hybrid minimalist theism as "thin theology," I aim to demonstrate that it is nonetheless sufficiently "thick" to defeat, neutralize or otherwise pose a serious challenge to atheism, assuming that my hybrid minimalist process-liberationist theism evades the array of philosophical objections to traditional Christian theism.

In the spirit of William of Ockham, then, I seek to supplant the highly cumbersome and excessively thick orthodox Christian theism with a philosophically and theologically palatable propaedeutic, ridding theism of its numerous contested beliefs that fall prey to numerous atheological objections. In this way, Ockham's Razor is used to excise several rationally problematic beliefs from theism as it also trims atheism of its dubious tenets. Indeed, I do not intend to multiply theological beliefs beyond necessity. Rather, it is my intent to clear the thicket of traditional religious beliefs from the forest of philosophical discussion in order to create a more sparse, but a more solid, intellectual field of inquiry about the problem of God's existence.

It will no longer do to rest content with the idea that the defeat of the orthodox Christian notion of God suffices for atheism's self-proclamation of victory. Epistemically speaking, each position has the burden to bear and each must stand or fall on the merits of its own argumentation. The ecumenical consortium of theologies that my hybrid minimalist theism brings to bear must itself be defeated in order for atheism to even have a reasonable ground for beginning to establish itself as the most plausible position in this arena of philosophical discussion. In the end, to the extent that this challenge is not met by my hybrid minimalist process-liberationist theism, the New Agnosticism stands as the most plausible, even if temporary, position on the question of God's existence.

There are some inconclusive elements of this hybrid of radical theisms (whether taken individually or collectively), ones that until adequately answered leave significant, but not necessarily insoluble, questions in the minds of serious and not overly biased thinkers. Thus it appears that the best position to adopt for the time being is the New Agnosticism. This is not a default position, as so many theists and atheists often dismissively assert of agnosticism. Rather, it is the position that seeks to take seriously both the best of theistic arguments and analyses, as well as atheistic challenges to them. It is because of the significant and reasonable doubt that persists concerning each position that lands one in the New Agnosticism. But the philosophical dynamics of the New Agnosticism are such that, should the balance of evidence and of human reason justify strongly either theism or atheism, then the proponent of the New Agnosticism is honest enough to embrace that view. Thus the New Agnosticism is neither dogmatic nor ideological, but rather Socratic in its desire to follow the best arguments and analyses wherever they may lead. And this includes the possibility that the New Agnosticism might well end up, all relevant things considered, to be the final resting place for those most serious about the question of God.

This implies that *The Errors of Atheism* is not written as a definitive philosophical analysis of the problem of God. Rather, it is a prolegomenon to the philosophy of religion. More precisely, it is a philosophical prolegomenon to the study of the problem of God's possible existence. Given the rich and complex[31] history of the debate about God, it is naïve, if not foolhardy, to think that one has the final word on the subject as so many theists and atheists seem to do in their dogmatic pronouncements. What one can hope, however, is that one has made a substantial and important contribution to the discussion, wanting of merely polemical dismissals of either of the three possible general positions taken on the matter. What one can do is to provide a fair-minded approach to the problem of God, while having high regard for proponents of each view. This is easy enough, as each position has a wealth of worthy and devoted apologists. What I seek herein is to place the reader a little closer to the end of the discussion without embracing or assuming claims that automatically rule out the most respectable forms of theism, on the one hand, or atheism, on the other.

While *The Errors of Atheism* is a prolegomenon to the study of the problem of God, it is not a typical one. Rather than tread over the terrain of the traditional "proofs" for the existence of God, the controversial nature of these alleged proofs is taken as a starting point of discussion. The reason for this is that a new and significantly more plausible conception of God is considered, having given the orthodox Christian idea centuries of defense, and it having seemingly struggled with limited success in passing that test. It is time to advance the discussion about God's possible existence,

---

[31] For an incisive account of the differences in approach between analytic philosophers of religion (mostly orthodox Christian theists) and theologians in addressing the problems of God, see Phillips, "Religion, Philosophy, and the Academy." Phillips notes how analytic theists tend to "distort religious concepts by assimilating them to contexts which obscures them," (p. 141) thereby creating and sustaining a "hermeneutics of suspicion," while theologians often sustain a relativism that allows them to wallow in a "hubbub of voices" that remain to a large extent unconvincing except to those who already believe.

absent the numerous orthodox Christian dogmas that have plagued the problem of God from its very inception in the Western world. As one popular author notes, "The problem of religion . . . is the problem of dogma itself."[32] There is no need to spend time wondering first whether or not God exists, only then to have to defend ideologies of "faith" such as the virgin birth of Jesus, the resurrection of Jesus, the trinity, the *parousia*, the legitimacy and infallibility of the pope as a special spokesperson for God (for Catholics), the infallibility of the canonical Christian scriptures (but no others), and the omniscience[33] and omnipotence of God (strictly understood).

Our best efforts ought instead to be devoted to the most plausible conceptions of God. If there is a God, certainly God deserves to be taken seriously, rather than having the nature and function of God obscured and obfuscated by centuries of orthodox Christian fideism and its *apologia*. The focus of discussion herein, then, shall be the existence of a more plausible notion of God and Her functions in the world, absent unnecessary articles of "faith" devised by church leaders. After all, of what good is it to defend all manner of theological beliefs such as those just noted if the existence of God is in serious doubt and cannot itself be justified? The words ascribed to God in *Isaiah* 1:18:[34] "Come now, and let us reason together," apply to theists, atheists, and agnostics alike. And we should

---

[32] Sam Harris, *Letter to a Christian Nation* (New York: Alfred A. Knopf, 2006), p. 43.

[33] Whether or not omniscience is taken to mean simple foreknowledge or middle knowledge, I concur with process theists that neither is indicative of the knowledge of God, properly construed, as it attributes to God a hyperbolic property of sovereignty, threatens human autonomy, and seems to make God the author of human evils. Each attempts to capture an orthodox conception of divine knowledge. For discussions of God's omniscience (including simple foreknowledge and middle knowledge), see Robert Adams, "Middle Knowledge and the Problem of Evil," *American Philosophical Quarterly*, 14 (1977), pp. 109–117; Dennis Ahern, "Foreknowledge: Nelson Pike and Newcombe's Problem," *Religious Studies*, 15 (1979), pp. 475–490; David Basinger, "Divine Omniscience and Human Freedom: A 'Middle Knowledge' Perspective," *Faith and Philosophy*, 1 (1984), pp. 291–302; Nelson Pike, "Divine Foreknowledge, Human Freedom and Possible Worlds," *The Philosophical Review*, 86 (1977), pp. 209–216; *God and Timelessness* (London: Routledge, 1970); Alvin Plantinga, *The Nature of Necessity* (Oxford: The Clarendon Press, 1974); William Rowe, "The Problem of Divine Sovereignty and Human Freedom," *Faith and Philosophy*, 16 (1999), pp. 98–101.

[34] Also see *Job* 13:3; 15:3.

take them with utmost seriousness. For it is the key to any hope for a plausible answer to the problem of God.

For their incisive comments on parts of or whole drafts of this book, I thank the following philosophers and theologians: James H. Cone, Robert Francescotti, Thomas Maloney, and Burleigh T. Wilkins. They provided a rather splendid array of criticisms that sharpened the arguments in this book. I have made every effort to address various of their most central concerns in light of the general aim of this project. I am also grateful to the *Humboldt Journal of Social Relations* for permission to use much of "Political Integration and Political Separation: Martin Luther King, Jr. and Malcolm X on Social Change," *Humboldt Journal of Social Relations*, 21 (1995), pp. 191–208 in Chapter 6. I am also grateful to Springer for the use of "Dawkins' God*less* Delusion," *International Journal for Philosophy of Religion* (2009) as Chapter 3. I would like to thank Mrs. Lorraine Corlett and Ms. Marisa Diaz-Waian for their assistance in proof-reading and indexing the manuscript.

INTRODUCTION

We need not be forced to religion, against our reason—against what we reasonably believe about the world—to make sense of our lives.

—Kai Nielsen[1]

A question arises for the honest, open-minded, truth-seeking fallibilist: Is there an idea of God that enhances the otherwise atheistic picture of reality, one that refuses to attribute hyperbolic properties to God such as omniscience and omnipotence insofar as these properties are understood strictly and literally? Can theism "come of age" as Dietrich Bonhoeffer[2] urges and no longer believe in a transcendent realm of the divine, refusing to seek refuge in orthodox Christian dogma in order to attempt to dodge genuine and legitimate philosophical questions about the problem of God? Can the debate about God be revisited without many orthodox Christian theists demanding a supreme *sacrificium intellectus* of those who accept the claim: "God exists"? And can the debate take place without the underlying empirical influences of a certain brand of analytical philosophy going unchallenged and having an undue influence on the outcome of our reasoning about God?[3]

These questions are vital in that centuries of debate about the problem of God have issued numerous credible objections to the traditional Christian conception of God. From the concepts of divine goodness, power and knowledge, to the natural theological ontological, cosmological and teleological arguments for God's existence to the arguments from religious experience[4] and morality, each of these notions and arguments have met with formidable challenges so much so that the very idea of God is rightly

---

[1] Kai Nielsen, *Naturalism and Religion* (Buffalo: Prometheus Books, 2001), p. 13.

[2] Dietrich Bonhoeffer, *Letters and Papers from Prison* (London: SCM Press, 1953).

[3] Paul M. van Buren, *The Secular Meaning of the Gospel* (New York: The Macmillan Company, 1963), pp. 13f.

[4] I have in mind here the recognition of such experiences found in William James, *Varieties of Religious Experience* (New York: New American Library, 1958) and Rudolf Otto, *The Idea of the Holy*, J. W. Harvey (trans.) (Oxford: Oxford University Press, 1950).

considered to be an essentially contested concept.[5] But does it follow from this that "the time has come for theology openly and fully to confront the death of God"?[6]

In order to focus my discussion, I shall not enter into a dialogue with orthodox Christian theism—even though I mention it throughout this book. My mention of it assumes the credibility of many, though not all, of the atheistic objections to it, making it overly problematic for further consideration. My main interlocutor is philosophical atheism. So while some of my arguments and claims pertain indirectly to orthodox Christian theism, my intended target of criticism throughout is atheism.

Is God Dead?

Besides erring in the form of a kind of "presentism" in its "immolation of history,"[7] radical theology's statement that "God is dead" is peculiarly ambiguous. First, it might mean that, sociologically speaking, there is no idea of God. But this implies the denial of an obvious fact of most, if not all, societies, namely, that some idea of God is alive and well in influencing several people in this or that way. Second, it might mean that "God is dead" in the sense that God is no longer alive for people. While this claim seems to make some sense by pointing to the utter discouragement that many people experience when facing problems in the world, wondering where God is to make meaning of it all, strictly speaking the claim makes no sense. The reason for this is that any being worthy of the name "God" cannot die, as by definition God is, among other things, everlasting. Thus something else other than God must be dead, but not God, if in fact God ever existed in the first place. Third, "God is dead" might have the intended meaning that, say, the orthodox Christian notion of God is no longer viable in light of the knowledge of our times. Thus the concept of God[8] is no longer plausible because of our enlightened situation. But strictly

---

5   For a philosophical analysis of the notion of essentially contested concepts, see W. B. Gaillie, "Essentially Contested Concepts," in Max Black (ed.), *The Importance of Language* (Englewood Cliffs: Prentice-Hall, 1962), pp. 121–146.
6   Thomas J. J. Altizer, *The Gospel of Christian Atheism* (Philadelphia: The Westminster Press, 1966), p. 15.
7   Harvey Cox, *The Feast of Fools* (New York: Harper & Row Publishers, 1969), pp. 148, 150.
8   For a discussion of the distinction between the concept of God and conceptions of God, see Eberhard Herrmann, "On the Distinction Between the Concept of

speaking, it makes no sense to say that "God is dead" in this sense either. For if the orthodox Christian idea of God is incoherent, then this implies that *that* very conception of God is implausible. But this just implies that that notion of God has no referent, which implies that there never was a God corresponding to that idea. But then it might be asked how such a God could be dead when She never existed in the first place? What the death of God theologian or philosopher (such as Friedrich Nietzsche) is entitled to proclaim here is that there has been a set of discoveries over time that reveal to the reasonable and informed person that it is not the case that God exists, assuming that what is under discussion is an orthodox Christian notion of God.

The foregoing suggests that the question of meaning (what we mean when we engage in God-talk) is intimately related to the question of God's existence. I shall not attempt to dissect these questions, but instead address the problem of God's existence. But in doing so, I recognize that this question implies questions of what we mean by "God." Even more important, the question of the existence of God is really one of how we *ought* to think of God, should God exist.[9] So the problem of God is a deeply normative question insofar as meaning is concerned. What exactly is God? That is, what conception of God is viable, e.g., evades all significant rational objections? To answer that God is omnipotent, omniscient, omnibenevolent, and the like runs afoul of the problem of evil, but to say that God is "ultimate concern," the "ground of being," or the divine spirit of the oppressed is vague, as many philosophers and theologians have already noted.

Hybrid Minimalist Theism

However, the discussion in question has in the Western world focused mostly on the orthodox Christian idea of God. What is needed is a novel approach to this important discussion. As Kai Nielsen implores of analytical *apologia* of orthodox Christian theism in particular, "It is high time that we stop playing that game—put that old horse out to pasture."[10] In concurring with Nielsen on the implausibility of orthodox Christian

---

God and Conceptions of God," *International Journal for Philosophy of Religion*, 63 (2008).

[9] This point is recognized in John Hick, *Who or What is God?* (London: SCM Press, 2008).

[10] Nielsen, *Naturalism and Religion*, p. 21.

theism, I propose that we jettison the orthodox Christian idea of God. And I agree somewhat with Nielsen that "If we must do metaphysics, what we need to realize is that physicalism or something close to it is the only meta-physical game in town, if there are any metaphysical games in town."[11] In light of this observation, I suggest that the discussion proceed along the lines of replacing the orthodox Christian idea of God that is subject to centuries of abuse with a conception of God that understands God in generally demythologized, but primarily in process and liberationist, terms. In short, I shall argue for an unorthodox theism that blends what I take to be some (but not all) of the basic features of process and liberationist the-isms, as well as Western radical and secular theism more generally. This is not to discount the possibility that certain Eastern notions of the nature and function of God are of use in this discussion. But my focus shall be on a Western conception of divinity, one that stems in large part from Rudolf Bultmann's call to demythologize primitive Christian theology.[12]

Just as Bultmann seeks to make the mythology of the Christian scrip-tures comprehensible to contemporary folk, ridding the *kerygma* of its underlying multistoried universe of transcendent notions of "heaven" and "hell," for instance, so too will be my approach of attempting to locate a version of theism that can truly engage us today in light of advanced and enlightened scientific and political outlooks. It is a version of theism that

---

[11] Nielsen, *Naturalism and Religion*, p. 20.

[12] For an excellent philosophical articulation of Rudolf Bultmann's programme of demythologization of the Christian *kerygma* by a former student of his, see Hans Jonas, *Philosophical Essays* (Englewood Cliffs: Prentice-Hall, 1974). My adoption of the general demythologization scheme of Bultmann, however, is not insensitive to finest points of criticism articulated in Dorothee Soelle, *Political Theology*, John Shelley (trans.) (Philadelphia: Fortress Press, 1974). Also see Ernst Bloch, *Atheism in Christianity*, J. T. Swan (trans.) (New York: Herder & Herder, 1972). But neither of these authors' criticisms denounces the general programme of demythologization itself, e.g., of translating the genuine *kerygma* from mythological language to the language of science, for example. Soelle's objections include the one that Bultmann does not go far enough. In "existentializing" the *kerygma*, Bultmann fails to politicize it and thus fails to capture part of the genuine message of the historical Jesus, namely, that of lib-erating the oppressed: ". . . a political interpretation of the gospel is not anti-thetical to the essential intentions of Bultmann's theology" (Soelle, *Political Theology*, p. 55). Indeed, as she argues, a truly Bultmannian perspective would provide ways of criticizing political structures such that wars, hunger, aggres-sion, etc., can and ought to be explained in the demythological terms of political criticism rather than simply seen as matters of fate (Soelle, *Political Theology*, pp. 61f.).

I call "minimalist" in that it sheds many of the trappings of orthodox Christian theology in favor of a pared-down conception of divinity that evades the objections to the idea of God it seeks to replace. My hybrid theism resembles in some ways the "secularist" approaches to Christian theism, though it recognizes no special status for Christian revelation. In this way, my version of theism that I refer to as "hybrid minimalist theism" (or, more cumbersomely, "hybrid minimalist process-liberationist theism") departs from Bultmann's which is Christian at least in some minimal sense. Indeed, my theism is not Christian at all, not even in the senses that process and liberation theologies typically are. For it rejects most, if not all, Christian doctrines. It does not even accept the special divinity status of Jesus of Nazareth, arguably the most central Christian doctrine. My hybrid theism evades the numerous and powerful objections to Christian theisms and has a more plausible conception of God. Nonetheless, it is religiously and theologically meaningful despite its thinness.

My hybrid theism is minimalist in at least the following ways. As just noted, it is pared down with respect to orthodox Christian theism's maximalist set of religious dogmas, a few of which were noted earlier. But my hybrid theism is also minimalist with respect to process and liberationist theisms. That is, it borrows from each what it considers to be of fundamental importance with the goal of both evading objections to classical Christian theism and providing a meaningful account of God and the world. But it does not concur with, for instance, process and liberationist theism's assent to the doctrine of the authority of the Christian scriptures, or in the doctrine of the immortality of the soul. No doubt there are other beliefs with which my minimalist hybrid theism disagrees vis-à-vis process and liberationist theisms. Nonetheless, the subject of my hybrid version of theism is, as we shall see, quite worthy of the name "God" even if it might be rejected by most Christian theists. The theology that underlies it replaces the supernaturalistic notion of divinity of orthodox Christianity with an idea of God that we can "live with," both literally and figuratively, that is, if we can live with any idea of God. It is a conception of God's nature and function that passes, I believe, the test of reason at least better than the orthodox Christian theistic notion of God does.[13]

---

[13] My hybrid minimalist theism is not to be confused with David Ray Griffin's revisionist theism, according to which an explicitly and robust Whiteheadean process "dipolar" conception of God is appropriated in order to answer atheistic charges against a version of Christian theism. Griffin's theism seeks to revise what is implausible about orthodox Christian theism, and retain the rest of it. But my hybrid minimalist theism, though it draws from process and liberationist

On the question of the possible proper relationship between science and religion, my minimalist hybrid theism concurs with Ian G. Barbour's integrationist perspective[14] which is sympathetic to and consistent with the process theist approach as is mine. But my view makes no appeal to Christianity as having any privileged authority such that its particular doctrines require or even deserve defense.[15] Furthermore, unlike most process and other progressive thinkers on the science-religion question, I provide far more than the *en passant* remarks that are infrequently—if ever—offered by such thinkers concerning questions of justice.[16]

Hybrid Minimalist Theism and God-Talk

I have referred to Bultmann's programme of demythologizing the Christian *kerygma*. But it is important to have a better understanding of

---

theisms that are somewhat Christian, and though it emanates from the call for the demythologization of the Christian *kerygma*, nonetheless is not revisionist as it does not desire to be associated with Christian theism in any significant theological manner. It is a revolutionary theism that jettisons various Christian dogmas, and without apology. While Griffin's revisionist theism seeks to employ various Whiteheadian process notions to preserve panexperientialism and the afterlife, my hybrid minimalism has no such aim, though my appropriation of certain process and liberationist theistic ideas seeks to evade the classic objections to the traditional Christian theistic "proofs" as well as the problem of evil. Thus it is plain that, unlike the theology of Griffin, my theism is unorthodox and revolutionary, rather than merely revisionistic. Perhaps this is due in large part to the fact that Griffin is a Christian theologian who, unlike many orthodox Christian theists, seeks quite honestly and sincerely to preserve what he can of the Christian faith veritistically by way of revising it responsibly, while I am an agnostic philosopher who wants to get to the truth of the matter of God's possible existence, *come what may*. This is hardly intended to be a criticism of Griffin's work. Instead, my point here is simply to draw attention to the differences between Griffin's revisionist approach and my revolutionary one.

14 For discussions of the approaches to the possible relationship between science and religion, see Ian G. Barbour, *Religion in an Age of Science* (New York: Harper & Row Publishers, 1990), Chapter 1; *When Science Meets Religion* (New York: Harper & Row Publishers, 2000); S. L. Bonting, *Creation and Double Chaos* (Minneapolis: Fortress Press, 2007), Chapter 1.

15 Thus I see as highly problematic the presumptuous attempt to rescue Christianity that we find in Christian process apologists such as Philip Clayton, *God and Contemporary Science* (Grand Rapids: Wm. B. Eerdmanns Publishing Company, 1997).

16 Here I have in mind the words made in passing in Barbour, *Religion in an Age of Science*, pp. 76–77.

his conception of demythologization insofar as it inspires part of my own conception of how to approach the problem of God. Bultmann's existentialist call to demythologize the primitive Christian *kerygma* involves the task of interpreting the Christian scriptures in a way that does not offend a modern scientific worldview while still retaining the most essential message of the *kerygma*. In short, the language of the scriptures must conform to contemporary knowledge-bases, understood in fallibilistic terms. And because of the fallibilist assumption of demythologization, each era will need to perform the task of demythologization for itself. Assumed here is a great degree of intellectual honesty between the self and God. But God is not otherworldly. Rather, God is with us ("Emmanuel") and seeks to work through us, as we are God's "ultimate transmuting" subjects. Thus there is a fundamentally existentialist core to Bultmann's programme: God acts in the world, not as a transcendent being, but as an immanent one.

Nonetheless, some have argued, it remains to be seen the extent to which the Bultmannian translation of ancient Christian myths into contemporary scientific language and concepts results in a genuine referent for "God" and other theistic concepts.[17] And this question holds as a challenge to theism whether or not basic theistic claims are linguistically reducible to non-theistic ones. For more than a simple yet comprehensive linguistic reduction is required for eliminability to occur here.

The reason why mere linguistic reduction of religious language to the language of, say, science, cannot straightaway entail the meaninglessness of religious language is due to the fact that G. Frege's Law of Substitutivity of Co-Referential Proper Names implies that such a reduction requires an identity relation between the informational contents of a religious claim, on the one hand, and the reductionist language, on the other. But it is precisely such an identity relation that shows that each claim or set of claims is substitutable for the other in co-referential proper names contexts. This implies that if "God" is meaningful, then the set of reductionist claims that capture "God" are meaningful, and vice-versa. But in no way does this automatically reduce "God" to meaninglessness.[18] A further argument is

---

[17] R. Hepburn, "Demythologizing and the Problem of Validity," in A. Flew and A. MacIntyre, Editors, *New Essays in Philosophical Theology* (London: SCM Press, 1955), pp. 227f.

[18] Assumed here is that the principle of substitutivity preserves not only truth-value, but meaning between the terms substitutable one for another under the terms of substitutivity.

required in order to demonstrate that feat.[19] Until this argument is given, there is insufficient reason to reject outright the sense or reference of religious language.[20]

Minimalist Theism

While my aim herein is not to defend to the end this hybrid minimalist theism, the view will be meant to stand the test of internal coherence as well as to evade the many objections to the traditional Christian idea of God. If this is successful, then major progress will be made concerning the problem of God, though not without the significant assistance of those philosophers and theologians cited along the way.

But for my hybrid minimalist theism to have any possible philosophical significance for the problem of God, it must be at least relatively clear at this preliminary stage of the discussion what God is supposed to be, and how God functions in the world. Moreover, this conception of God must be intuitively and rationally coherent. Otherwise, confusion will result.

I shall attempt, then, to provide a minimalist conception of God and theism that rests on no worse linguistic foundations than secular language. Of course, my hybrid minimalist theism accomplishes this in part by rejecting what it understands as inessential theistic beliefs, many of which are said to be found in traditional Christian theism. Nonetheless, some basic theistic claims remain, and must be shown to have at least as much sense and reference as do nontheological statements. I shall attempt to do this in devising my hybrid minimalist theism as a challenge to atheism. Unlike orthodox Christian theism, I shall employ language that uses a minimum of oblique terms so as not to obscure their truth-values. For "statements which fail to pay the necessary price for factuality . . . cannot be counted as statements of fact."[21] The language of hybrid minimalist theism, I shall argue, is indeed informative in the sense that "God exists" is more plausible than so many leading atheists seem to believe.

---

[19] An argument regarding the possible eliminability of collectivist language is provided in J. Angelo Corlett, *Analyzing Social Knowledge* (Totowa: Rowman & Littlefield Publishers, 1996), pp. 120–122.

[20] A helpful discussion of religious language is found in van Buren, *The Secular Meaning of the Gospel*, Chapter IV.

[21] Peter Donovan, *Religious Language* (New York: Hawthorne Books, Inc., 1976), p. 20.

The question is whether or not in the end it constitutes a successful challenge to atheism.

In arguing thusly, I am not committed to the empiricist position that all religious language must be completely free of nonempirical meanings or implications. For such a view begs the question against theism. Given the nature of theism, one expects to reasonably believe that it might not accommodate well all empirical restrictions on the use of language in order for it to be informative.[22] Nonetheless, theism cannot philosophically afford to make too many nonempirical claims as not every theological claim is likely to be provided with empirical grounding. And my hybrid minimalist theism does not. My assumption here is that "Oblique language may well be tentative, vague and easily misunderstood, yet can nonetheless be capable of pointing us in the right direction, and thus carrying genuine informativeness."[23]

The following, then, is my minimalist conception of God. In a sense, it is an attempt to provide a minimalist answer to the factual challenge (by Antony Flew,[24] John Hick,[25] among others) to all religious discourse, namely, that its essentially oblique language be shown to possess informative content. If God, being non-corporeal spirit, is anything in addition to truth and justice, it seems, God is, as Boethius states, good.[26] This I shall not dispute with the traditional Christian theist, though understandings of exactly what God's goodness amounts to might be a bit unclear.[27] Moreover, it would seem that if God exists, then God is omnipresent because She[28] is spirit, and the most perfectly loving, just, and true being who is the

---

[22] This point is based on the arguments of Ian Ramsey, *Religious Language* (London: SCM Press, 1957).

[23] Donovan, *Religious Language*, p. 65.

[24] Antony Flew, "Theology and Falsification," in Antony Flew and A. MacIntyre, Editors, *New Essays in Philosophical Theology* (London: SCM Press, 1955), pp. 96–98.

[25] John Hick, *Philosophy of Religion* (Englewood Cliffs: Prentice-Hall, 1963), p. 93.

[26] Boethius, *The Consolation of Philosophy*, Richard Green (trans.) (Indianapolis: The Bobbs-Merrill Company, Inc., 1962), p. 62. It is reason that demonstrates this fact about God, according to him.

[27] For example, is God's goodness to be found in cancerous illnesses that bring excessive pain to humans and nonhumans? Is God's goodness to be found in human or other natural evils? Or, is it the case that there is some other origin of the goodness in spite of such evils? Is all goodness such that it originates from God, because, as many theologies have it, God is Good?

[28] I use the female pronoun to refer to God because it is my general writing style to use this pronoun in reference to entities that are genderless, or those that might be of mixed gender, or to refer to a generic someone who is either male

subject of our ultimate concern, the ground of being in the Tillichian senses of these expressions. But is God really omnipotent and omniscient in their strict senses as the Christian tradition suggests? Is God so powerful that She can at any time and in any epistemic circumstance believe both conjuncts of a logical contradiction without violating the law of noncontradiction? Can God make it rain in a particular place and at a particular time while making it not the case that it is raining there and then? The fact is that God is not powerful in this hyperbolic sense, as has already been noted or argued by several philosophers and theologians such as Thomas Aquinas, Duns Scotus, Ockham,[29] Paul Tillich, John A. T. Robinson, John Cobb, Jr., and David Ray Griffin.

In reply to these kinds of points, it might be noted that even the conservative Protestant Christian orthodox position on the nature of God admits that "It is no more a limitation of power that it cannot effect the impossible, than it is of reason that it cannot comprehend the absurd, or of infinite goodness that it cannot do wrong."[30] Nonetheless, though, it is said that "God cannot contradict Himself, He is able to do whatever He wills, . . ."[31] The precise nature of the power of God, then, is an open question. It is also unclear whether God is omniscient in some absolute sense. For if the problem of nonnatural evil is telling, then God's omnibenevolence and omnipotence cannot make it such that God could permit evil if She knew

---

or female. I am attempting to avoid complicity in centuries of sexist bias in referring to God, though I suppose I am participating in an opposite kind of sexism, or perhaps even a kind of patronizing of theological feminism as some might aver. But in light of the deeper problems facing the God hypothesis, this is the very least of the problems with which one ought to be concerned. If the God hypothesis is resolved in favor of some version of theism, then I surely will begin to address the nature of God in terms of gender, and if or how God ought to be refereed to along those lines. It is beyond the purview of this book to look beyond the most fundamental of theistic concerns, namely, whether or not God exists. Thus issues of gender are not considered, not even in the discussion of liberatory theisms. For it is assumed that whatever liberation theologies might bring to bear on the matter of God's existence entails the freedom of the truly oppressed, regardless of gender.

29   Indeed, the Catholic theological tradition, with few exceptions, holds to a notion of "relative omnipotence." By this is meant that God is omnipotent relative to the things God cannot possibly do due to logical limitations. I owe this insight to Thomas Maloney.

30   Charles Hodge, *Systematic Theology*, Volume 1 (Grand Rapids: Wm. B. Eerdmans Publishing Company, 1977 reprint), p. 409. Originally published in 1871.

31   L. S. Chafer, *Systematic Theology*, Volume 1 (Dallas: Dallas Seminary Press, 1947), p. 210.

about it in advance. As James Baldwin poignantly asks about God's omnibenevolence and the plight of blacks in the U.S.: "If His love was so great, and if He loved all His children, why were we, the blacks, cast down so far?"[32]

Of course, "It is not simply evil, but pointless and irredeemable evil, which would be incompatible with the character of God as Christians conceive him."[33] However, this being so, it is not the case that the agnostic critic of theism has the burden of showing "that there could be no way of justifying evil in the world" and that "it is logically impossible that God should have a morally sufficient reason to allow evil of the sort that we encounter in the world."[34] Philosophically speaking, the theist makes the claim that God exists. Against the truth of this claim, critics offer as evidence that evil exists and pose a challenge to the ideas of divine omnipotence, omnibenevolence, and omniscience, all properties that are attributed to God by most theists. Contrary to Basil Mitchell, then, it would seem that it is the theist rather than the atheist who has the burden of explaining the existence of various sorts of evil given the orthodox Christian definition of "God." This is not to deny, however, that the atheist has the burden of her own claims to defend, as we shall see in a subsequent chapter.

So there is serious question concerning the exact meaning and limits of God's omnipotence and omniscience, contrary to traditional Christian doctrine, assuming the idea of divine omnibenevolence. But does this spell doom for theism? Is there no retreat to a more plausible and viable form of belief in God that would render atheism dubious? Is the open-minded theist forced by logic and reasonableness to simply accept the self-contradictory nature of what I am calling the orthodox Christian religious belief in the nature of God? If so, does this spell the demise of orthodox Christian theism? Must it mean that the honest theist should become an atheist? Or, is it the case that theism worthy of the name (perhaps even Christian theism worthy of the name) can be rescued from the onslaught of criticisms that plague traditional Christian theism, for example? Is a nontraditional theism possible, one that reconceptualizes God in more philosophically viable and minimalist terms? Might God really be "less" (in terms of the quantitative content of the divine attributes are concerned) than so many seem to think She is? If so, might it imply that such a notion

---

[32] James Baldwin, *The Fire Next Time* (New York: The Dial Press, 1963), p. 45.
[33] Basil Mitchell, *The Justification of Religious Belief* (Oxford: Oxford University Press, 1973), p. 10.
[34] Mitchell, *The Justification of Religious Belief*, p. 10.

of God would make God "too small"[35] to be worthy of prayer-offerings and worship? And even if it turns out that God is not what orthodox Christian theisms say She is, does this imply insurmountable conceptual trouble for theism? Or, is it rather the case that orthodox theism proclaimed and defended a hyperbolic conception of the nature and function of God? And if so, then surely theism itself cannot be blamed for such poor understanding on the part of many of its most spirited and most intelligent adherents.

Hybrid Theism

I shall delve into some of the depths of radical Christian theology, especially process and liberation theologies, in order to provide what I take to be the strongest defense of theism against the assault of objections to God's existence proffered over centuries by some of the most highly respected philosophers. I do not here recount those criticisms, or the traditional proofs for the existence of the God of traditional Christian theism. That is quite well-trodden philosophical and theological terrain, and I have little, if anything, to add to those discussions. However, in reconsidering the nature and function of God via theologies of process and liberation, I, like them, follow the call to demythologize the nature and function of God from what most think God is to what God actually is, should She exist at all. In so doing, it might turn out that there is a notion of God that, unlike that of the notion of deity often defended by traditional Christian theists, is plausible enough to evade the vast and powerful objections confronting the notion of God of traditional Christian theism. To the extent that this dialectical move succeeds, it will, all relevant things considered, represent an important step forward in the discourse about God's existence.

In drawing on some of the conceptual resources of process and liberation theologies in providing answers to some important atheistic concerns, I am aware of the disagreements between these two approaches to theology. In fact, some liberation thinkers have distanced themselves from what they consider to be European theorizing altogether, including the secularization of Christian theology and its roots in the theological programme of Bultmann.[36] For example, while Griffin has done much especially in recent

---

[35]   J. B. Phillips, *Your God is Too Small* (New York: The Macmillan Company, 1961).

[36]   José Miguez Bonino, *Doing Theology in a Revolutionary Situation* (Philadelphia: Fortress Press, 1975), Chapter 4.

years to set forth the case for process theism,[37] and liberation theologians such as James H. Cone and Gustavo Gutiérrez have done the same for their respective views,[38] my approach shall be ecumenical insofar as it seeks to bring these theologies into the forefront of discussion in analytical philosophy of religion. This is significant not only because most liberation theologians do not find process theology as friendly to their enterprise perhaps due to liberationist commitments to the authority of scripture and some of the orthodox doctrines of God, but also because most process theologians tend to merely mention the importance of racism and oppression in the world. In contrast, I shall employ key elements of each of these theistic perspectives and combine them into one voice that can supplant traditional Christian theism and thereby pose serious challenges to atheism's claim that it is not the case that God exists.[39]

Attacking Atheism

One main purpose of my philosophical investigation into the problem of God is to discover whether or not atheism is sufficiently well-founded for

---

[37] David Ray Griffin, "Process Philosophy of Religion," *International Journal for Philosophy of Religion*, 50 (2001), pp. 131–151; *Reenchantment without Supernaturalism* (Ithaca: Cornell University Press, 2001).

[38] James H. Cone, *Speaking the Truth* (Grand Rapids: Wm. B. Eerdmans Publishing Co., 1986); *Risks of Faith* (Boston: Beacon Press, 1999); Gustavo Gutiérrez, *Essential Writings* (Maryknoll: Orbis Books, 1996).

[39] I am also cognizant of at least some of several other thinkers whose views about the nature of God seem remarkably similar to those found in the radical theologies I shall employ, especially with regard to my appropriation of process thought. F. Schleiermacher, for example, holds that God is that which is recognized by way of human experience and wherein God is the universe and the unity underlying it. The "Meliorist" theologians, also called "social theologians," of the 19th century held immanentist conceptions of God. And Josiah Royce called God "the immanent spirit of the community." One question facing such conceptions of God is whether E. G. Brightman was correct in thinking that they expand the notion of God so that we have "too much of God," including God as being responsible for evil in the world, thus posing conceptual difficulties for the idea of divine omnibenevolence. And at least as far back in the history of ideas as B. Spinoza, known among other things as that "God-intoxicated man," divine immanentism is defended. Thus my philosophical investigation into God's nature and function is cognizant of the fact that other immanentist thinkers predate those discussed herein. But since this project is not one in the history of ideas, but rather focused on particular problems related to the question of God, I beg the reader's forgiveness in not having paid due tribute to what other of the great minds throughout history have written on the subject.

us to call into question its rejection of theism on the basis of its allegedly refuting orthodox Christian theism. For if theism worthy of the name can answer or evade plausibly some or all of the objections to the traditional Christian notion of God, then this would appear to cast doubt on atheism's claim to plausibility insofar as it asserts (by definition of "atheism") that it is not the case that God exists. Indeed, it would expose the "God*less* delusion," which is the delusional spell under which an atheist suffers when she mistakenly—often arrogantly—believes that the self-proclaimed refutation of one particular form of theism, such as traditional Christian theism, spells the justification of atheism. This delusion, it turns out, rests on the cluster of "errors of atheism," which are discussed in Chapter 2. What is needed are not more atheists who are as guilty of uninformed, dismissive, and bellicose dogmatism as are many orthodox theists.[40] What we need, as Harvey Cox states in reference to Umberto Eco, are "thinkers who know what they are talking about when they disagree with theologians, interlocutors who are incredulous but not principled skeptics." We need those who "may not themselves believe in God, but realize how arrogant it would be to declare . . . that God does not exist."[41] Like Eco, what we need are atheists who are genuinely open to the deepest questions of religious faith.[42] Why? Because not only is the question of God's existence "still viable and valuable, but that respectful disagreement on very basic issues is still possible."[43] This is precisely what I seek to bring to analytical philosophy of religion at this juncture.

So the contributions of this book are multifarious. Unlike most discussions within analytical philosophy of religion today that either constitute *apologia* of traditional Christian theism and assume a set of controversial ontological, epistemological, and metaphysical assumptions about the nature of God and what constitutes acceptable Christian faith, or simply assume with many atheists, on the other hand, that God does not exist, I shall challenge atheism (as it is set forth by some of its most philosophically sophisticated proponents) by revealing some fundamental logical and conceptual flaws some such philosophers have committed, and I shall not do so by defending traditional Christian theism. Rather, the theism I set

---

[40] A similar point is found in David Lack, *Evolutionary Theory and Christian Belief* (London: Methuen, 1957), p. 18.

[41] Harvey Cox, "Introduction," in Umberto Eco and Carlo Maria Martini, *Belief or Nonbelief?* M. Proctor (trans.) (New York: Arcade Publishing, 1997), p. 4.

[42] Cox, "Introduction," pp. 5–6.

[43] Cox, "Introduction," p. 10.

forth is one that does not depend for its plausibility on any particularly or uniquely Christian doctrine as it seeks to be theologically neutral in the sense that its theology proper is minimalist, absent the rather burdensome conceptual baggage of most theologies whether Western or Eastern.

Moreover, on the assumption that, in the main, the objections of Immanuel Kant, David Hume, J. L. Mackie, and some others to the traditional theistic "proofs" for God's existence are telling *against orthodox Christian theism*, it does not follow that atheism is justified in more than a rather weak sense as the justification of atheism is only as strong as the strength of the theism that it defeats. On the other hand, exposure of the fallacious reasoning of some leading atheists does not provide relief for defenders of orthodox Christian theism, as the latter cannot be resurrected merely by the interpolation of unorthodox theologies which themselves condemn orthodoxy in crucial ways.

The most plausible position at this juncture of the debate about God is the New Agnosticism. Its respect for certain radical theologies does not allow it to commit the atheist's errors. But nor does it (blindly or otherwise) accept orthodox Christian faith or orthodox theism of any kind. If there is a future for God in the world, it must be at least the God of process and liberation theologies. Among other things, it must be a God whose workings in the world are reconcilable with sound science and justice for oppressed peoples. While this might not provide a complete account of a plausible or sound theism, it certainly points us in the right direction. In secularist theological terms, we might say that the matter of attempting to resurrect a viable conception of God in the contemporary paradigm "lies not in the stars, and not with God, but with ourselves."[44] By this is meant that we must cast off the mantle of orthodox Christian theological antiquity and rethink the nature and function of God in terms that speak truth to power politically, socially, ethically, and scientifically. Hiding behind the masks of orthodox ideologies does no one any good. In particular, it does God (should She exist) no good to be misrepresented by such orthodox theological and religious arrogance and presumptuousness as is often the case. The time has truly arrived to discard the veriphobia[45] that prohibits most from following the arguments wherever they lead us. This applies to theists, atheists, and agnostics alike.

---

[44] Cox, *The Feast of Fools*, p. 34.
[45] I borrow this term from A. I. Goldman, *Knowledge in a Social World* (Oxford: Oxford University Press, 1999), pp. 7–9.

The New Agnosticism

As a philosopher, I must conduct my investigation honestly and rigorously, and with as little bias as possible. Dissenting voices—even those that provide discomfort to us and, as Tillich might say, "shake our foundations"[46]—must be considered with all of the seriousness we can muster. Only then can we make intelligent and fair-minded decisions about the existence of God. Only then will we take (the problem of) God seriously. There are plenty of traditional Christian theists who believe this or that without honest and adequate reflection and consideration of evidence. On the other hand, there are numerous atheists who deny the existence of God but without having in a serious way considered alternative theologies to the traditional one in the Western tradition,[47] or even beyond that.[48] The world can certainly do without impudently nescient minds, regardless of their ideological persuasion. Perhaps what are most needed now are epistemically responsible cognizers, rather than close-minded atheists, theists, or agnostics.

It is understandable why popular Christianity would mistake God for a personal, supernatural, and transcendent being. But what is particularly opprobrious is that many leading atheists, including respected philosophers, continue to do battle with theists as if traditional Christian theism articulated the *only* notion of God that requires refutation in order to establish atheism. Yet this ignoring of more plausible theisms by atheists has, curiously, endured for generations, as noted by Ian Ramsey: ". . . 'popular Christianity has always posited such a supreme personality'. But those who think in this way include not only ordinary Christians but also 'our contemporary linguistic philosophers' in so far as 'for all their sophistication' they still 'continue to do battle'. . . for the existence or non-existence

---

[46] This phrase is taken from Paul Tillich, *The Shaking of the Foundations* (New York: Charles Scribner's Sons, 1948).

[47] For further ways in which to construe Christianity, see Ninian Smart, *In Search of Christianity* (New York: Harper & Row Publishers, 1979).

[48] For just a few discussions of alternative ways of understanding God and religion, see Emile Durkeim, *The Elementary Forms of the Religious Life* (New York: The Free Press, 1915); Lewis M. Hopfe, *Religions of the World* (Beverly Hills: Glencoe Press, 1976); Robert E. Hume, *The World's Living Religions* (New York: Charles Scribner's Sons, 1959); John B. Noss, *Man's Religions*, 5th Edition (New York: Macmillan Publishing Co., Inc., 1974); Ninian Smart, *The Religious Experience of Mankind*, 2nd Edition (New York: Charles Scribner's Sons, 1976); *Worldviews* (New York: Charles Scribner's Sons, 1983); Huston Smith, *The Religions of Man* (New York: Harper & Row Publishers, 1958).

of such a being."[49] So not only is traditional Christian theism epistemically and religiously irresponsible for not taking dissenting theological voices sufficiently seriously, atheist philosophers are guilty of proclaiming that atheism is justified when they, considered collectively, have not even taken at most more than an occasional glance at the ongoing and sophisticated attempts to reconcile the most fundamental elements of Christianity with good science and philosophy. This reveals atheism (as it is argued by many leading atheists) to be presumptuous, ignorant, and superficial. How can so many atheists confidently proclaim that it is not the case that God exists, or even as some "more careful" atheists do, that it is probably not the case that God exists, if only one (popular) notion of God is defeated? Is that not a bit too akin to an athlete's outperforming one (albeit popularly supported) contender, and then loudly and seriously proclaiming that she is the world's best at that competition, without even attempting to recognize—much less compete against—other major competitors? Would we not refer to such a person as a rogue, foolish, misinformed, or even witless? And how much more embarrassing would it be if it turned out that the defeated athlete was not even close to being one of the best at that competition? I suggest that this is analogous to the situation that we have in philosophy of religion regarding atheism and its self-proclaimed defeat of theism.

However, as the agnostic Bertrand Russell implies, one need not be either a Christian in the traditional sense, or an atheist. Indeed, one ought not to be either, given the difficulties faced by each. Inspired not only by a host of Christian theologians of the past and present, but also by the most "profane" of agnostic philosophers such as Russell[50] and atheists like Mackie, I seek to clarify what is at stake in the debate concerning the existence of God, and to provide the most reasonable answer to the question of God's existence given the main points of what has been argued thus far in the history of the debate about God's existence. This is a tall order indeed, as many a thinker in centuries past attempted the same, and with limited results.

What is needed is a clarification of the basic issues and a clearing of the conceptual table in the debate about God, one that neither seeks to defend the existence of a particular notion of God come what may, nor one that

---

49 Citing John A. T. Robinson, *Honest to God*, (Philadelphia: The Westminster Press, 1963), pp. 11, 12, 13, 40 [Ian Ramsey, *Christian Discourse: Some Logical Explorations* (Oxford: Oxford University Press, 1965), p. 63].

50 Bertrand Russell, *Atheism: Collected Essays: 1943–1949* (New York: Arno Press, 1972).

seeks to boldly infer (however equivocally) that because one major notion of God is defeated that this somehow, by some mystical feat of logic, proves atheism. What we need is a New Agnosticism, one that seeks to evaluate the problem of God's existence only after seriously considering the various options before us, philosophically and theologically speaking. In the end, the New Agnosticism might lack sufficient reason to affirm some meaningful form of theism. But this does not mean that it fails to leave open the door for further inquiry. So it denies for the time being atheism's claim that it is not the case that God exists because the atheist has failed to demonstrate this in her haste to disprove a most implausible set of hypotheses in traditional Christian theism. But as clarified in the Preface, the New Agnosticism also disagrees with the claim that "God is dead"[51] insofar as this statement makes reference to the traditional Christian theistic idea of the nature and function of God. For this would appear to imply that that notion was alive to begin with. If the traditional notion of God is implausible, then that "God" never existed to begin with! And it is time that we become at least honest enough about God to recognize this as a theological datum.[52] As Robinson, following the demythologization programme of Bultmann and the existentialist theology of Tillich, argues, the crude notion of God being supernaturalistically "out there" or "up there" must be rejected as it is an obstacle to healthy religious faith.[53]

Suffice it to say that the New Agnosticism, with its serious consideration of an unorthodox hybrid minimalist theism, picks up where the "death of God" and radical theology movement entered Christian theology decades ago. Without apology, it seeks to bring with some depth various of the ideas of radical theology from the periphery of theological debate into the core of the philosophical discussion about God's existence. Only then, and if the evidence affords it, can atheists claim without equivocation and with more epistemic authority and trustworthiness that it is not the case that God exists. Only then, and if the evidence supports theism, can theists commit themselves to belief in God without uttering irresponsible nonsense.

---

[51] By this I mean that the conceptual content of the sentence is empty.

[52] For more on these issues, see J. L. Ice and J. J. Carey, Editors, *The Death of God Debate* (Philadelphia: The Westminster Press, 1967); D. L. Edwards, Editor, *The Honest to God Debate* (Philadelphia: The Westminster Press, 1963). Also see Gabriel Vahanian, *The Death of God* (New York: George Braziller, 1957). For a philosophical perspective on the death of God idea, see, of course, Walter Kaufmann, Editor, *The Portable Nietzsche* (New York: The Viking Press, 1954).

[53] Robinson, *Honest to God*, pp. 41f.

It is time to take the problem of God more seriously than ever before. We need a synthesis of philosophy of religion and some of the central themes of some radical theologies into dynamic conflict for the sake of discovering the truth about the question of God's existence and functioning in the world. But unlike the typical Western theistic approach, the one adopted herein assumes no starting point that affirms the existence of God, as does the fideist philosophy of religion of Alvin Plantinga.[54] But it also fails to deny the possibility of God, at least until all plausible options are seriously considered. For it is believed that the bringing of radical theologies into the forefront of philosophy of religion will effect a dramatically more fruitful and engaging dialectic in philosophy of religion that will challenge in tremendous ways atheism and theism alike to reconsider their respective pre-theoretical commitments. Unless all (or at least, many more) reasonable proposals about the existence of God are taken into serious consideration and analyzed, we are in no position to take leave of God[55] once and for all, whether this means to finally deny the existence of God, or to affirm the most plausible and adequate notion of the divine reality in the world.

One might wonder whether some form of agnosticism is the best answer to the problem of God and if it is even possible to encourage philosophers to consider more seriously the plausibility of radical theologies. Would it not be reasonable to think that as a result of this enterprise either theism or atheism will stand as the more plausible position on God? While this is a reasonable position to take, I shall take a more aporetic one, consistent with Socrates' arguments as represented in Plato's dialogues.[56] In other words, I shall take whatever meaningful progress can be made in answering plausibly criticisms of the traditional Christian theistic notion of God to warrant an invigoration of agnosticism rather than a simple acceptance of theism. And since in the end the investigation might eventuate in the repudiation of any theism worthy of the name, atheism cannot be ruled out absolutely. Hence, the New Agnosticism serves as a call to rethink the question of God, but in terms that have never been at the forefront of discussions in analytical philosophy of religion.

---

[54] Alvin Plantinga, *Warranted Christian Belief* (Oxford: Oxford University Press, 2000).

[55] This phrase refers to the traditional Christian notion of God, and is borrowed from Don Cupitt, *Taking Leave of God* (New York: Crossroad, 1981).

[56] For more on Plato's dialogues and *aporia* in them, see J. Angelo Corlett, *Interpreting Plato's Dialogues* (Las Vegas: Parmenides Publishing, 2005). Also see, of course, J. M. Cooper and D. S. Hutchinson, Editors, *Plato: Complete Works* (Indianapolis: Hackett Publishing Company, 1997).

So the question remains: Can theism remake itself in order to evade the daunting problems raised against it by some atheists, or will it retreat into the comforts of the orthodox or neo-orthodox fideist Christian theologies of the likes of Augustine,[57] Karl Barth,[58] and Emil Brunner[59] who insist on effectively discontinuing or even blocking these vital discussions with appeals to the primacy of faith and revelation?

Unlike these thinkers, I assume a kind of evidentialist posture throughout, wherein "evidentialism" means that "there is a moral duty to proportion one's beliefs to evidence, proof or other epistemic justifications for belief"[60] or acceptance. But reason, not revelation, must be our primary guide along the way. And whatever the challenges evidentialism faces because of the limits of reason, it nonetheless stands as the best hope we have in answering questions about God or other matters falling within the range of philosophical discourse and method. That reason is imperfect is surely no good reason to deny its legitimate role (during its better moments) as the arbiter of debates about the existence of God. As Allen Wood argues, "There are no matters in which letting factors other than the evidence influence our beliefs do not violate both our self-respect and to the legitimate claims our fellow human beings make on us as rational beings."[61]

If God exists, then God expects us to be honest in our quest for truth about the problem of Her existence. And while it may be unreasonable for the atheist to demand that we understand everything there is to know about God in order for it to be reasonable to accept the claim that "God exists,"[62] it is equally unreasonable for the theist to conveniently assign

---

57 Augustine, *Confessions*, J. K. Ryan (trans.) (New York: Image Books, 1960).

58 Karl Barth, *Anselm* (New York: Meridian Books, 1960); *Church Dogmatics*, Volumes 1–2, G. T. Thomson (trans.) (New York: Charles Scribner's Sons, 1955); *Evangelical Theology*, G. Foley (trans.) (Grand Rapids: William B. Eerdmans Publishing Company, 1963).

59 Emil Brunner, *Dogmatics*, Volumes 1–2, O. Wyon (trans.) (Philadelphia: The Westminster Press, 1952).

60 Allen Wood, "The Duty to Believe According to the Evidence," *International Journal for Philosophy of Religion*, 63 (2008), pp. 7–24.

61 Wood, "The Duty to Believe According to the Evidence," p. 24.

62 Even on a significantly modified and non-hyperbolic idea of God's nature and function, it is reasonable to expect that some aspects of divinity might remain beyond our understanding, at least for the time being until we discern them by reason. But this assumes that most of what is purported about God's nature and function is quite understandable to the honest thinker. And it is not to say that there are some aspects of God that are by necessity beyond our comprehension, and that we ought to accept them nonetheless. Reasonable religion, and I might add any acceptable and healthy theology, ought to pass the test of reason at

everything we fail to understand to the mysteriousness of God. As Alfred North Whitehead argues, "The task of reason is to fathom the deeper depths of the many-sidedness of things. We must not expect simple answers to far-reaching questions. However far our gaze penetrates, there are always heights beyond which block our vision."[63] Contrary to Søren Kierkegaard, Christian faith properly understood is not a blind leap into the dark backward.[64] Instead, it is *pistis*, an act of commitment to God.[65] It is neither contrary to reason nor the acceptance of dogma or creed, nor, as Thomas J. J. Altizer puts it, "radical inwardness or subjectivity,"[66] but rather an act of reasonable dedication to the will of the divine in the world. Religious faith ought, moreover, to be based on an honest search for truth from whatever quarters truth can be discovered.

The general aim of this prolegomenon of sorts to the philosophy of religion is the philosophical pursuit of truth as it pertains to matters of God's existence. It is vital that this all-important issue be examined with both clarity and respect for responsible positions from various and opposing quarters.

Some Basic Assumptions

At the close of *The Feast of Fools*, Cox writes of Tillich as the "most brilliant practitioner of the theology of culture"[67] and notes that ". . . no one

---

every turn. As Kai Nielsen states: "We cannot have faith in or accept on faith that which we do not at all understand" [Kai Nielsen, *Philosophy & Atheism* (Buffalo: Prometheus Books, 1985), pp. 23–24]. Again, he writes: "Faith presupposes a *minimal understanding* of what you take on faith" (Nielsen, *Philosophy & Atheism*, p. 94).

[63] Alfred North Whitehead, *Process and Reality* (New York: The Humanities Press, 1929), p. 519.

[64] Søren Kierkegaard, *Fear and Trembling* and *The Sickness Unto Death*, W. Lowrie (trans.) (Princeton: Princeton University Press, 1954).

[65] Fred L. Fisher, *Jesus and His Teachings* (Nashville: Broadview, 1972). For contrary conceptions of faith, see William Ladd Sessions, *The Concept of Faith* (Ithaca: Cornell University Press, 1994); Kenneth W. Kemp, "The Virtue of Faith in Theology, Natural Science, and Philosophy," *Faith and Philosophy*, 15 (1998), pp. 462–477. For a taxonomy of conceptions of faith, though not related so much to the orthodox Christian faith, and how faith relates to belief and acceptance, see Robert Audi, "Belief, Faith, and Acceptance," *International Journal for Philosophy of Religion*, 63 (2008), pp. 87–102.

[66] Thomas J. J. Altizer and William Hamilton, *Radical Theology and the Death of God* (Indianapolis: The Bobbs-Merrill Company, Inc., 1966), p. 97.

[67] Cox, *The Feast of Fools*, p. 196.

writes without premises or a point of view. How to be aware of one's premises without being paralyzed by them remains one of the most persistent and fascinating problems with which any writer, theological or otherwise, must learn to contend."[68] It is in this spirit that I lay out the following philosophical assumptions on which I base my approach. I am a realist, ethically, epistemologically, and metaphysically. It is not my purpose to argue for these positions in this book. While as a philosopher I take skepticism seriously at every turn, I do not subscribe to strong forms of skepticism that are logically self-defeating, but rather to the Socratic attitude of continually doubting what I consider for possible acceptance. Epistemologically, I subscribe to a blend of coherentism and reliabilism.[69] Unlike some who deny the relevance and even utility of the laws of logic, I openly but not uncritically embrace them as philosophical advances in human knowledge. Logic and philosophical analysis, I believe, are the primary but not exclusive keys to human understanding, and this includes our understanding about the truth about the problem of God. They are the chief components of reason, which I assume shall be the primary arbiter of human discourse about the problem of God.

While my philosophical commitments are analytically mainstream, my theological commitments are minimalist. Since I was also trained in the Protestant Christian theological tradition, my entire discussion presupposes this framework of discussion. As an agnostic, I want to remain open to the possibility that "God exists" is true, or "It is not the case that God exists" is true. However, I do share some ideas in common with theological moderates and liberals within Christendom. First, I assume that the Christian scriptures are roughly accurate testimonials of some of the beliefs of some of the earliest followers of Jesus, though I do not grant special authority to them beyond that essential aim. I have insufficient reason to believe that these documents, utterly fascinating as they are to study, are divinely inspired, or have any special ethical, religious, or theological authority beyond that of revealing what some early Christians believed about matters of their religious faith. The balance of human reason at its best is a far better guide to ethics and truth than the contents of Christian scriptures.

Second, I assume with Boethius that, if God exists, God is omnibenevolent, but that God is also perfectly just and perfect truth. By this I mean that God would never do or support anything that is not good (I do not mean this in some utilitarian way), but that God always does or supports

---

[68]   Cox, *The Feast of Fools*, pp. 209–210.
[69]   Corlett, *Analyzing Social Knowledge*, Chapters 5–6.

the right thing under any circumstance. In other words, God is morally infallible. Moreover, I mean that God is always on the side of justice and righteousness, so that to know God is to do justice. That God is truth means that She does not accept any false beliefs, or as Aunt Ester in August Wilson's play, *Gem of the Ocean* exclaims, "God don't know nothing but the truth."[70] Furthermore, whatever can be known is known by God, excluding the future. God is not fallible, epistemically speaking, though Her knowledge is limited. I assume that the love of God is or can be made to cohere with these and other truths about God's nature and function in the world.

Another of my assumptions is that there are, in principle, correct all relevant things considered answers to the questions of whether or not God exists and the nature of God. Truth, though context-sensitive, is objective, though not absolute. Furthermore, reason must be our primary guide in approaching and resolving these difficulties. No amount of anti-intellectualism can continue to guide us. Nor can question-begging appeals to the authority of what is deemed by sectarian bias to be divine revelation serve to reveal the truth of the matters for us. If there is a God, then—as most religious people believe—God gave us reason and a brain in which to use it effectively. To refuse to use reason in attempting to understand God is to become derelict in one's religious and epistemic duties. It is time that religious folk own up to the fact that if God exists, then reason is one of Her many and several gifts to humans and some nonhumans. And reason is that primary means by which God is to be understood—even when consulting revelation! After all, revelation admits of interpretation, and that requires the judicious use of reason. Are we to insult God by not using reason, especially regarding the most important questions in life and death? Besides, reason might well be precisely that gift from God by which we can best understand Her, an instrument that can and ought to guide the emotional aspects of human being in the world. Thus a search for the truth about God without reason is a mistake waiting to happen. Indeed, it is a fideistic error that has left many a theist mired in confusion. While it may be true that reason without faith is incomplete, it is surely true that faith absent reason is shallow theology disguised as genuine religiosity!

So reason can and ought to guide religious folk in asking in prayer to God for only what is reasonable because God is reasonable. If God exists, She is not some genie who grants things to those who request them whether

---

[70] August Wilson, *Gem of the Ocean* (New York: Theatre Communications Group, 2006), p. 54.

or not the requests are reasonable. This is especially true in a world in which reason and religion are all too often alienated from one another, often resulting in unjust wars, mass suicides, monetary fraud, and the like. The careful and proper use of reason, I suggest, can often lead us to truth, justice, and the good. And if there is a God, God possesses at least these properties.

But what precisely *is* reasonable or the right thing to do or believe? This is where we can gain much assistance from Socrates, who in Plato's *Euthyphro*[71] reveals for many a startling truth about what later became known as the divine command theory. To paraphrase the passage: Is something right because God says it is right, or does God say something is right because it is right? In other words, who or what makes something the right thing to do? If God makes something right, then God could have simply declared that everyone ought to become what we would deem evil. What if, as the puritans, Catholics, and other European invaders of the Americas believed, God declared that the "savages" of the Americas be destroyed and their lands stolen in the name of the doctrine of discovery and manifest destiny? What if, as many of these same folk sincerely believed, God declared that African persons ought to be enslaved in order to build a New World? Would this make genocide and slavery the right things to do?

Socrates asks us to think deeply about this problem, concluding that God, being reasonable, could never make such pronouncements as that would run counter to reason. God's judgments must be reasonable, and the implication is that if we do not use reason we are unlikely to understand what God wants us to do. Reason is what reveals whether or not something is correct, and God cannot, being omnibenevolent and omniscient (though not in the strict sense), act contrary to reason and do the right thing. So if God is to act in and through us, we must also act according to reason. This rationalistic theology is not new. But it has important implications for those who believe that they are genuinely religious. This implies that moral obligation finds its source in what the balance of human reason dictates about this or that circumstance.

Richard Swinburne is incorrect, then, to state that "God is thus a source of moral obligation—his commands create moral obligations."[72] This is to misunderstand fundamentally the nature of moral obligation. If God exists,

---

[71] John M. Cooper and Hutchinson, Editors, *Plato: Complete Works* (Indianapolis: Hackett Publishing Company, 1997).

[72] Richard Swinburne, *Is There a God?* (Oxford: Oxford University Press, 1996), p. 15.

then God is or ought to be the source of *religious* obligations, should there be any. But in light of the failure of divine command theory, God's commands are verifically subject to moral standards that are discovered by way of reason. It is not, as Swinburne claims without supportive argument, that "some moral truths are moral truths quite independent of the will of God."[73] Rather, if Socrates is correct, then it is that all moral truths and obligations are that way.

With this rather concise list of presuppositions in mind, we can surge forward into a new discussion about the possibility of God's existence in analytical philosophy of religion. Further assumptions will be clarified as the discussion progresses and as they are relevant to certain points of argument or analysis. Assuming that many of the arguments of some leading atheists have posed serious and yet inadequately unanswered questions for orthodox Christian theism, my discussion continues the debate about God's existence with an analysis of atheism, followed by a refutation of it, followed by a discussion of the New Agnosticism, and ending with a statement and defense of my hybrid theism as a challenge to atheism.

Can theism withstand atheistic criticism? Can it be shielded from the "wolves of disbelief"[74]? Or, in the end, is atheism the most plausible position on the problem of God? Or, is there for the time being a more plausible, albeit tentative, position that serves as the inference to the best explanation about the most central theistic claim, "God exists"?

Part I of this book explores some of the many errors of atheism, while Part II discusses how the concept of God might be well-grounded in light of orthodox Christian theism's failure to provide an adequate foundation over the course of almost two centuries. In Part II, I graft some features of process and liberation theisms into a minimalist hybrid theism that evades the problems of orthodox Christian theism, posing a new challenge to atheism's claim that it is not the case that God exists, whether this claim is made explicitly or implicitly. The New Agnosticism employs this hybrid minimalist theism as a challenge to atheism and traditional Christian theism.

---

[73] Swinburne, *Is There a God?* p. 15.
[74] Nielsen, *Naturalism and Religion*, p. 14.

Part I

The Errors of Atheism

The man who wants to sow a fertile field must first clear the ground of brush, then cut out the ferns and brambles with his sharp hook, so that the new grain may grow abundantly.

—*Boethius*

Chapter 1

Analyzing Atheism

Definition is, therefore, essential here. But we need now to try to look at the long familiar words of standard definitions with fresh and foreign eyes, ready to notice any incongruities in the combination of the various elements that are there combined.

—Antony Flew[1]

In fact, "atheism" is a rather elusive concept in the history of Western thought—more something of which one has been accused than a mantle proudly assumed.

—Steve Fuller[2]

In light of the recent history of the debate about God's existence, atheism has received a great deal of attention. While a cadre of popular authors contributes to what is often called "the new atheism,"[3] my primary focus shall be on philosophical atheism. But as the above epigraph from Antony Flew urges, definitions of key categories are crucial in getting to the truth of the matter about God's possible existence. So it is important to be clear about the precise natures of atheism, theism, and agnosticism, especially since the majority of those involved in the discussion concerning the problem of God seem to function under the explicit or implicit assumption that the only viable contenders for our assent are theism of a particular sort and its denial.

In analyzing atheism, it is important to bear in mind a distinction between at least the following two questions: "What is atheism?" and "What is adequately justified atheism?" The first question, of course, concerns the nature of atheism itself, while the second concern is one of justification. While these questions are separable, it is significant that they are also mutually dependent. For the question of justification depends on adequate conceptions of the

---

[1] Antony Flew, *Atheism and Humanism* (Buffalo: Prometheus Books, 1993), p. 23.

[2] Steve Fuller, *Science vs. Religion* (Cambridge: Polity, 2007), p. 25.

[3] Some of the critics of the new atheism include Tina Beattie, *The New Atheists* (Maryknoll: Orbis, 2007); John Cornwell, *Darwin's Angel* (London: Profile Books, 2007); John F. Haught, *God and the New Atheism* (Louisville: Westminster John Knox Press, 2008); Kathleen Jones, *Challenging Richard Dawkins* (Norwich: Canterbury Press, 2007); Keith Ward, *Is Religion Dangerous?* (Oxford: Lion Hudson, 2006).

nature of atheism, and vice-versa. It is also true that an adequate definition of "atheism" depends on adequate definitions of "theism" and "agnosticism," respectively. As we shall see, mistakes in the construal of one category lead to errors in how the others are portrayed.

Generally, I follow tradition in defining "theism" as the view that "God exists," and "atheism" as the position that "It is not the case that God exists." This is consistent, of course, with the idea that "A person is an atheist . . . if he adopts an attitude of rejection toward all three theistic positions . . .—belief in a metaphysical God, in an infinite anthropomorphic God, and in a finite anthropomorphic God."[4] Yet in no case is "theism" to be construed solely in supernaturalistic terms as so many seem to assume or claim without supportive argument. For while orthodox Christian theists concur with the idea that "Regard for the correct usage of the term requires that religion be defined in such a way as to include supernaturalistic belief,"[5] an entire history of panentheistic thought[6] holds roughly that "the best religion must inevitably become increasingly finite, i.e., restricted in scope and limited in function"[7] and that a century ago it was urged that "few men, if any, can honestly deny that in some sense the supernatural is passing."[8] Indeed, naturalistic theism is not just the idea of certain contemporary theologians, but of a history of philosophical and theological thought.[9]

Naturalistic theism, as I use the category, is theism that makes no reference to the supernatural in explaining anything—even the nature and function of God. It employs the sciences and reason to account for all of

----

[4] Paul Edwards, "Atheism," in Paul Edwards, Editor-in-Chief, *The Encyclopedia of Philosophy*, Volume 1, Reprint Edition (New York: Macmillan Publishing Co., & The Free Press, 1972), p. 176.

[5] W. R. Wells, "Is Supernaturalistic Belief Essential in a Definition of Religion?" *The Journal of Philosophy*, 18 (1921), p. 275.

[6] John W. Cooper, *Panentheism: The Other God of the Philosophers* (Grand Rapids: Baker Academic, 2006).

[7] H. C. Ackerman, "The Differentiating Principle of Religion," *The Journal of Philosophy*, 19 (1922), p. 320.

[8] A. H. Lloyd, "The Passing of the Supernatural," *The Journal of Philosophy, Psychology, and Scientific Methods*, 7 (1910), pp. 533–534. A. H. Lloyd also states: "So the supernatural is passing and the religion of the future must do without it, but also the supernatural still lives, being reborn in the human and natural. The supernatural is becoming immanent in the natural and is inspiring or animating the natural with unlimited freedom and possibility" (p. 550).

[9] For arguments in favor of the idea that a supernaturalistic theism must give way to a naturalistic one, see G. Fulmer, "The Concept of the Supernatural," *Analysis*, 37 (1977), pp. 113–116.

reality, recognizing the fallibility of each method of inquiry. It is, as we shall see in Chapter 5, panentheistic. But it also employs reason-based ethics to explain the political and moral dimension of justice and fairness. Much more will be made of this notion in Part II.

Thus atheism is properly understood as the logical denial of theism, just as theism is the logical denial of atheism. One important benefit of construing these categories in this way is that it avoids conceptual confusion about what theism and atheism amount to, and it does not somehow minimize or rule out agnosticism in some self-serving theistic or atheistic manner.

While atheism accepts the claim that it is not the case that God exists, and theism accepts the logical denial of the atheistic claim, and vice-versa, agnosticism accepts neither of the claims of these positions. But this rather general construal of these categories requires more explicit taxonomical precision.

A Taxonomy of Approaches to the Problem of God

There is much confusion regarding the understanding of the concepts of theism, atheism, and agnosticism. Until there is conceptual clarity along these lines, there will remain much lost in the very important discussion about whether or not God exists. One of several such examples is found in the following words: "Eighteenth century deism subjected any conception of transcendence so exhaustively to the control of reason that the distinction between immanence and transcendence lost much of its meaning. In so doing they inevitably paved the way to atheism."[10] However, one problem with this statement is that it makes the issue of transcendence the defining feature of theism, which it is not, at least not without careful qualification. For there are theisms without transcendent notions of God, and they do not lead to atheism as the above words claim.

Thus it is important that when we discuss the problem of God's existence that we are clear about precisely which views are being discussed in light of their complexities. This requires a taxonomy of views about the existence of God.

First, there are ontological versions of theism, atheism, and agnosticism. In its strong form, *ontological theism* states that God exists, while its weaker version holds that it is possible that God exists. Note that the

---

[10] Louis Dupré, "On the Intellectual Sources of Modern Atheism," *International Journal for Philosophy of Religion*, 45 (1999), p. 4.

strong version of theism logically entails the weaker one, but not vice-versa. For one cannot hold that God exists without also affirming the possibility of God's existence, while one might hold that it is possible that God exists without also affirming that God exists.

Ontological atheism, on the other hand, denies the truth of the claims of ontological theism. In its weak form, it states that it is not the case that God exists, and its strong form holds that it is not the case that God's existence is even possible. As with strong and weak versions of ontological theism, the strong version of ontological atheism logically entails the weaker one, but not vice-versa. For one cannot hold that God's existence is not even possible without also denying that God exists, while one might deny that God exists without denying the possibility of God's existence.

Ontological agnosticism, in its positive version, states that it is probable that God exists, while its negative version states that it is probable that it is not the case that God exists. The ontological agnostic claims that there is insufficient reason to affirm or deny with certitude (at least for the time being and lacking further evidence) either theism or atheism, all relevant things considered. It is a stance adopted by an agnostic who understands that the opposite sets of evidence offered by theism (on the one hand) and atheism (on the other) might well turn out to be incomparable and leave one in a state of being unjustified in accepting the claims of either theism or atheism.

Whereas ontological theism and atheism each have weak and strong versions, ontological agnosticism admits of a wide array of versions contingent on the extent to which the ontological agnostic believes, fallibilistically, that there is a probability of it being true that God exists. One might, then, be an ontological agnostic strongly, moderately, or weakly. A strong positive ontological agnostic might accept the claim that "It is (highly) probable that God exists"; a strong negative ontological agnostic might accept the claim that "It is (highly) improbable that God exists"; a weak positive ontological agnostic might state that "It is somewhat probable that God exists"; a weak negative ontological agnostic might claim that "It is somewhat improbable that God exists"; a moderate positive ontological agnostic might claim that "It is more or less probable that God exists"; while a moderate negative ontological agnostic might claim that "It is more or less probable that God does not exist." Under no circumstance would an ontological agnostic affirm belief or disbelief in God's existence *per se*. Thus the categorical difference between agnostics and theists, on the one hand, and atheists, on the other.

Moreover, there is *epistemological theism*, according to which one knows that God exists (strong version), or that one knows that it is possible that God exists (weak version). A justificatory species of epistemological theism states that I am justified in accepting the belief, "God exists."[11] By "justification" and its cognates is meant that one has and can supply reasons for her belief, reasons that, on balance, objectively outweigh the denial of her belief.[12] As Richard Swinburne argues, "When beliefs are true and well justified, they constitute knowledge."[13] Contemporary orthodox Christian theists tend to be either foundationalists[14] or coherentists[15] insofar as the justification of theistic belief is concerned.

Moreover, *epistemological atheism* states that one knows that it is not the case that God exists (weak version), or one knows that it is not the case that God's existence is even possible or that God can exist (strong version). The reason the latter atheism is stronger than the former one is that the weaker version allows for the possibility that God did at one time exist or might exist at some time in the future, but does not now exist. As with the theistic version of this position, there is a justificatory species which holds that I am justified in accepting the proposition, "It is not the case that God exists."

Epistemological agnosticism, on the other hand, holds that I know neither that "God exists" nor its denial, nor that "It is possible that God exists," nor its denial. And there is a positive version of epistemological agnosticism according to which it is justified to affirm the claims of both strong epistemological theism and strong epistemological atheism, or both weak versions of these epistemic views. And the justificatory kind of epistemological agnosticism states that I am justified in accepting either that "God exists," or its denial, or that "It is possible that God exists," or

---

[11] There is a doxastic version of epistemological theism according to which one simply believes in God. But this seems to amount to a version of ontological theism without epistemological foundations (pure faith without reason). And there is also a verific version of epistemological theism that states that "God exists" or "God is possible." But without the justificatory element, this verific version amounts to an ontological theism. Similar points can be made of atheism and agnosticism.

[12] This reason-giving conception of justification is found in Lehrer, *Theory of Knowledge*, 2nd Edition (Boulder: Westview Press, 2000). A hybrid reason-giving and non-reason-giving conception of epistemic justification is found in J. Angelo Corlett, *Analyzing Social Knowledge* (Totowa: Rowman & Littlefield Publishers, 1996), Chapter 4.

[13] Richard Swinburne, *Is There a God?* (Oxford: Oxford University Press, 1996), p. 5.

[14] Alvin Plantinga, *Warranted Christian Belief* (Oxford: Oxford University Press, 2000).

[15] Richard Swinburne, *The Coherence of Theism* (Oxford: Clarendon Press, 1977).

its denial. Each of these views holds that we can know whether or not there is a God. The theist affirms it, the atheist denies it, and the agnostic believes that in light of the available evidence, she simply does not know.[16]

Implicit in all forms of agnosticism is the probability of God's existence or nonexistence, making agnostic any position short of an affirmation or denial of God's existence. Thus it is agnostic to affirm that it is probable that God exists, or that it is probable that God does not exist. This is what separates agnosticism from theism and atheism, properly construed. Self-described atheists or theists who cast their positions in terms of probabilities are conceptually confused. If either position could be legitimately defined in terms of the probability of God's existence, then the category of agnosticism would rightly be eliminated. But then so would theism and atheism as each would become blended with the other in terms of a wide range of belief/unbelief based on probabilities. The result would be conceptual muddlement and there would be no way of nonarbitrarily distinguishing between theism, atheism, and agnosticism.

So there are at least two questions that must be carefully distinguished here. One is the ontological question of whether or not God exists or is possible. Another is the epistemological question of the extent to which God's existence is or can be known or justified. Yet another question is the iterative one, namely, how does one know that one knows God exists or can exist. But this latter question seems less important for our primarily ontological purposes of whether or not God exists, and so will be set aside. For if the answer to the other questions is negative and ends in atheism, then the iterative question becomes irrelevant, ontologically speaking.

Furthermore, it is crucial to understand that God can exist without one's knowing that God exists, though one cannot know God exists without God existing. In answering the epistemological question, then, we must understand that the discussion of the epistemic coherence of theism, atheism, and agnosticism is much more complicated than one might think.

---

[16] A general point similar to this is made by Russell in Al Seckel, Editor, *Bertrand Russell on God and Religion* (New York: Prometheus Books, 1986), p. 73. I make this point to draw the reader's attention to the fact that my taxonomy of positions on God's existence is consistent with Russell's agnosticism in the sense that it preserves Russell's position as what he stated it to be: agnostic. Also see, Bertrand Russell, *Why I am Not a Christian*, Paul Edwards, Editor (New York: Simon and Schuster, 1957).

There are different coherence theories of epistemic justification.[17] I shall employ the one advanced by Keith Lehrer, and use it as a measurement by which theism, atheism, and agnosticism might be assessed. Rather than succumb to the regress argument to which fallibilistic or unfallibilistic foundationalisms fall prey, Lehrer's complex version of coherentism divides justification into two kinds: personal and complete. While personal justification requires only that one accept a belief that accords well with the beliefs already in one's own doxastic system, complete justification requires the objective element of having one's beliefs be true, thus accepting into one's own doxastic system those beliefs that are coherent with the true beliefs in one's system. This is facilitated by the presence of a keystone belief regarding one's trustworthiness. To the extent that one can trust oneself epistemically and cognitively, one can justify the beliefs in one's doxastic system by some set of beliefs each of which is true and each of which is linked to the keystone belief of self-trust. Thus the infinite regress facing foundationalisms is avoided and doxastic coherence evades the charge that competing coherent systems make coherence insufficient for human propositional knowledge. Also crucial to Lehrer's coherentism is the idea that what one accepts as true must "match" the way the real world is, thus avoiding the problem that coherence is unnecessary for knowledge.[18] Lehrer's epistemology is helpful in understanding the extent to which atheism, theism, or agnosticism are justified, not merely within themselves, but in accordance with the way the world is.

It is important to understand that there are a variety of ways in which these ontological and epistemological views might be combined or distinguished. For instance, one might be an ontological theist but not an epistemological theist. That is, she might assert that God exists, but not believe that she has (or that there is) sufficient warrant to demonstrate her justification for her belief. This view is a species of "fideism." It states that where reason ends and cannot take us any further toward an answer to the problem of God's existence, faith must complete the journey. Of course, one can hardly be an epistemological theist and hold that she is able to provide sufficiently good reasons for the existence of God without also being an ontological theist. But the most respectable theistic position, philosophically at any rate, is the one that is both ontological and epistemological: that one believes one has sufficiently good reasons to ground her belief in the existence of God.

---

[17] W. V. O. Quine, *The Web of Belief* (New York: Random House, 1978).
[18] Lehrer, *Theory of Knowledge*, Chapters 6–7.

As far as atheism is concerned, one might be an ontological atheist while not being an epistemological atheist, holding, in effect, that it is not the case that God exists but without proper warrant for doing so. If fideism is dogmatic insofar as it places faith in God over reason, so too is "anti-fideism" insofar as it dogmatically avers that God does not exist even though there is insufficient reason to do so. One cannot be an epistemological atheist without also being an ontological one. And the most respected form of atheism is one which is both epistemological and ontological: that one believes that she has sufficiently good reason to hold that it is not the case that God exists, and indeed accepts this proposition. But even here there are variations as there are deductive and inductive ways to be an atheist.

The agnostic might be one who out of faith is unsure of the existence or possibility of God, but not because of the evidence she has or does not have. Rather, it is in a sense an article of faith that she is an agnostic. This is certainly not the meaning of the New Agnosticism. On the other hand, an agnostic is hardly one who is an epistemological agnostic while at the same time she might not be an ontological one. And just as with her theistic and atheistic counterparts, the New Agnosticism is one that believes that the evidence for and against the existence or possibility of God is such that she can neither affirm nor deny theistic belief. In fact, this is what drives the New Agnostic to seek the deeper truth about whether or not God exists, by examining and reexamining alternative theisms and their plausibility statuses. Much more is devoted to the New Agnosticism in Chapter 4.

As noted previously, just as theism entails the claim that "God exists," atheism finds itself in denial of this claim. In other words, atheism accepts "It is not the case that God exists." But just as there is a weaker version of theism that holds to the mere possibility of God's existence, or "It is possible that God exists," there is a stronger version of atheism that denies even this humble claim. Strong atheism accepts the claim that "It is not the case that it is possible that God exists," or "It is impossible that there is a God." Part of my focus of criticism has been, of course, on the version of theism which accepts the actual, not merely the possible, existence of God. In the end, I shall arrive at an acceptance of the claim of agnosticism as the one view that deserves our acceptance. For strong theism's claim that God exists is highly problematic in the traditional Christian sense, and alternative conceptions of the nature and function of God, though more plausible than that traditional Christian idea of God, require additional examination before they can be made sufficiently reasonable for rational acceptance.

In Chapters 5–6, I shall provide a challenge to atheism that renders it problematic as a viable solution to the problem of God.[19] By this I do not mean that it will be rendered dubious in a permanent way. Rather, it is that, given certain factors, atheism worthy of the name cannot claim to be well-grounded unless and until certain theistic issues are adequately addressed. In the meantime, I shall clarify the major categories under discussion.

Analyzing Atheism

Consider an argument proffered by a self-described atheist. After refuting the various arguments for the conception of God of traditional Christian theism, and after clarifying that he only intends to address that very notion of the nature of God, Nicholas Everitt states:

> . . . the defining attributes of God are either individually self-contradictory (omnipotence) or cannot be coinstantiated (omniscience and omnipotence, omniscience and eternity, eternity and personhood, eternity and creatorship, etc.). It thus follows that not only does God not exist, he *cannot* exist. For ignorant agnostics who unthinkingly proclaim that it is impossible to prove or disprove the existence of God, here is a putative set of disproofs.[20]

But the haughtiness of Everitt's atheism turns to embarrassment when it is pointed out both that Bertrand Russell (hardly "ignorant," as Everitt implies) was an agnostic because he believed that he could not disprove the existence of God,[21] and from the supposition that traditional Christian theism is badly flawed it surely fails to follow without further argument "that not only does God not exist, he cannot exist." Yet it is precisely this

---

[19] In Chapter 4, I shall provide a more detailed taxonomy of positions relative to the problem of God in an effort to distinguish the New Agnosticism from other views.

[20] Nicholas Everitt, *The Non-Existence of God* (London: Routledge, 2004), p. 303. See also: ". . . on balance, the empirical evidence tells against theism; . . . theism is an ultimately self-contradictory doctrine" (p. 304). Further: ". . . the balance comes down heavily against theism. Overall, there are good reasons for thinking that theism can be *proved* false; and even if those reasons are found not to be compelling, overall there are further good empirical grounds for the falsity of theism" (p. 305). This latter claim, of course, contradicts Bertrand Russell's reason why he is an agnostic instead of an atheist, namely, because he is unable to disprove the existence of God (see the next chapter).

[21] See Chapter 3 of this book.

kind of arrogant and erroneous reasoning that motivates so many atheists, past and present, to declare victory over theism.[22] As David Ray Griffin notes:

> Most anti-theistic philosophies of religion are directed against traditional [Christian] theism. Although their exponents often give the impression that they have shown *all* "belief in God" to be irrational, they seldom devote serious attention to any of the revisionary forms of theism. Much that passes for "philosophy of religion" in the contemporary scene, therefore, consists simply of arguments for or against the truth of traditional Christian theism.[23]

One of Griffin's goals as a process philosopher-theologian of religion is to show that "(nonsupernaturalistic) theistic explanations are not necessarily excluded from the academic study of religion."[24] However, this is a rather weak claim. It is not, contrary to Griffin, simply that nonsupernaturalistic (or naturalistic) theisms should not necessarily be excluded from philosophy of religion. Rather, it is that they are conceptually superior to at least orthodox Christian theism, which in its supernaturalistic hyperbole, commits the theist to numerous dubious and false assertions. This atheistic

---

[22]   Another example of a contemporary atheist whose argument for atheism rests exclusively on the refutation of traditional Christian theology is found in Michael Martin, *Atheism, Morality, and Meaning* (Amherst: Prometheus Books, 2002). Also see the bulk of the writings in Michael Martin, Editor, *The Cambridge Companion to Atheism* (Cambridge: Cambridge University Press, 2006) for a collection of articles that does not seriously delve into alternative theisms before proclaiming the soundness of atheism.

[23]   David Ray Griffin, *Reenchantment without Supernaturalism* (Ithaca: Cornell University Press, 2001), pp. 8–9. While David Ray Griffin's point here is similar to my argument that atheism's attack on theism is sufficient, at best, to justify a refutation of orthodox Christian theism, my point goes beyond his in various respects. First, I challenge atheism directly and point to its conglomeration of errors in reasoning about God. Second, I in no way seek to defend any particular version of Christian theism, but rather to investigate a minimalist notion of theism more generally. Third, in my appropriation of some of the basics of process thought, I do not adopt many of the more robust notions that Griffin does in his revision of Christian orthodoxy. Thus while his is rightly categorized as a revisionist position of orthodox Christian theism, mine is an unorthodox view of theism more generally. Nonetheless, while my hybrid minimalist process-liberationist theism is better termed "unorthodox" rather than revisionistic, there is much about Griffin's revisionist Christian theism that is consistent with my hybrid minimalist theism.

[24]   Griffin, *Reenchantment without Supernaturalism*, p. 18.

(on the one hand) and traditional Christian theistic (on the other hand) mode of inquiry makes the current state of affairs in analytical philosophy of religion mostly parochial. Because of this, I challenge atheism's implied or explicit claim that it is not the case that God exists, as such a claim seems to be based on an inadequate number of "samples" of theism refuted, or rendered dubious. And this challenge succeeds also against the probabilistic kinds of "atheism" that have emerged. For how can one claim with high probability that it is not the case that God exists if only a paucity of theistic samples are tested and found wanting?[25]

Furthermore, it is of interest to note that the atheist wants us to succumb to a sort of bifurcation fallacy that is related to the fallacy of hasty conclusion mentioned in the previous paragraph: Either the God of orthodox Christian theism (replete with maximal and hyperbolic attributes) is sound, or there is no God. And the admission of atheists (such as Everitt) that there may be more plausible conceptions of God than that found in traditional Christian theism does not suffice to rescue this kind of atheist from the logical error to which her argument falls prey. One might concur with Everitt's arguments against traditional Christian theism, yet not be logically entitled to or epistemically justified (in a strong or robust sense) in embracing atheism. This is true especially since Everitt only hints at certain suggestive ways in which traditional Christian theism might be revised to evade atheistic concerns, but never explores them.[26] His failure to explore these possibilities leaves one with the impression that Everitt's atheism is, like so many others in the West, presumptuous and superficial. Everitt's discussion focuses mainly on the traditional Christian *apologia* of Alvin Plantinga and Richard Swinburne, respectively. While this is understandable because these two philosophers have done more than others in recent years from within the analytical philosophical tradition to defend philosophically various of the traditional Christian ideas of God, both Everitt's discussion and his bibliography demonstrate that he is unaware of the writings of, for example, process theists who attempt to address each of the atheistic concerns with the traditional Christian doctrine of God. Until Everitt takes such theologies as seriously as he has taken the works of Plantinga and Swinburne, he is at best only minimally justified in concluding that his strong version of atheism is sound. That is, he is merely

---

[25] In Chapter 3, I shall expose Richard Dawkins' commission of this particular atheistic fallacy. So the treatment of the complexities of those errors is deferred until then.

[26] Everitt, *The Non-Existence of God*, pp. 268, 300, 305.

personally or subjectively justified. By that is meant, per the epistemology of Lehrer, that Everitt is personally justified in light of the evidence that he currently possesses. But this is only one (necessary, but insufficient) element of full justification and knowledge.[27] Since Everitt has given us no indication that he is even familiar with competing and alternative theisms, we can rightly assume that his justificatory base for grounding his assessment of theism and acceptance of atheism is inadequate (or, perhaps to borrow Everitt's own description of agnostics, "ignorant"). Indeed, besides nontraditional Christian theologies, there may be other, say, Eastern theologies that have conceptions of God worthy of the name "theism" that evade atheistic objections. And some or all of these theologies may work with a viable notion of divinity so as to avoid mere verbal disputation.

Precisely how does it follow from the fact that some beliefs held by traditional Christians may be nonsensical that the very notion of God cannot be made reasonable? But is this not precisely what the atheists assert in claiming that "there is no God" or "It is not the case that God exists"? In refuting a certain notion of God, they apparently think that it follows logically from this point that no conception of God is reasonable to accept. Otherwise, they would not be atheists who by proper definition accept the claim that "It is not the case that God exists," but agnostics who as a matter of principle leave open the possibility or probability of the existence of God for whatever reasons. At most, the atheists in question could claim to be atheists *relative to orthodox Christian theism*. It is epistemically irresponsible[28] for atheists like Everitt, Kai Nielsen, J. L. Mackie, and Flew to describe themselves without qualification as atheists when the most they can claim, for all they have argued, is that orthodox Christian theism is implausible. In short, they are at best partially justified in accepting the general atheistic position. But they are hardly robustly justified in doing so.

Now atheism worthy of the name might be a reasonable inference had "atheists" such as Everitt actually examined alternative notions of God and demonstrated through reason that they too are implausible. But Everitt demonstrates the same kind of carelessness in reasoning. He simply assumes (perhaps out of a Western bias that if traditional Christian beliefs about God are unsound, then surely unorthodox or non-Western theisms cannot fare any better) that a defeat of the notion of the traditional Christian idea

---

[27] For a complete analysis of Lehrer's coherentist analysis of knowledge, see Lehrer, *Theory of Knowledge*, Chapters 5–6.

[28] For an analysis of the concept of epistemic responsibility, see J. Angelo Corlett, "Epistemic Responsibility," *The International Journal of Philosophical Studies*, 16 (2008), pp. 179–200.

of God implies the plausibility of atheism. Or, perhaps it is because of the double-duping by orthodox Christian theism: Not only has it duped many millions to believe in its brand of theism, but it has also duped many atheists into believing that orthodox Christian theism is the only theism worth addressing, or at least the only version of theism worthy of the name! A notable example here is Mackie, whose atheism amounts to a kind of probability claim to the effect that the "balancing of probabilities" favors atheism over the God hypothesis:

> This conclusion can be reached by an examination precisely of the arguments advanced in favour of theism, without even bringing into play what have been regarded as the strongest considerations on the other side, the problem of evil and the various natural histories of religion . . . the extreme difficulty that theism has in reconciling *its own* doctrines with one another in this respect must tell heavily against it. . . . The balance of probabilities . . . comes out strongly against the existence of a god.[29]

Thus Mackie is an atheist who commits one of the errors of atheism in thinking that the refutation of traditional Christian theism logically and epistemically entitles him to adopt even a probabilistic version of atheism. In the end, probabilistic statements about God's existence relative to, say, orthodox Christian theism, are really versions of agnosticism as "atheism" implies that no concept of God worthy of the name "God" is viable.

But even if probabilistic notions of atheism were legitimate kinds of atheism, they are deeply problematic in that the number of theisms refuted by atheists is so few that the most they can establish (given the number of theisms available) is that a small percentage of them are implausible, making the probability of atheism rather low unless and until numerous other theisms are rendered implausible. Thus the probabilistic notion of atheism is not only confused conceptually because it conflates itself with agnosticism or fails to adequately distinguish itself from it in a non-question-begging way, but it is also poorly supported by the evidence of argumentation about God's existence.

Clearly the most notable living atheist philosopher is Nielsen. Unlike Flew whose empirical falsification theory[30] has been criticized as being

---

29 J. L. Mackie, *The Miracle of Theism* (Oxford: Oxford University Press, 1982), p. 253.

30 Antony Flew, *The Presumption of Atheism* (Buffalo: Prometheus Books, 1976).

insufficiently grounded by supportive and independent argument,[31] Nielsen adopts a verification theory[32] to support his brand of atheism and to criticize orthodox theism. Although other critics of theism mentioned above focus their primary attention on the core doctrines of traditional Christian, Judaic, and Islamic theisms, Nielsen seeks to address his concerns to traditional theism as a whole, though he does spend some energy and time on nontraditional forms of belief in the existence of God.

Nonetheless, Nielsen's conception of atheism is a bit confusing. While he distinguishes his own atheism from the "militant" brand that dogmatically asserts with *certitude* that "theism is either false or incoherent," he also claims that the naturalist is not an agnostic.[33] This is puzzling since atheism clearly is the position that it is not the case that God exists, while agnosticism, properly construed, can and does hold that it is uncertain that theism is false or incoherent, wherein the notion of uncertainty captures probabilistic ideas of God's existence. Moreover, Nielsen wants to insist that atheism holds that "theism is either false or incoherent or in some other way unbelievable."[34] But it is unclear what the issue of certitude from the previous quotation from Nielsen has to do with the classification of atheisms, as all the while Nielsen affirms a kind of epistemic fallibilism. Moreover, according to Nielsen, agnostics believe that "we do not know, or perhaps even cannot know, whether or not God does or does not exist."[35]

However, there are problems with Nielsen's construal of agnosticism. First, there are different kinds of agnosticism, just as there are different kinds of atheism and theism, respectively. There are, for example, ontological and epistemological versions of each, as have been noted above and explicated in Chapter 4. Nielsen needs to clarify to which kind of agnosticism (as well as theism and atheism) he refers in order to adequately ground his point.

Second, Nielsen's imputing to agnostics both the descriptively epistemic claim that "we do not know" whether or not God exists *and* the categorical epistemic claim that we "cannot know" whether or not God exists is confused. These are two very different claims. As such, this conflation amounts to a fallacy of equivocation. While I as an agnostic can and do

---

[31] Kai Nielsen, *Philosophy & Atheism* (Buffalo: Prometheus Books, 1985), Chapter 7.

[32] Kai Nielsen, *Naturalism and Religion* (Buffalo: Prometheus Books, 2001), pp. 470f.

[33] Nielsen, *Naturalism and Religion*, p. 30.

[34] Nielsen, *Naturalism and Religion*, p. 30.

[35] Nielsen, *Naturalism and Religion*, p. 30.

without confusion or conceptual absurdity accept the former, it is the latter claim that, according to Russell, is precisely why the agnostic is not an atheist. Nielsen owes us an explanation as to how the agnostic *qua agnostic* cannot know that God, most plausibly construed, does or does not exist. Otherwise, he uncharitably imputes to agnostics an unacceptable position, epistemically speaking. Thus as many other atheists, Nielsen is playing fast and loose with the categories of "atheism," "theism," and "agnosticism," and to the rhetorical advantage of atheism.

Some leading atheists seem to recognize at some level that atheism is inadequately grounded. So they employ the ploy of redefining "atheism" in terms of agnosticism, or a strong version of agnosticism, to make it seem to the unsuspecting reader that they are atheists when they are not true atheists. But a more careful study of atheistic categorizations reveals that atheism is not adequately justified, and that it cannot justify itself by wittingly or unwittingly co-opting some version of agnosticism, properly construed, in order to confuse others into accepting atheism, improperly construed.

While Nielsen is correct to note that there are dogmatic and nondogmatic expressions of atheism (the same is true of theism and agnosticism, I would add), this does not imply that atheism can be legitimately construed as a form of agnosticism, as we will explore in Chapter 4. That is, any atheism that would assert as its main reason for its position that theism is uncertain is indistinguishable from agnosticism worthy of the name, and hence is misled or confused. Indeed, atheism itself, for all Nielsen's discussion of error theory, is confused and as such "rooted in massive error," a charge Nielsen himself levels against theism.[36]

To his credit, Nielsen recognizes that "the dividing line between atheism and agnosticism is not sharp."[37] And he goes on to describe the atheist as:

> Someone who rejects belief in God either (a) because she believes that it is false or highly unlikely that God exists, (b) believes that the concept of God is incoherent or so problematic as to make such belief impossible or irrational, or (c) because she believes that the term "God" is being used in such a manner that it is so devoid of substance as to make religious belief, rhetorical effects aside, indistinguishable from purely secular beliefs except for the fact that religious beliefs are associated with certain religiously distinctive stories which in turn are stories which (on such an account) the religious believer, though she must entertain them in a vivid and lively way, may or may not believe. . . . The kind of atheist I am rejects (i) anthropomorphic conceptions

---

[36] Nielsen, *Naturalism and Religion*, p. 50.
[37] Nielsen, *Naturalism and Religion*, p. 56.

of God on the basis of (a), (ii) belief in the God of Developed Judaism, Christ-
ianity, or Islam on the basis of (b), and (iii) purely symbolic conceptions of
God such as Richard Braithwaite's and R. M. Hare's on the basis of (c).
(Nielsen 1985, 9–13)[38]

However, the probabilistic phrase "highly unlikely that God exists" in (a)
misconstrues atheism as a kind of agnosticism. Again, as an agnostic,
I hold without conceptual embarrassment that it is unlikely, highly or
otherwise, that God exists. Thus this part of Nielsen's definition of "atheism" is misleading, if not false, though he is correct to state that atheism
holds that it is false that God exists, which is equivalent to my characterization of atheism as claiming that "It is not the case that God exists." Thus
Nielsen again seems to commit a fallacy of equivocation in conflating
atheism and agnosticism. Simply put, atheists cannot win the debate about
God by appending agnosticism to atheism and thereby declaring victory
whenever one form of hyperbolic theism is rendered highly dubious. For it
might well be the case that atheism, properly construed, is also indefensible, thereby making agnosticism the most plausible position, *ceterus
paribus* and for the time being.
     But Nielsen and Mackie are not the only self-proclaimed atheists who
are confused about the nature of atheism. Following John Gaskin's definition of "atheism," Flew characterizes atheism in terms of a three-fold
notion of "comprehensive unbelief":

> First comes "lack of belief in supernatural agents—God, gods, demons, or
> any abstraction intended as a substitute for these, for example, Tillich's
> 'ground of our being.'" Next is "lack of belief in miracles, interventions in
> the natural order by supernatural agents." And the third is "lack of belief in
> a future state, in the continuance of any individual person after that person's
> real bodily death."[39]

I concur that this three-fold characterization of atheism is generally comprehensive. The locution "lack of belief" throughout Flew's description of
atheism is captured well by my locution "It is not the case that," making
the first element of Flew's construal of atheism equivalent to mine.
     But there are difficulties with Flew's notion of atheism. Flew dismisses
but fails to refute unorthodox conceptions of divinity such as Paul Tillich's.
In doing so, Flew's "defeasible" "atheistic humanism" does not provide

---

[38] Nielsen, *Naturalism and Religion*, pp. 56–57.
[39] Flew, *Atheistic Humanism*, pp. 17–18.

any reason whatsoever for disbelief in unorthodox theisms, of which there are some well-respected varieties. Furthermore, Flew's notion of atheism need not be as comprehensive as it is. For one might be an atheist and yet believe in "interventions in the natural order by supernatural agents," but not agents as defined hyperbolically as in orthodox Christian theism. Indeed, this is the burden of the final chapters of this book, namely, to explain via my hybrid minimalist theism how divine (though not super-natural in the traditional theistic sense) forces can influence the workings of the world. If my strategy is plausible, then this implies that Flew's notion of comprehensive unbelief requires too much of the atheist. All the atheist needs to establish is that it is not the case that God (properly construed) exists. For these reasons, I believe Flew's notion of atheism to be overly strong and is rejected for purposes of determining the overall plausibility of atheism.

Nielsen's atheism is grounded in his naturalism,[40] according to which "all forms of supernaturalism" are rejected,[41] and which "denies that there are any spiritual or supernatural realities."[42] In other words, there are "no purely mental substances and there are no supernatural realities transcendent to the world or at least we have no sound grounds for believing that there could be such realities."[43]

It would be a mistake, however, to think that Nielsen's naturalism embodies either scientism, eliminativism, or reductionism. For his is a naturalism that also rejects the metaphysical individualism of physicalism as "social relations are partly constitutive of what it means to be a human being."[44] Nielsen rejects by implication, it appears, methodological individualism as a metaphysical doctrine. But he also rejects scientism which holds that science has a privileged position in our inquiries about reality. Whereas scientism asserts that "what science cannot tell us humankind cannot know," Nielsen rejects this scientific dogma,[45] seeking to avoid all kinds of metaphysical dogmas, both religious and scientific:

> Talk of the one correct explanation of the world or of science (or anything else) telling us what "ultimate reality" is like or what human beings really

---

[40]   As Nielsen states, "Naturalism, where consistent, is an atheism" (Nielsen, *Naturalism and Religion*, p. 30).

[41]   Nielsen, *Naturalism and Religion*, p. 57.

[42]   Nielsen, *Naturalism and Religion*, p. 29.

[43]   Nielsen, *Naturalism and Religion*, p. 29. Also see p. 30.

[44]   Nielsen, *Naturalism and Religion*, p. 57.

[45]   Nielsen, *Naturalism and Religion*, p. 57.

are—to say nothing of providing a "final theory"—is scientific mythology and not a rational activity continuous with science. Reductionist, eliminativist, or functionalist physicalism is not part of science or even continuous with science. Rather we have with them an activity coming up with metaphysical pictures that are without rational warrant.[46]

Instead, Nielsen's is a "social naturalism," which is for him a fallibilistic atheism or agnosticism.[47] Yet it is this latter claim that is problematic insofar as it broadly characterizes his position as fallibilistically atheistic or agnostic. It makes a great difference whether a position is atheistic, on the one hand, or agnostic, on the other. And for Nielsen to refer to his own position as fallibilistically atheistic seems to concede to the theist that atheism might be incorrect.

Epistemically, the element of fallibilism is already implied in each of the positions under discussion. Thus it is either redundant or misleading to refer without clarification to atheism as being fallibilistic. Again, I as an agnostic can and do without conceptual absurdity accept precisely the claims from Nielsen quoted above. Thus Nielsen's description of social naturalism is, to be sure, equivocal concerning atheism and agnosticism. What indeed separates these two positions is not their social naturalism, but that atheism affirms that it is not the case that God exists, while agnosticism does not affirm this claim. Rather, agnosticism properly construed entails a range of positions ranging from, say, "It is highly probable that God exists" to "It is highly improbable that God exists." Contrary to Nielsen's ambiguous characterization of atheism and agnosticism, these two positions are quite distinct from one another. And no atheistic conflation of the two views will work to the rhetorical advantage of atheists.

Nielsen's social naturalism is also a thoroughgoing secularism, employing no supernatural or religious ideas. As he puts it, it is secularism "all the way down."[48] This position is further described by him in terms of D. A. Armstrong's view that "the whole of being is constituted by the space-time world" and that "over and above space-time, there is nothing further that exists."[49] While this kind of language may lead many to think that Nielsen has violated his antiscientistic, antireductionistic, anti-eliminativistic theoretical commitments, this is untrue. Nielsen can be a social and secular naturalist through and through while not succumbing to the ideologically

---

[46] Nielsen, *Naturalism and Religion*, pp. 60–61.
[47] Nielsen, *Naturalism and Religion*, p. 61.
[48] Nielsen, *Naturalism and Religion*, Chapter 2.
[49] Nielsen, *Naturalism and Religion*, p. 436.

dogmatic attitudes of others who accept the very same propositions about reality and space-time. Humans, according to Nielsen, are more than just physical machines. They are persons with interests and such. To the extent that this is true, and to the extent that interests and the like are not physical realities, then Nielsen can affirm a social naturalism and secularism without adhering to a kind of scientism in how we know reality or to sub-doctrines of it that do not recognize anything nonphysical in the world.[50]

Even considering the nuances of Nielsen's social naturalism, it appears that more conceptual precision is required of it if it is to avoid critical ambiguity. For it seems to be a species of scientific naturalism, however social. Yet there are various ways in which one might be a scientific naturalist. One way is minimally, another is maximally. While Nielsen seems to distance himself from the maximalist version of scientific naturalism in that his is not reductionistic, eliminativist, or deterministic, it is unclear whether or not Nielsen's naturalism fits well into the minimalist mold insofar as it rejects supernatural interventions in the world. In brief, Nielsen's atheistic naturalism seems to disallow the possibility of a theism that affirms the existence of a spiritual being exerting real influences in the world through divine persuasion. So while Nielsen's naturalism is minimalist, it nonetheless fails to take seriously this theistic possibility. Some theists will charge this kind of theistic possibility ("thin theism") with vacuity and thinness.[51] The theoretical alternatives seem to be controversial and unsubstantiated (though perhaps not scientifically disproven): Parapsychological doctrines about the mind-body problem and the afterlife, or maximally naturalistic atheism which to this point is dubious until all most viable theisms are found wanting.

Moving from atheistic misconstruals of atheism and the naturalism of atheism to atheistic critiques of theism, one of the difficulties with Nielsen's criticism of theism is that it focuses on the hyperbolic properties ascribed to God by traditionalists. While most of the atheistic criticisms of such theologies are on target, Nielsen makes some common atheistic errors. One is that he states that "Anything that could actually be encountered or experienced could not be an eternal transcendent reality."[52] But this claim is dubious. First, it depends on what is meant by "eternal" and "transcendent." If the former means that God exists beyond time, it is hard to

---

[50] Nielsen, *Naturalism and Religion*, pp. 436f.

[51] David Ray Griffin, *Religion and Scientific Naturalism* (Albany: SUNY Press, 2000), p. 108.

[52] Nielsen, *Philosophy & Atheism*, p. 16.

understand exactly what that means and it might be that Nielsen's statement is plausible. But if it is meant that God has always existed insofar as time has, and will continue to exist so long as time persists, then why would the possibility of humans experiencing God as a being in time be so incomprehensible? And if transcendence means not that God is above and beyond our empirical reality as orthodox Christian theism asserts, but rather that God is beyond or greater than any one of us or all of us combined, then why is this notion considered to be such a difficulty? Why should it be deemed conceptually absurd? It is worth noting here that various ancient religions conceived of God in precisely such terms.

That God is on most every theological account a spiritual presence or being (rather than or as well as physical), there is a large sense in which God cannot be directly observed, empirically speaking. While God Herself is spirit and cannot be directly and fully verified by empirical methods, God's workings in and through humans are observable empirically. When we feed the poor and hungry, educate the ignorant, provide medical care for the ailing, etc., we do God's work as the spirit of God (or God, who is spirit) works through us whether or not we are admittedly religious, using us as vehicles of Her love and compassion for humankind and the world in which it lives. This is even part of popular Christian doctrine, and is based in part on Jesus' statement that what you do to the least of these, you do to me (*Matthew* 25:15). So it seems problematic for Nielsen to draw the quick inference that there is "neither empirical nor *a priori* knowledge of God, and talk of 'intuitive knowledge' is without logical force."[53] Moreover, it renders doubtful his claim that ". . . when we consider what kind of transcendent reality God is said to be, . . . there is an implicit *logical* ban on the presence of empirical evidence (a pleonasm) for His existence."[54] Contrary to Nielsen's dogmatic insistence that "We do not know what we are talking about in speaking of such a transcendent reality,"[55] unorthodox theism can rearticulate a meaningful notion of God that is not in violation of common sense and empirical observation. Refusing to see God as transcendent in the sense of being supernaturalistic, an unorthodox theism can meet Nielsen's demands head-on.

Unlike most atheists, Nielsen considers a certain kind of nontraditional theism, namely, what he refers to as the "nonanthropomorphic" notion of the nature of God. But as quoted above, he seriously doubts that this

---

53   Nielsen, *Philosophy & Atheism*, p. 19.
54   Nielsen, *Philosophy & Atheism*, p. 19.
55   Nielsen, *Philosophy & Atheism*, p. 20.

approach is promising, as "we do not know what it would be like to specify the denotation (the referent) of a nonanthropomorphic God."[56] But this dubiety is due to the poverty of Nielsen's theological imagination and his apparent ignorance of the contributions of process theologies that seek precisely to devise what Nielsen and so many other atheists doubt can be done. So the power of Nielsen's denial of God's existence will depend on how well an unorthodox theology can deliver on the promise to describe God in meaningful terms that are not anthropomorphic and otherwise exaggerated. This matter is taken up in Chapters 5–6, so I shall not belabor it here.

The unsound reasoning of so many atheists in the West is understandable if it originated from those who do not understand the basics of logic and informal reasoning. But Mackie, Flew, and Nielsen are distinguished philosophers. One wonders, then, how they reach atheism by such illogical means. Perhaps it is as Russell notes: "Men tend to have the beliefs that suit their passions"[57] regardless of their orientation vis-à-vis the question of God's existence. And as Basil Mitchell points out with equal profundity: "A man's position is comparatively rarely affected by explicit argument and the more profoundly religious, or indeed anti-religious, the less likely is he to be argued out of it."[58] We must be careful, then, not to fall prey to passionate discourse that temporarily (or not) discards reason. More specifically, we must remain on guard to not commit the errors of atheism.

However, there is yet another reason why atheism is problematic. It stems from Russell's hesitance to adopt atheism because he could not prove that it is not the case that God exists. And this relates to the problem of the burden of argument concerning the problem of God.[59]

Let us assume that the atheist manages to educate herself in the depths of all kinds of theologies, East and West. And let us assume that the atheist succeeds in demonstrating that each of them is sufficiently problematic

---

[56] Nielsen, *Philosophy & Atheism*, p. 20. Also see Nielsen, *Naturalism and Religion*, p. 33.

[57] Seckel, Editor, *Bertrand Russell on God and Religion*, p. 91.

[58] Basil Mitchell, *The Justification of Religious Belief* (Oxford: Oxford University Press, 1973), p. 1. Chapters 1–2 of Mitchell's book provide fine cursory accounts of arguments against and in favor of theism.

[59] For a philosophical discussion of this problem in relation to theism, atheism, and agnosticism, see R. McLaughlin, "Necessary Agnosticism?" *Analysis*, 44 (1984), pp. 198–202; T. V. Morris, "Agnosticism," *Analysis*, 45 (1985), pp. 219–224; P. J. McGrath, "Atheism or Agnosticism," *Analysis*, 47 (1987), pp. 54–57; L. Stubenberg, "The Principle of Disbelief," *Analysis*, 48 (1988), pp. 184–190.

such that it is unreasonable to accept any one or combination of them. Under such circumstances, precisely what is the atheist epistemically justified (in the robust sense) in accepting? Does the failure of such theisms entitle her to accept atheism in the strict and proper sense? Or is the atheist really bound only to accept some probability idea pertaining to the existence of God? Perhaps this is why Russell refused to accept atheism. He understood what it entails, and refused to accept what he knew he could not prove. Simply because all available theisms are disproven, it hardly follows from this that atheism is justified in any robust sense. For one could yet be in a poor epistemic position to be justified in accepting "It is not the case that God exists" or its equivalent. Under such conditions, then, agnosticism seems to be the most reasonable position to adopt, however tentatively. This appears to be Russell's agnostic contribution to philosophy of religion, one that has seemed to be lost on many atheists.

Why does not atheism follow from the defeat of theisms worthy of the name? Because it might be that there are other theisms that are not implausible and are rationally acceptable, but have yet to be discovered. Taken to an extreme, this philosophical point seems to amount to the claim that atheism requires the rejection of all possible conceptions of theism, which is in turn impossible. But my claim is more subtle than this. It is one of epistemic justification. If only one of many competing theisms is defeated by atheists, then atheism is hardly justified except in some weak sense for the reasons noted above. But even if a probability notion of atheism is adopted, far more than one or two popular versions of theism must be rendered problematic for atheism to be more than minimally justified. Hence the wisdom of Russell's agnosticism that stopped short of adopting atheism, and the significance of the New Agnosticism which goes further than Russell's agnosticism by actually investigating certain forms of theism[60] that seem to be much more plausible than those that have been refuted in the past few centuries of discussion in the philosophy of religion.

In the next chapter, I shall set forth varieties of theism, atheism, and agnosticism in order to clarify the complexity of these perspectives and thereby the complexity of the discussion between these interlocutors. In doing so, I point out a pervasive and complex array of errors committed by atheists, ones that eventuate in the inadequate grounding of that viewpoint on the problem of God.

---

[60]   See Chapters 5–6.

Chapter 2

The Errors of Atheism

We commit intellectual blunders because it suits our interests to do so, or because our blunders are of such a nature that we get pleasure or excitement from committing them.

—*Aldous Huxley*[1]

Most every person has at least at one time or another pondered the question of the existence of God. Religious people claim that God exists, while atheists deny such a claim, and agnostics remain cautiously skeptical, and each for a variety of reasons. But in order for the question of God's existence to be answered responsibly and to prevent conceptual confusion, we must have in mind a proper understanding of what, should God exist, God is and what God is not, as well as precisely what is being claimed by each possible position concerning the existence of God. In fact, the question of God's existence cannot be adequately answered apart from answering the question of who or what God is. If God exists, who (or what) is She (or it)? What properties or qualities does God possess should God exist?

Methodological Considerations

If Thomas Aquinas and some other medieval Scholastics are correct, sometimes God is best understood in negative terms, or *via negativa*.[2] By definition, then, God is neither evil, nor unjust, nor a holder or promoter of falsehoods, nor an adulterer, nor petty, nor unconcerned with human and nonhuman life, etc. And of course there are well-known positive attributes of God, at least, according to orthodox Christian theism: omniscience, omnipotence, omnipresence, omnibenevolence, eternality, perfection, and so on. However, one must be careful to not think that God can be defined into existence, as Immanuel Kant accused proponents of the

---

[1] Aldous Huxley, "Words and Their Meanings," in Max Black, Editor, *The Importance of Language* (Englewood Cliffs: Prentice-Hall, 1962), p. 11.

[2] Other ways in which God is known include the *via causalitatis* and the *via eminentiae*. Roughly, by causal relations in the world we can know something about God's nature, as it were. Also, by considering ourselves we can discover certain other aspects of God's nature.

ontological argument of doing.[3] That, of course, is simply one of the criticisms of the ontological argument. Others argue that one or more of the properties traditionally ascribed to God by orthodox and neo-orthodox Christian theologies are problematic.[4]

I concur with atheists that many Christian theists are incorrect that God, should She exist, is exactly who or what they claim She is. But it hardly follows from this that atheists are correct in inferring, as they typically do and must in order to rightly qualify as atheists, that it is not the case that God exists. Indeed, it will not even do to argue, as self-described atheist and popular evolutionist Richard Dawkins does, that "there almost certainly is no God."[5] For as I argued in Chapter 1, the defeat of the traditional Christian notion of the nature of God does not imply the nonexistence of God in categorical or highly probabilistic terms. Nor does it show that any more plausibly construed God is less likely to exist than for God to exist. In other words, the defeat of traditional Christian theism fails to show the unreasonableness of theism itself, which is requisite for the plausibility of any credible notion of atheism. More exactly, the defeat of orthodox Christian theism's notion of God does not even entail the refutation of nontraditional Christian theism. For it is not enough to justify any position that its denial is not able to be grounded in reason. This is true because it might be the case that the sufficient reasons that would ground that denial might exist but remain undiscovered.[6] And this applies to both theism and atheism alike. God could be something different such that objections to the existence of what God was thought to be by traditional Christian theism miss the mark insofar as they are meant to establish the truth of atheism, legitimately construed. I believe that this is what has taken place in the ongoing debates between theists in the Christian tradition, on the one hand, and atheists, on the other, at least in the analytical philosophical tradition. It is the failure of atheists to adequately

---

[3] Immanuel Kant, *Religion and Rational Theology*, Allen Wood (ed. and trans.) (Cambridge: Cambridge University Press, 1996); *Religion within the Bounds of Mere Reason and Other Writings*, Allen Wood and George Di Giovanni (eds. and trans.) (Cambridge: Cambridge University Press, 1998).

[4] Among the several defenses of the ontological argument, see Charles J. Klein, "On the Necessary Existence of an Object with Creative Power," *Faith and Philosophy*, 17 (2000), pp. 369–370.

[5] Richard Dawkins, *The God Delusion* (New York: Houghton Mifflin Company, 2006), Chapter 4.

[6] I am not arguing that such reasons that would ground the denial might exist and therefore God exists as this would amount to an argument from silence, a fallacy that we must avoid.

ground their belief that it is not the case that God exists, or that the existence of God is not very likely, that leads me, in Chapter 4, to state and
defend the New Agnosticism.

In the meantime, it is important to come to terms with how the discussion about the possible existence of God ought to proceed. Orthodox
Christian theists, at least of the conservative variety,[7] blatantly engage in
question-begging in their appeals to the authority of revelation in order to
resolve the question of God's existence. And it is fallacious to characterize
atheism in uncharitable terms, as most conservative Christian orthodox
thinkers tend to do:

> In view of the *semen religionis* implanted in every man by his creation in the
> image of God, it is safe to assume that no one is born an atheist. In the last
> analysis atheism results from the perverted moral state of man and from his
> desire to escape from God. It is deliberately blind to and suppresses the most
> fundamental instinct of man, the deepest needs of the soul, the highest aspir-
> ations of the human spirit, and the longings of a heart that gropes after some
> higher Being. This practical or intellectual suppression of the operation of
> the *semen religionis* often involves prolonged and painful struggles.[8]

It is important that this inquiry into God not employ *ad hominem* rhetoric
to address one of the most important questions we face. Too much depends
on our proper mode of this important inquiry to allow it to be clouded
with poor reasoning.

Nor is it appropriate for philosophical theists to invoke the authority of
revelation (construed in infallibilistic, inerrant, or merely in ultimate
authoritative terms) in order to address quandaries where reason itself fails
to provide sufficiently adequate answers. It is unacceptable to state that
"The only proper way to obtain perfectly reliable knowledge of the divine
attributes is by the study of God's self-revelation in Scripture."[9] For there
are a number of problems with this approach. First, it constitutes blatant
question-begging in favor of a revelatory-based theism when part of the
very question is whether such a divine author of the revelation exists in the
first place. Second, what makes the orthodox Christian theologian think
that there are no other religious scriptures (Christian or not) worthy of due
consideration? And what if they contradict what the canonical Christian
scriptures tell us? Since there appears to be no non-question-begging way

---

[7] L. Berkhof, *Systematic Theology* (Grand Rapids: W. B. Eerdmans Publishing Co.,
   1939), pp. 41f. Also see footnotes 21–22 of the Introduction.
[8] Berkhof, *Systematic Theology*, p. 22.
[9] Berkhof, *Systematic Theology*, p. 54.

of establishing the orthodox (or even neo-orthodox) Christian appeal to the sacred authority of revelation, it is properly considered to be overly contested to be trusted as a reliable source of testimony regarding the question of God's existence.[10] So in the search for the divine attributes, whether they are moral or natural, absolute or relative, immanent or transitive, or communicable or incommunicable, religious revelation is not an unproblematic method of philosophical investigation. The most to which it can speak is how some early Christians thought about various religious matters.

Nor is Alvin Plantinga's question-begging theologically "reformist" notion that the idea of God is "properly basic"[11] a philosophically unproblematic way of proceeding. The very foundationalist nature of such a view has been repudiated by numerous epistemologists throughout the years, as it suffers from a myriad of conceptual difficulties beyond repair.[12] A simple coherentist approach to defending theism also fails so long as the claims it makes do not match reality independent of the theistic perspective, a point that is made later on in this book.

Yet traditional Christian theists are not the only ones to employ faulty rhetoric in order to become victorious in the debate about God. One fallacious objection to orthodox Christian theism is that the evils of the church and of many Christians more generally speak against the existence of God. This point is made repeatedly by many atheists and agnostics alike. But precisely what does the fact that several millions of self-proclaimed Christians throughout the ages have not lived up to their religious faith and even committed evils say against the existence of God? One must be careful not to commit the fallacy of thinking that a person's unjust actions repudiate the truth-value of their ideals. While Christians are commended to do good in the world, their failure to do so hardly entails or even implies the nonexistence of God for the simple reason that they are not obeying God when they do the wrong things. If God exists, She condones only that

---

10 This does not mean, however, that the canonical Christian scriptures do not serve as a reasonably accurate guide to the founding and history of the early Christian church.

11 Alvin Plantinga, *Warranted Christian Belief* (Oxford: Oxford University Press, 2000). Also see Alvin Plantinga, "Advice to Christian Philosophers," *Faith and Philosophy*, 1 (1984), pp. 253–271. For a critical discussion of this fideist position, see Peter van Inwagen, "Some Remarks on Plantinga's Advice," *Faith and Philosophy*, 16 (1999), pp. 164–172.

12 Keith Lehrer, *Theory of Knowledge*, 2nd Edition (Boulder: Westview Press, 2000), Chapters 3–4; John Pollock, *Contemporary Theories of Knowledge* (Totowa: Rowman & Littlefield Publishers, 1986), Chapter 2.

which is, for instance, just and good. Anything that is not just or good cannot be an act of obedience to God. So one must not fall prey to the temptation of thinking that simply because so many millions of those who profess to be on God's side are failing (for whatever reasons) to do just and good things that God fails to exist. So the existence of God is not affected by the fact that most people who claim to be followers of God do not in significant ways represent God.

But just as revelation cannot serve as the ultimate source of authority in our metaphysical query, neither can science serve as the sole and final authority. For science is incapable of investigating that which is nonempirical in nature. And to foist the scientific method on the debate about God's existence as its sole authority is inappropriate because it is unfair insofar as it is believed that science ought to have the final word on matters—even on matters nonempirical. That too would beg at least one important question, namely, about whether or not God could exist as spirit and not as mere matter. So neither revelation nor science are the sole authorities in determining whether or not God exists, though each can and ought to play important roles regarding, for instance, what certain religions say about the matter, in the case of revelation, and the extent to which certain processes in nature are observed, in the case of science. Thus while revelation and science cannot serve as sole guides to our investigation into God, they serve as essential albeit limited sources by which we can gleam information about the possible nature and function of God. Reason must serve as our ultimate arbiter of truth here. By "reason" I mean argument and analysis in terms of the Socratic method of inquiry.[13]

The Errors of Atheism

Now atheists might argue that theism bears the burden of argument in its insistence that God exists, and since it fails to do so in light of the many criticisms made against the traditional arguments for the existence of God, atheists are justified in accepting the proposition that it is not the case that God exists.[14] In other words, the arguments for "God exists" cannot bear

---

[13] By "Socratic method" I do not refer to some formal method of investigation. Rather, I refer to the general way in which Socrates, according to Plato's dialogues, approaches problems through the use of reason [J. Angelo Corlett, *Interpreting Plato's Dialogues* (Las Vegas: Parmenides, 2005), Chapter 3].

[14] Nielsen, *Philosophy & Atheism* (Buffalo: Prometheus Books, 1985), p. 14. Also see Antony Flew, *The Presumption of Atheism* (New York: Barnes & Noble,

critical scrutiny and fail to satisfy the burden of argument. Thus, according to many leading atheistic philosophers, "God exists" is false. But this is unsound reasoning because the discussion centers on the traditional Christian theistic conception of the nature and function of God. Again, we ought not to countenance the bifurcation fallacy that either the God of traditional Christian theism exists, or there is no God at all. This is part of what I refer to as the "errors of atheism," as noted in the previous chapter.

As we shall see in Chapters 5–6, there are alternative and much more plausible conceptions of God that must be proven to be problematic prior to any well-justified atheistic declaration of victory in the debate about God. Otherwise, honest deniers of God's existence would not in fact embrace atheism worthy of the name. Even if the atheist insists without supportive and plausible argument that atheism is properly construed in terms of the probability of God's existence, atheism still falls prey to the fallacy of bifurcation, as well as that of having a grossly inadequate sample of refuted theisms to warrant acceptance of the atheistic hypothesis.

Other aspects of the errors of atheism include the atheist's strong tendency, in light of the vast literature on the problem of God, to commit a version of the straw person fallacy in supposing that the orthodox Christian notion of the nature and function of God is actually the one that is most worthy of our most serious philosophical attention, and to oftentimes equivocate between atheism and agnosticism.

Finally, the atheist's errors involve the hasty conclusion that, in light of the vast numbers and kinds of theisms articulated over centuries, the falsity of traditional Christian theism spells the demise of theism itself. So the

---

1976), p. 15; *Atheistic Humanism* (Buffalo: Prometheus Books, 1993), p. 29. For Flew, atheism is the presumed starting point of inquiry concerning discussions of theology, though it is a "methodological assumption" that is defeasible (pp. 13–14, and 31). It is supported by his "Agnostic Principle" which states that one's beliefs ought to be proportioned to the evidence in support of them (pp. 7, 32, 35). Flew argues that the available evidence places the onus of proof on the theist (p. 14). Flew's presumption of atheism is not atheism itself. For that would entail the proposition that it is not the case that God exists. Rather, it amounts to what might be referred to as "negative atheism": that one not assume theism or take a theistic stance (until theism is adequately supported to warrant our assent according to the Agnostic Principle). Flew's Rationalistic Principle requires that a belief, in order to be legitimately accepted, must have adequate grounds for acceptance (p. 22). While Nielsen objects that this scheme of evaluating theisms requires independent argument in order to be helpful in adjudicating the debate about the existence of God (Nielsen, *Philosophy & Atheism*, pp. 139–140), I do not share Nielsen's concerns along these lines.

atheist's errors typically involve the implicit or explicit committing of a cluster of related errors of reasoning: bifurcation, straw person, equivocation, and hasty conclusion. Whether or not the atheist's errors also involve a kind of Western or specifically Christian chauvinism is unclear as the fallacies noted could have been committed by atheists quite external to the Western tradition in their thinking about the problem of God.

The atheist might respond to my argument that atheism typically commits the above cluster of errors by insisting that if no one can be a true atheist unless she has examined every plausible theism, does this imply that atheism is irrational because there will always remain the possibility of some other yet undiscovered plausible theism? But this seems absurd.[15]

In reply to this point, it might be argued that such a scenario would not rule out atheism in principle, but that it might not be a fully epistemically justified position to adopt due to the incompleteness of such an inquiry into God's possible existence (the same might be said of theism, for that matter, as a theist is only as fully justified in her belief in God's existence to the extent that defeaters to her arguments for God's existence are sought and neutralized or defeated). Yet one might become and remain a more or less reasonable atheist depending on the extent to which she can or has refuted the most plausible conceptions of God and theism available to her as a truth-seeking epistemically responsible agent. Thus atheism is not ruled out in principle, nor does it face a merely semantic problem.

It might also be argued in defense of atheism that there exist legitimate probabilistic versions of it, contrary to my claim that atheism, strictly speaking, amounts to the claim that it is not the case that God exists. If this is true, however, the atheist still bears the burden of proof concerning her claim, which will require much more to establish as being reasonably justified than the refutation of orthodox Christian theism. Moreover, this weakening of the concept of atheism requires the atheist to provide a non-question-begging and non-self-serving rationale for the distinction between atheism and agnosticism, and by parity of reasoning, between theism and agnosticism. As argued in the previous chapter, the reason for this is because agnosticism, properly construed, just is a probabilistic position vis-à-vis the problem of God. For the atheist to not be able to carry out this task would be to court conceptual confusion.

However, this prolegomenon to philosophy of religion is in part an attempt to rescue the atheist from this conglomeration of errors by revisiting the discussion about God in terms of a more plausible notion of God in order to discover whether or not this more plausible notion of God

---

[15]   This concern is raised by Thomas Maloney.

withstands the test of reason, and permits atheists who are genuinely
serious about the problem to examine critically this notion absent problems of bifurcation, straw person, hasty conclusion, or any other fallacies.
Simultaneously, it seeks to draw honest and open theists into the discussion to critically examine theism yet again, absent precommitments to
doctrines theological or otherwise.

Throughout the contemporary history of the discussion of the existence
of God in the philosophy of religion, much has been insisted by certain
members of one party or another. Some agnostics and atheists insist that
theists must make their arguments conform to the best findings of scientific
investigation. As we found in the previous chapter, some of them have even
imposed some version of scientific verificationism[16] or falsificationism[17] on
the arguments of theists. The basic point here is that since God is not an
object of empirical observation, there is no falsifiable or verifiable conception of God. Thus the idea of God is not a matter of human knowledge.[18]
This assumes, of course, that all human knowledge reduces to that of
scientific knowledge, a claim that many theists and even some atheists have
challenged.

Many theists, most notably those of the traditional Christian variety,
argue directly or in effect that the belief that God exists is innocent until
proven guilty and that scientific investigation is ill-equipped to either
confirm or disconfirm theistic belief. Others, like E. Gilson, argue that the
scientific method "rests upon the assumption that nothing can be rationally known unless it be scientifically known, which is far from being an
evident proposition." Gilson continues: "The simple truth may be that
while human reason remains one and the same in dealing with different
orders of problems, it nevertheless must approach these various orders of
problems in as many different ways."[19] Indeed, this view seems to place the
question of the existence of God outside of the realm of scientific investigation: "If, speaking in the order of pure natural knowledge, the proposition
'God exists' makes any sense at all, it must be for its rational value as a

---

16   Al Seckel, Editor, *Bertrand Russell on God and Religion* (New York: Prometheus
     Books, 1986), pp. 57–91. Also see Nielsen, *Philosophy & Atheism*.
17   See Flew, Hare, and Mitchell, "Theology and Falsification: A Symposium," in
     A. Flew and A. MacIntyre, Editors, *New Essays in Theological Theology*
     (London: SCM Press, 1955).
18   E. Gilson ascribes this view to I. Kant and A. Comte, respectively [E. Gilson,
     God and Philosophy (New Haven: Yale University Press, 1941), pp. 111f.].
19   Gilson, *God and Philosophy*, p. 118.

philosophical answer to a metaphysical question."[20] Thus science ought to answer questions of empirical knowledge, while questions of God's existence are the proper domain of metaphysics (philosophy). So ". . . natural theology is in bondage not to the method of positive science but to the method of metaphysics, . . ." because ". . . the highest metaphysical problems in no way depend upon the answers given by science to its own questions."[21] Yet this theistic perspective seems to assume that God is a reality other than the world. If this were all there could be said about the matter, the discussion would be mired in a dialectical stalemate. Although I do believe that discussions between theists and atheists in the philosophy of religion are somewhat forestalled, they need not end in a stalemate as there are yet alternative approaches to the resolution of the problem of God, as I am in the process of articulating.

However, one difficulty with Gilson's position about religion and science is that it seems to disallow for the idea that—whatever else God may be—God is in this world. Furthermore, even according to Christian orthodoxy, God works the divine will through humans to effect positive change. Insofar as this notion is plausible, it would appear that the sciences can in principle at least investigate some truth-claims relevant to God's workings in the world. It ought not to be assumed that God and the world are totally alienated from one another, or that there exists a multitiered universe wherein God exists apart from Her creation which is the world.

One thing that seems reasonable to believe is that the theist owes sufficiently good reasons for her belief in God or God's possible existence. Lacking such reasons, however, the atheist is not automatically justified in inferring that there is no God or that the existence of God is impossible. And assuming that Thomas Reid was incorrect in thinking that beliefs are innocent until proven guilty,[22] each position (whether theistic, atheistic, or agnostic) must bear its own burden of proof. This view, of course, rejects what is called "Stratonician atheism": The idea that the theist bears the sole burden of proof related to matters of the existence of God.[23] However tempting this view might be, it seems to commit the fallacy of assuming that if *p* is false, then –*p* must be true. But it might be the case that there is,

---

[20] Gilson, *God and Philosophy*, p. 119.

[21] Gilson, *God and Philosophy*, p. 120.

[22] Thomas Reid, *The Works of Thomas Reid, D.D.*, W. Hamilton, Editor (Edinburgh: James Thin, 1895); Keith Lehrer, *Thomas Reid* (London: Routledge & Kegan Paul, 1989).

[23] Antony Flew, *The Presumption of Atheism* (Buffalo: Prometheus Books, 1976).

at t_n, adequate justification for neither p nor $-p$, making agnosticism the only position that is justified under the relevant epistemic circumstances. Thus neither a presumption in favor of theism nor one in favor of atheism is epistemically justified in more than a weak sense at best.

Distinguishing Atheism, Theism, and Agnosticism

What if it can be shown that there is a reasonable alternative to traditional Christian theism (on the one hand) and atheism (on the other)? Among other things, this would suggest that the defeat of orthodox Christian theism does not necessarily and in itself spell doom for theism. Further, just as theism bears the argumentative burden of proof in establishing its claim that God exists, so too does atheism bear a burden of argument in establishing the logical denial of theism's central claim. Each position requires evidentiary support. And should the evidence for theism, on the one hand, and the evidence for atheism, on the other, each turn out to be supported strongly and coherently by evidence that is incomparable to one another and hence unable to be weighed against each other except from an unduly biased (question-begging) perspective, then agnosticism becomes a tentative position of reasonable acceptance for those who take the issue of the existence of God seriously. Assumed here is the idea that atheism is not properly understood to be the position that theists of this or that kind cannot prove beyond reasonable doubt their central claim: the God hypothesis. As Kai Nielsen writes: "To be atheists we need to deny the existence of God."[24] It is the logical denial of theism which holds that "God exists," just as theism is the logical affirmation of the denial of atheism. And just as the responsible theist will be a fallibilist, so will the thoughtful atheist.[25] While it is crucial to see the atheist's error of bifurcation implicit in atheism these days, it is not fallacious for the atheist to infer from the history of argumentation about the God of orthodox Christian theism that it is not the case that the God of traditional Christian theism exists, as pointed out in the previous chapter.

---

[24] Nielsen, *Philosophy & Atheism*, p. 10.
[25] Nielsen, *Philosophy & Atheism*, p. 15. One way in which atheism expresses its fallibilism is by stating the denial of God's existence in probabilistic terms, just as the theist might express the existence of God inductively. In this way, there is a certain agnostic tempering of theism and atheism, respectively. Only their infallibilist cousins seem to be quite different from agnosticism.

As we saw in Chapter 1, agnosticism can take different forms. It is often understood to mean that one cannot in light of the relevant evidence make up one's mind about the existence of God, e.g., that one can neither responsibly affirm nor deny God's existence in light of the relevant available evidence. In epistemological terms, it means that given the evidence I cannot accept the proposition, "God exists." But it also means that in light of the evidence I cannot accept the claim that "It is not the case that God exists."

However, we must delve deeper into agnosticism in order to better grasp its true nature as it has often been the victim of misrepresentation. For as we saw in the previous chapter, there are at least two ways to take these agnostic claims. One is to admit that one cannot make up one's mind about the existence of God because one thinks that, all relevant things considered, one wishes to embrace both that "God exists" and its denial in that the evidence justifies accepting this contradiction. I shall refer to this position as "positive agnosticism." But another way to be an agnostic is to deny that either opposing claim about the existence of God possesses sufficient evidence to warrant our assent. I call this "negative agnosticism." Of course, a variant of these positions, one I refer to as "mixed agnosticism," is one where I cannot decide between theism and atheism because of some of the evidence that is comparable between these competing views, though other parts of the evidence profile for each position cannot possibly be weighed against each other without undue bias. This might occur in a case where the balance of reason in light of available evidence might represent a genuine dialectical stalemate between theism and atheism.

As we will see in Chapter 4, the New Agnosticism does not, however, call for a détente between atheism and theism that amounts to "the suspension of both theistic and atheistic belief, coupled with official neutrality between them."[26] Rather, it calls for a reexamination of the problem of God from a new perspective, untainted by the conceptual perils of orthodox Christian theism and atheism's seemingly pathological focus on its vanquishing this brand of theism. More will be said in Chapter 4 about

---

[26] David O'Connor, *God and Inscrutable Evil* (Lanham: Rowman & Littlefield Publishers, Inc., 1998), p. xii. Indeed, O'Connor's work addresses only the problem of evil as an objection to theism of the orthodox variety. So it is difficult to know whether what is established is a détente between atheism and theism at all. For even if orthodox theism survived the objection from evil, it might still be the case that it failed to withstand the objections to the traditional "proofs" for the existence of God. Moreover, even if orthodox theism failed to provide plausible replies to such objections, there might be unorthodox theisms that can answer them.

atheism, theism, and agnosticism. Now I want to clear the conceptual way for the taxonomy of these views that is to follow.

It is instructive to point out that agnosticism has been mischaracterized even by judicious thinkers. Yet a careful examination of some such portrayals of it reveals that it is defined in terms that conflate it with atheism or conveniently support the plausibility of atheism in the attempt to stifle further discussion about the God hypothesis.

Consider Nielsen's description of agnosticism as asserting that "we can neither know nor have sound reasons for believing that God exists . . ."[27] Again: "We do not know and cannot ascertain whether 'God' secures a religiously adequate referent. . . . The agnostic, . . . is not led to faith, but he does believe that such questions cannot be answered."[28] The problem with Nielsen's construal of agnosticism is that it describes the agnostic as one who states that we "cannot know" that God exists or that God-talk is meaningful. The reason this is problematic is that this position is essentially indistinguishable from atheism, epistemically speaking. Contrary to Nielsen, agnosticism need not and is not most charitably seen as the view that we cannot know or ascertain the truth-value of "God exists." Rather, it is either the view that the central theistic claim appears to be neither true nor false because of lack of adequate supportive evidence on either side of the debate, or that it is at the present time unable to be decided with adequacy due to certain factors of ambiguity, an evidentiary nature, or conceptual confusion. But nothing about agnosticism, properly understood, entails the idea that we *cannot* know that or whether God exists, as Nielsen suggests. *That* the agnostic simply is not, by proper definition of "agnostic," entitled to accept. The reason for this is the essentially open-ended and fallibilistic position of the true agnostic as one who is open to the possibility that the evidence for "God exists" might someday be found, or that in the future sufficient evidence will be discovered to discount it.

Agnosticism worthy of the name is not an inferior and confused form of atheism, as so many seem to think. Rather, it is not a form of atheism at all, nor is it a kind of theism. It is, rather, a position distinct from these two opposing views. Most certainly, the genuine agnostic cannot subscribe to Nielsen's atheistic claim that

> . . . there are no good intellectual grounds for believing in God and very good ones, perhaps even utterly decisive ones, for not believing in God; and

---

[27]   Nielsen, *Philosophy & Atheism*, p. 22.
[28]   Nielsen, *Philosophy & Atheism*, p. 24.

there is no moral or human need, let alone necessity, for a nonevasive and informed person in the twentieth century to have religious commitments of any kind.[29]

One reason why this statement is problematic is that Nielsen has not taken into serious consideration nontraditional theisms that non-evasively attempt to restate the nature and function of God in terms that seem to evade the many criticisms of traditional Christian theism, and suggest a divine nature that the rationalist and empiricist can accept. Unless and until this stage of the argument is conducted, the scientific and rationalistic enterprise of atheism remains incomplete, and thus found wanting in a serious way. In fact, to the extent that atheism for whatever reasons fails to address nontraditional theisms that explicitly attempt to answer atheistic concerns with traditional Christian theism, atheism is guilty of a kind of epistemic irresponsibility.

In light of the attempts of process and liberation theologies to address various concerns with traditional Christian theism, unless and until such views are successfully refuted, the best position then open to the honest inquirer into God's possible existence is the New Agnosticism (or agnosticism, properly understood). In Chapters 5–6, such views will be given serious consideration in order to provide more ample reason to affirm or deny the existence of God.

It will not do to resort to an implicit form of the fallacy of *ad hominem*, as Nielsen does at one point in his defense of atheism, referring to one such attempt as a "ploy":

A standard ploy at this moment in the dialectic is to maintain that utterances like "God is all merciful," "God is the Creator of the heavens and the earth" or "God loves all His creation," are symbolic or metaphorical utterances which manifest the ultimate or Unconditioned Transcendent but are themselves not literal statements which could be true or false. They hint at an ineffable metaphysical ultimate which is, as Tillich put it, "unconditionally beyond the conceptual sphere . . ." On the remarkable assumption that such verbosities are helpful explications, some theologians, addicted to this obscure manner of speaking. . . .[30]

Granted, existentialist Christian theologians like Paul Tillich often express their notions of God in terms somewhat difficult to understand. In fact, their descriptions of God's nature and function can at times become downright incomprehensible, especially for us analytic philosophers who strive for

---

[29] Nielsen, *Philosophy & Atheism*, p. 40.
[30] Nielsen, *Philosophy & Atheism*, pp. 88–89.

clarity of thought and language as well as sound argumentation. But Nielsen's interpretive claim of Tillich's view that "Given the proper experience, the reality they obliquely attest to will, while remaining irreducibly mysterious, be humanely speaking undeniable" hardly indicates a serious attempt to generously understand Tillich's words in a way that might further the discussion.[31] As such, it is questionable and seems to violate the principle of charity[32] in the interpretation of texts and the ideas they express.

Nothing about analytical philosophy prevents us from conducting such fair interpretations and assessments of views we find hard to grasp. What the debate about God needs is not dismissiveness of new ideas from either theists or atheists, but honest and open-minded inquiry about views of sufficient seriousness that they deserve our undivided scrutiny. Precisely this attitude is found, by the way, elsewhere in Nielsen:

> What we need to recognize is that the concept of God is very problematic indeed. What is crucially at issue is to ascertain, if we can, whether sufficient sense can be made of religious conceptions to make faith a live option for a reflective and concerned human being possessing a reasonable scientific and philosophical understanding of the world he lives in, or whether some form of atheism or agnosticism is the most nonevasive option for such a person.[33]

This challenge is essentially the same one issued both by Bertrand Russell and J. L. Mackie, and as noted earlier it is the one I shall undertake in later chapters of this book. But one wonders whether a self-described atheist is really an atheist after all if, as Mackie and Nielsen, they are truly open to the possibility of there being an alternative and plausible theism. Perhaps they are atheists in a rather restricted sense such that they deny the claim "God (as understood by traditional Christian theism) exists," while remaining agnostic about theism more generally. If this is true, it is a bit misleading to refer to such a position as being atheistic as "atheism" denotes a denial of the existence of any God. As one who has gone to great lengths

---

[31] Indeed, many orthodox Christian theologians are unsympathetic with Tillichian theology, perhaps due to their bias against the reconceptualization of anything theistically orthodox. But not having sympathy for a view does not amount to understanding it sufficiently to refute it.

[32] More on the principle of charity can be gleaned from Jorge Gracia, "History and the Historiography of Philosophy," in Donald M. Borchert, Editor, *Encyclopedia of Philosophy*, 2nd Edition (London: Macmillan Publishing Company, 2006).

[33] Nielsen, *Philosophy & Atheism*, p. 28.

to criticize theism for its abuses of religious language,[34] Nielsen stands condemned by his own words.

Was Bertrand Russell an Atheist or an Agnostic?

Agnosticism is hardly a novel position, as it can be traced in the 20th century to philosophers like Russell, known to the public at large as "that atheist philosopher." Yet agnosticism rarely, if ever, has received a sustained philosophical defense. A close study of Russell's position reveals him to be an agnostic, not an atheist. In "Am I an Atheist or an Agnostic?" (1949) he writes: "As a philosopher, if I were speaking to a purely philosophic audience I should say that I ought to describe myself as an Agnostic, because I do not think that there is a conclusive argument by which one can prove that there is not a God."[35] Perhaps Russell is implying that atheists as well as theists have the burden to prove their own position.[36] Why indeed ought theists be the only ones to have the argumentative burden of proof in the debate about the problem of God? Besides, even if it turned out to be the case that theism is implausible, does it logically follow that atheism is? Or, might some version of agnosticism be the best all things considered position to accept on the matter?

Indeed, in "The Faith of a Rationalist" (1947) Russell does not rule out the possibility that there may be alternative conceptions of God that are indeed plausible answers to the problem of evil:

> There is a different and vaguer conception of cosmic purpose as not omnipotent but slowly working its way through a recalcitrant material. This is a more plausible conception than that of a god who, though omnipotent and loving, has deliberately produced beings so subject to suffering and cruelty as the majority of mankind. I do not pretent [sic] to know that there is no such purpose; my knowledge of the universe is too limited.[37]

---

[34] Nielsen, *Philosophy & Atheism*, Chapters 1–5.
[35] Seckel, Editor, *Bertrand Russell on God and Religion*, p. 85.
[36] This point is raised in the form of a question in Piers Benn, "Some Uncertainties about Agnosticism," *International Journal for Philosophy of Religion*, 46 (1999), p. 175.
[37] Seckel, Editor, *Bertrand Russell on God and Religion*, p. 90. See also Russell's claim that "Many people who say they believe in God no longer mean a person, or a trinity of persons, but only a vague tendency or power or purpose immanent in evolution. Others, going still further, mean by 'Christianity' merely a system of ethics which, since they are ignorant of history, they imagine to be

Such epistemological humility on Russell's part serves as a caution to atheists as well as theists. It is consistent with his agnostic statement that "... in matters as to which men disagree, or as to which our own convictions are wavering, we should look for proofs, or, if proofs cannot be found, we should be content to confess ignorance."[38]

The willingness to acknowledge that theism might assume a different and more plausible form than that of traditional Christianity is found in the probabilistic atheism of Mackie. Subsequent to his refuting the traditional arguments for the existence of God, Mackie gives significant attention to the "extreme axiarchism" of John Leslie[39] according to which the world exists because it ought to exist.[40] And Mackie, I believe, provides sufficient criticism of Leslie's theory to render it dubious. However, it is Mackie's rather brief admission that Tillich's notion of God as ultimate concern might prove plausible that leads me to explore in some detail an alternative conception of the nature and function of God in order to better test the God hypothesis. Tillich, of course, means by "God" that thing or principle which is objectively of ultimate concern and is the ultimate reality,[41] an idea of divinity that Mackie insists traces back to the idea of the Form in Plato's dialogues.[42] Even more striking is Mackie's statement that:

> In short, all forms of the free will defence fail, and since this defence alone had any chance of success there is no plausible theodicy on offer. We cannot, indeed, take the problem of evil as a conclusive disproof of traditional theism, because, as we have seen, there is some flexibility in its doctrines, and in particular in the additional premises needed to make the problem explicit.

---

characteristic of Christians only" (Seckel, Editor, *Bertrand Russell on God and Religion*, p. 76). Careful philosophers and theologians must remember that Russell wrote "Why I am not a Christian," not "Why I am not a Theist." The difference demonstrates how cautious Russell was in his reasoning, unlike many atheists who slip, unwittingly, from agnosticism to atheism without regard to what the balance of human reason supports.

38   Seckel, Editor, *Bertrand Russell on God and Religion*, p. 88.
39   John Leslie, *Value and Existence* (Oxford: Basil Blackwell, 1979).
40   J. L. Mackie, *The Miracle of Theism* (Oxford: Oxford University Press, 1982), Chapter 13.
41   Paul Tillich, *Systematic Theology*, Volumes 1–3 (Chicago: The University of Chicago Press, 1951).
42   Mackie, *The Miracle of Theism*, p. 230. For an argument to the effect that what is found in Plato's dialogues is not attributable to Plato, see Corlett, *Interpreting Plato's Dialogues*.

There *may* be some way of adjusting these which avoids an internal contradiction without giving up anything essential to theism. But none has yet been clearly presented, and there is a strong presumption that theism cannot be made coherent without a serious change in at least one of its central doctrines.

It leaves open several possibilities for revised religious views.[43]

I believe that Mackie's reasoning here is correct, and shall take him up on his challenge to discover whether or not there is a viable alternative notion of God to the highly problematic one to which orthodox Christian theism incessantly clings. Mackie's challenge is echoed, though pessimistically, by Nielsen:

The doubt arises (or at least it should arise) as to whether believers or indeed anyone else, in terms acceptable to believers, can give an intelligible account of the concept of God or of what belief in God comes to once the concept is thoroughly de-anthropomorphized. It is completely unclear how we could give such a term any empirical foundation. We do not know what it would be like to specify the denotation (the referent) of a nonanthropomorphic God.[44]

Apparently, Mackie and Nielsen were unfamiliar with the Whiteheadian process theologies of Charles Hartshorne, John Cobb, Jr., and David Ray Griffin, respectively, or even of those of certain liberationists like James H. Cone and Gustavo Gutiérrez. I shall employ aspects of process and liberation theologies to explore the possibility that many of the concerns with traditional Christian theism might intelligibly and plausibly be evaded by the theist. Furthermore, I shall not consider certain attempts to rescue traditional Christian theism from the objections it faces, such as Hans Küng's "indeterminate and mysterious"[45] notion of God that amounts to nothing short of fideistic double-talk and incomprehensibility:

God cannot be grasped in any concept, . . . cannot be defined in any definition: he is the incomprehensible, inexpressible, indefinable.
   . . . he is nothing of that which is; he is not an existent: he transcends everything.

---

43 Mackie, *The Miracle of Theism*, p. 176.
44 Nielsen, *Philosophy & Atheism*, p. 20.
45 Mackie, *The Miracle of Theism*, p. 251.

God transcends all concepts, statements, definitions; but he is not separate
from the world and man; he is not outside all that is . . . God is, but he is not
an existent, he is the hidden mystery of being; . . .
. . . In God, therefore, transcendence and immanence coincide.[46]

Nor shall I engage Richard Swinburne or Plantinga in their (ultimately) fideistic efforts to defend traditional arguments for the existence of God. Much of their respective contributions to this field of inquiry have attracted great attention in analytical philosophy of religion, and I have nothing to add to some of the criticisms of their arguments in defense of God's exist-ence. I am convinced that, from Kant to David Hume to Mackie, that the ontological, cosmological, and teleological arguments are problematic for a variety of reasons. There is no being that exists which is simultaneously omnipotent, omniscient, omnibenevolent, and omnipresent in any strict senses of these categories. And some of the criticisms of the traditional "proofs" for God demonstrate this point.

Instead of reconceptualizing God in fanciful and yet incomprehensible terms that are self-contradictory or based solely and reportedly on divine revelation, I shall ask whether the basics of a more plausible, hybrid, and minimalist notion of God can solve the questions posed to theism by so many philosophers. In the end, this dialectical move will either strengthen Mackie's probabilistic conclusion that atheism is more reasonable than theism, or it will render it doubtful.

---

46 Hans Küng, *Does God Exist?* E. Quinn (trans.) (New York: Doubleday and Company, 1980), pp. 601–602; 632–633. For a Whiteheadian critique of some of the points made by Küng, see David Ray Griffin, "The Rationality of Belief in God: A Response to Hans Küng," *Faith and Philosophy*, 1 (1984), pp. 16–26.

CHAPTER 3

DAWKINS' GODLESS DELUSION

Heresies are systems that inherit all the claims of orthodoxy with only a part of its resources . . ..

The truth is often ugly or terrible, and almost always less simple and unqualified than our love of eloquence would wish it to be.

—*George Santayana*[1]

Most men prefer to go through this world with their eyes open—even though it may be true that many of us pride ourselves on having them open while they remain really closed.

—*P. A. Schilpp*[2]

There is something profoundly misanthropic in the belief that modern Western science has shown all religious believers to be deluded savages at best and immoral bigots at worst.

—*Tina Beattie*[3]

Having both set out the challenge of atheism to theism and laid the groundwork for proceeding in the debate about God's existence, and having also exposed some of the difficulties of contemporary philosophical atheism, it is important to address a recent putatively scientific version of atheism. I write "putatively scientific" in that as it turns out, the popular position is more scientistic than scientific.

In studying Richard Dawkins' *The God Delusion*, one is left with the impression that he is on an evangelical mission to "go into all the world and preach the gospel" of scientific atheism so that his readers might be delivered from the delusional tenets of theism.[4] However, it is unclear that Dawkins' self-described brand of atheism is genuinely atheistic in the first place. But even if it is atheistic, it is implausible. At most, what Dawkins' argument supports is an atheology relative to orthodox Christian theism.

[1] George Santayana, "Philosophical Heresy," *The Journal of Philosophy, Psychology, and Scientific Methods*, 12 (1915), p. 562.

[2] P. A. Schilpp, "A Rational Basis Demanded for Faith," *The Journal of Philosophy*, 21 (1924), p. 211.

[3] Tina Beattie, *The New Atheists* (Maryknoll: Orbis Books, 2007), p. 48.

[4] The rhetorical tone of Dawkins' verbiage seems to remind one somewhat of T. H. Huxley, who was referred to as "Darwin's Bulldog" [Arthur Peacocke, *Creation and the World of Science* (Oxford: Oxford University Press, 2004), p. 50].

But this is atheism only for those who are parochially Western in their thinking about God, a problem (ironically) with which Dawkins saddles orthodox Christian theism. So while it might be true that orthodox Christian theism is delusional, for all Dawkins argues, he himself suffers from the God*less* delusion of wrongly reasoning that the putative defeat of orthodox Christian theism justifies atheism, properly construed. Indeed, I shall argue that agnosticism is a more intellectually and scientifically responsible and respectable position than Dawkins' atheism. Thus I shall turn Dawkins' reasoning on its head, exposing his God*less* delusion.

While one might agree that orthodox Christian theism suffers from a level of delusion for reasons that Immanuel Kant, David Hume, Bertrand Russell, J. L. Mackie and Kai Nielsen, and some others have provided, I shall explain how atheism suffers from the delusion that it is not the case that God exists. What is not delusional is to embrace some version of agnosticism, which is a view quite unlike Dawkins' tirade against traditional Christian theism which shows no significant appreciation for the several rather respectable attempts to deal with various problems of God's existence.[5] What is not delusional is to take the question of God's existence sufficiently seriously that one does not simultaneously commit straw person, bifurcation, equivocation, and hasty conclusion fallacies in investigating philosophically these matters of ultimate concern. If it is true that in order to refute a view one needs to properly understand it, and if it is also the case that in order to properly understand a position one must have an appreciation and grasp of at least some of the depths of the most plausible and charitable version of the view, then Dawkins fails in his assessment of theism. It is, moreover, as a result of this failure that Dawkins' brand of atheism is problematic.

Various critics of Dawkins have raised a number of points about *The God Delusion*. For instance, one writes that while the book

> . . . is written with rhetorical passion and power, the stridency of its assertions merely masks tired, weak and recycled arguments.[6]
>   . . . The book is often little more than an aggregation of convenient factoids suitably overstated to achieve maximum impact and loosely arranged to suggest that they constitute an argument.[7]

---

[5] Some such attempts to bring greater philosophical and scientific respectability to theism are discussed in Chapters 5–6.

[6] A. McGrath and J. McGrath, *The Dawkins Delusion?* (Downers Grove: IVP Press, 2007), p. 12.

[7] McGrath and McGrath, *The Dawkins Delusion?* p. 13.

. . . The total dogmatic conviction of correctness which pervades some sections of Western atheism today—wonderfully illustrated in *The God Delusion*—immediately aligns it with a religious fundamentalism that refuses to allow its ideas to be examined or challenged.[8]

Dawkins's inept engagement with Luther shows how Dawkins abandons even the pretense of rigorous evidence-based scholarship. Anecdote is substituted for evidence; selective Internet trawling for quotes displaces rigorous and comprehensive engagement with primary sources. In this book, Dawkins throws the conventions of academic scholarship to the winds; he wants to write a work of propaganda and consequently treats the accurate rendition of religion as an inconvenient impediment to his chief agenda, which is the intellectual and cultural destruction of religion. It's an unpleasant characteristic that he shares with other fundamentalists.[9]

It is unfortunate that such a popular writer makes claims to represent the best of scientific inquiry on questions that, his underlying logical positivism notwithstanding, are far beyond the domain of his expertise and legitimate domain of inquiry.

Evidence of Dawkins' poor reasoning is found in his dealing with agnosticism by conveniently distinguishing what he declares are two forms of it: ". . . the legitimate fence-sitting where there really is a definite answer, one way or another, but so far we lack the evidence to reach it" from a more permanent kind of position of this sort of fence-sitting.[10] One might concur with Dawkins that the former position is more acceptable than the latter, as the latter leaves no room for the future discovery of the fact of the matter about God's existence one way or the other. But why Dawkins' reasoning does not lead him to adopt the former view instead of the one he · does adopt is mysterious in light of the evidence and his own arguments. One wonders, then, whether the title of that section of his book ("The Poverty of Agnosticism") ought rather to read: "The Plausibility of Agnosticism."

---

8   McGrath and McGrath, *The Dawkins Delusion?* p. 14.
9   McGrath and McGrath, *The Dawkins Delusion?* p. 24. See also p. 51: "One of the most melancholy aspects of *The God Delusion* is how its author appears to have made the transition from a scientist with a passionate concern for truth to a crude antireligious propagandist who shows a disregard for evidence."
10   Dawkins, *The God Delusion* (New York: Houghton Mifflin, 2006), p. 47. For a critical discussion of Dawkins as one of a contemporary cadre of "new" "soft-core atheists" as opposed to the alleged "hard-core atheism" of Albert Camus, Ludwig Feurerbach, Karl Marx, and Jean-Paul Sartre, among others, see John F. Haught, *God and the New Atheism* (Louisville: Westminster John Knox Press, 2008); John Cornwell, *Darwin's Angel* (London: Profile Books, 2007).

Moreover, he deliberately, or perhaps out of ignorance of alternative theisms developed by certain philosophers and theologians in recent decades, focuses his attention on one of the theologically weakest or most easily refutable of Christian theisms. While this tactic sells books among those unaware of the fallacies underlying such rhetorical shenanigans, it does nothing to advance serious discussion of the important issues at hand. No doubt a significant motivation for Dawkins' reasoning is activistic in that he is sincerely concerned with the well-being of societies (both human and nonhuman) and realizes that traditional Christian theism is so influential in the world and that it must be stopped because of its history of delusion and wrongdoing. But this is no excuse for fallacious argumentation, confused analysis, and weak scholarship. Even given Dawkins' general purpose in addressing the God hypothesis to a general audience as a public intellectual (in itself a rather admirable post), there is no justification for drawing poor inferences, especially amidst readers several of whom might be influenced by them. If what Dawkins writes is sound, then sound argument can be garnered to support it, regardless of his intended audience. But it is somewhat pernicious to use poor reasoning to attempt to persuade one's audience to adopt one view in place of another—even if it is true that the view targeted for criticism is for various reasons problematic and unworthy of continued acceptance. I believe, however, that Dawkins genuinely believes what he writes and argues. So he does not suffer from the fatal error of propagating views he believes to be false, being unconcerned with the truth of matters.[11] But some of his main arguments suffer from fundamental fallacies of reasoning.

Dawkins rightly insists that reason, not revelation, must guide our deliberations of the possible existence of God. But when we take reason sufficiently seriously, we shall find the weaknesses of Dawkins' atheism. Moreover, agnosticism, properly and not merely conveniently construed, is the best position to accept at this time, all relevant things considered. And this is true even though some like Dawkins are careful enough to define their positions in terms of probabilities. In this way, Dawkins commits the very same error that he accuses agnostics of committing, namely, that of conflating atheism with agnosticism. While Dawkins charges agnostics with not recognizing that they really are in practical terms atheists, it is Dawkins who is playing fast and loose with these categories given the proper and commonsense understandings of "atheism" and "agnosticism."

---

[11] Otherwise, that would constitute "bullshit," according to Harry G. Frankfurt, *On Bullshit* (Princeton: Princeton University Press, 2006).

In the end, Dawkins is the one who—we shall see—creates a seven-fold category scheme of theisms, agnosticisms, and atheisms that conveniently places himself as an atheist through linguistic and conceptual fiat.

Dawkins is careful to draw distinctions on a scale between "strong theism" ("100 per cent probability of God"); "*de facto theism*" ("very high probability but short of 100 per cent"); "agnostic but leaning towards atheism" ("higher than 50 per cent but not very high"); "completely impartial agnosticism" ("exactly 50 per cent"); "agnostic but leaning towards atheism" ("lower than 50 per cent but not very low"); "*de facto atheism*" ("very low probability, but short of zero"); and "strong atheism" ("I know there is no God").[12] Dawkins opts for *de facto atheism*, stopping short of but "leaning towards" strong atheism as he apparently believes that the existence of God cannot be disproven. Of course, Russell (one of the greatest public intellectuals of the 20th century) already made that point decades ago.

The reality is that Dawkins is a kind of agnostic, and even if he accurately portrays his own position as atheistic, his reasoning does not allow him to accept atheism in any meaningful sense of the term. This is the case for at least two reasons. First, from the supposition that traditional Christian theism is in the end implausible it hardly follows logically that atheism is sound. Second, while it is true that there are degrees of belief in general and degrees of belief or disbelief in God in particular, atheism, being the logical negation of theism which affirms "God exists," is the view that "It is not the case that God exists." This is the relatively uncontroversial and conventional understanding of theism and atheism in philosophy of religion and in theology, regardless of Dawkins' attempt to stipulatively redefine atheism in probabilistic terms. Dawkins leans toward but fails to embrace this construal of atheism, perhaps recognizing that his arguments do not adequately ground it.

There are different species of theism, agnosticism, and atheism. But Dawkins works explicitly with an epistemological version of atheism, namely, one that endorses the claim that "I know there is no God." But one might not *know* there is no God and yet God might also not exist, and this poses problems for Dawkins' position as it is substantially weaker than the traditional atheistic claim, unacknowledged by Dawkins: "It is not the case that God exists." First, Dawkins never explains what he means by "know," a rather technical term in epistemology and is loaded with conceptual possibilities and complexities. For instance, does it imply certainty about God's nonexistence, or probability (and how much?), or something else? Dawkins'

---

12 Dawkins, *The God Delusion*, pp. 50–51.

own words suggest a probability reading, but he provides no indication as to how high a probability is required for even his own atheism to be plausible. So his own position on what atheism amounts to suffers from a fatal case of ambiguity. For Dawkins to claim that he knows that it is highly unlikely that God does not exist is a bit misleading, then, without careful qualification.

Second, even if Dawkins did supply us with a workable and plausible notion of "know" for purposes of this category of strong atheism, it is unclear that his position is strong enough to warrant the label "atheism" for the reason noted above. This makes his position misleading, to say the least, especially since orthodox atheism is the claim that "It is not the case that God exists," with no epistemic qualifier. Also, Dawkins' own *de facto* atheism is indistinguishable from what an agnostic would hold, or could very well hold without misleading herself or others. The agnostic can easily embrace *de facto* atheism's claim that there is a "very low probability" of God's existence, "but short of zero." And this is because for the agnostic there are degrees of belief or lack thereof in God's existence, and hence a range of the extent to which one falls under the category "agnostic" based on the range of skeptical reasoning employed to reach agnosticism. Thus Dawkins' position that he conveniently labels "atheism" is a rather weak version compared to traditional atheism, and his own position is indistinguishable from what has traditionally and widely been understood as agnosticism, a position Dawkins believes is "poverty"-stricken. In this way, Dawkins commits a kind of fallacy of equivocation between "atheism" and "agnosticism." Dawkins demonstrates the tell-tale signs of someone who is unfamiliar with issues that have been a part of philosophy of religion and theology for generations. And this does not bode well for the credibility of his arguments or his authority in these fields of inquiry. He is quite unlike Russell who carefully steered clear of such hyperbole when he so often addressed the very same issues in public forums.

But neither does Dawkins' view that God most probably fails to exist enjoy adequate support in and of itself (whether or not it is atheistic or agnostic). As one philosopher-admirer of Dawkins' states, "As Dawkins himself would rightly say, one cannot generalize from a sample of one. . . ."[13] But *how then can Dawkins embrace with logical credulity a position of denying with high probability the existence of God when he has considered and refuted only the most obviously nonexistent but alleged divinity*

---

13   A. C. Grayling, "Dawkins and the Virus of Faith," in A. Grafen and M. Ridley, Editors, *Richard Dawkins* (Oxford: Oxford University Press, 2006), p. 243.

having hyperbolic attributes? What Dawkins' arguments support is the idea that a certain rather popular notion of God is implausible, and for a variety of reasons that have been noted (for the most part) for centuries by philosophers from at least Kant to Hume and beyond. But this neither defeats theism itself (not even the strictly supernaturalistic theism that Dawkins claims to refute) in its more plausible and interesting formulations nor adequately buttresses his alleged atheism—not even his probabilistic variety!

Even supposing that Dawkins defeats traditional Christian theism, he infers from some miraculous feat of "logic" that he has defeated all reasonable claims to God's existence (otherwise he would not call himself an atheist, but rather an agnostic). After disposing of the Thomistic proofs for God's existence,[14] Dawkins, in the span of only a few pages each,[15] discards the ontological argument and related arguments because they are essentially question-begging,[16] the aesthetic argument due to its questionable logic,[17] the existential argument because religious experience admits of psychological explanation,[18] the argument from religious texts due to its questionable veracity regarding certain crucial questions of theology and religion,[19] the argument from scientific authority because it constitutes a dubious appeal to authority,[20] Blaise Pascal's famous wager because it discount's the value of questioning,[21] and the probability argument in that the probability of God's existence is far less than is imagined by theists.[22] However, Dawkins omits several details of intricate argumentation and analysis (Why, after all, trouble folk whom you think are too simple to understand the details of such argument and analysis if they are sufficiently gullible to accept traditional Christian theism in the first place? Or, is it that Dawkins himself truly does not know the details? Or, is it both?). This leads Dawkins into a somewhat protracted discussion of the teleological argument.

---

[14] Dawkins, *The God Delusion*, pp. 77–79.
[15] Careful scholars of theology and philosophy of religion know that these and other arguments for God's existence usually attract much more serious attention from critics than Dawkins provides.
[16] Dawkins, *The God Delusion*, pp. 80–85.
[17] Dawkins, *The God Delusion*, pp. 86–87.
[18] Dawkins, *The God Delusion*, pp. 87–92.
[19] Dawkins, *The God Delusion*, pp. 92–97.
[20] Dawkins, *The God Delusion*, pp. 97–103.
[21] Dawkins, *The God Delusion*, pp. 103–105.
[22] Dawkins, *The God Delusion*, pp. 105–109.

The argument from design, being a particularized version of the cosmological argument, argues from the perception of intricate design in the
world to a Grand Designer. William Paley offered this argument along the
lines of a watch's requiring a maker, thus God being the Watchmaker of
the world. Dawkins has argued at length that the argument at best shows
that if there is a Watchmaker, that the Watchmaker is terribly "blind" or
defective in light of the many natural problems that exist.[23] But it is
Dawkins' more general assault on the God hypothesis that concerns me
here. For it is his response to the argument from design that for the most
part leads him to clarify and adopt his self-described atheism.

In short, Dawkins quite rightly argues that the creationist's almost
addictive habit of attributing natural complexity to God where there are
gaps in natural evolution (the "God of the gaps" way of thinking, a criticism that traces at least as far back as Alfred North Whitehead, as we will
see in Part II of this book) is highly problematic in that Charles Darwin's
theory of natural selection serves as the inference to the best explanation
of the creationist's illicitly bifurcative alleged dilemma (an *embarrass de
choix*, if you will) between natural evolutionary chance and the God
hypothesis.[24] In fact, Dawkins argues that it is more probable that natural
selection answers problems of evolution than the existence of God as
Creator does. And this is especially true, Dawkins argues, in light of the
phenomenon of accumulation in natural selection.[25] And while some
creationists might concede these points, they tend to argue that natural
selection cannot serve as the basis of a plausible cosmology.[26] Dawkins
points out that this is true, but unlike the orthodox Christian creationist
who simply offers the existence of God as the Creator of all things, including the universes,[27] the anthropic principle in physics serves as a viable
alternative to creationism. It is more likely to best explain the origin of the
universes than is the God hypothesis. Why? Because the God hypothesis,

---

23 Richard Dawkins, *The Blind Watchmaker* (Harlow: Longman, 1986). For a
    critique of Dawkins' treatment of William Paley's watchmaker argument
    from design, see Elliot Sober, "Intelligent Design and Probability Reasoning,"
    International Journal for Philosophy of Religion, 52 (2002), pp. 68–69.
24 Of course, this point is found in theists such as Peacocke, *Creation and the
    World of Science*, pp. 60–61.
25 Dawkins, *The God Delusion*, pp. 120f.
26 For example, see Kathleen Jones, *Challenging Richard Dawkins* (Norwich:
    Canterbury Press, 2007).
27 "Human beings are the inhabitants, not of one universe, but of many
    universes" [Aldous Huxley, "Words and Their Meanings," in Max Black Editor,
    The Importance of Language (Englewood Cliffs: Prentice-Hall, 1962), p. 2].

argues Dawkins, leads to an infinite regress,[28] as critics of the cosmological argument have pointed out long ago.[29] While it is understandable that humans attribute the origin of the universe and the goings on of nature to God, that hypothesis is far less probable than truly scientific ones. And it is not simply that the postulating of God as the Creator of the universe and all that is in it ends in an infinite regress. It is also that the nature of such a deity must be inordinately complex, contrary to traditional Christian theism: "A God capable of continuously monitoring and controlling the individual status of every particle in the universe *cannot* be simple."[30] Thus the orthodox Christian doctrine of divine simplicity is called into serious question.

While one might concur with Dawkins on several points he raises against traditional Christian or even traditional theistic thinking, he is not entitled to draw the inference that atheism is the most reasonable alternative explanation of fundamental issues of cosmogony and cosmology. For it might well be the case that either a non-Christian theism or an agnosticism is most reasonable, all relevant things considered.

One might concur with Dawkins that "it is a common error" of reasoning "to leap from the premise that the question of God's existence is in principle unanswerable to the conclusion that his existence and non-existence are equiprobable."[31] Indeed, one might even agree that "the existence of God is a scientific hypothesis like any other" in the sense that it can, in principle, be shown to be true or false.[32] And one might further grant him that "even if God's existence is never proved or disproved with certainty one way or the other, available evidence and reasoning may yield an estimate of probability far from 50 per cent."[33] One might even grant that the arguments, not necessarily the ones he offers, against the traditional arguments for the existence of God count heavily against the plausibility of those traditional "proofs." But in granting Dawkins all of this, one can still legitimately deny that he is entitled to infer that some credible version of atheism is sound. The reason for this is that he has brought into the debate a bifurcation fallacy.

---

[28] Dawkins, *The God Delusion*, p. 141. It is noteworthy, however, that an atheistic cosmology meets the same objection, as argued in Jones, *Challenging Richard Dawkins*, p. 24.

[29] One such account is found in Anthony Kenny, *The Five Ways* (Notre Dame: University of Notre Dame Press, 1969).

[30] Dawkins, *The God Delusion*, p. 149. The core of Dawkins' case for atheism is found on pp. 157–158.

[31] Dawkins, *The God Delusion*, p. 51.

[32] Dawkins, *The God Delusion*, p. 50.

[33] Dawkins, *The God Delusion*, p. 50.

While on occasion Dawkins seems to admit that there might be alternative theisms that might plausibly evade powerful criticism, he has nonetheless presumed that they are for some reason not worthy of addressing (perhaps because he is totally ignorant of them and too busy to study them, or perhaps because he is so driven by his emotive brand of atheistic propaganda and ideology that he is fearful of pursuing theism to its more plausible depths).[34] Whatever the case, Dawkins is not warranted in inferring strongly atheistic conclusions until he has, like a good scientist, conducted a more in-depth investigation into the alternative theistic hypotheses that would render theism significantly more plausible than its traditional Christian version. If such an investigation is conducted thoroughly and fair-mindedly, and if theism is still found wanting, *then* Dawkins is in a suitable epistemic position to claim that atheism, properly construed, is the most reasonable position about the God hypothesis. Until that time, however, Dawkins' atheism is unwarranted because it is based on a complex fallacy of a hasty conclusion based on inadequate data and a bifurcation fallacy that assumes that either the God of orthodox Christian theism exists, or atheism is sound.

For those who might think that Dawkins' position of *de facto* atheism makes his position immune from my criticism, I would ask how can it be said plausibly that "there is a very low probability" of God's existence if one has not investigated much more plausible notions of the nature and function of God? Is that not akin to refuting a truly bad idea and concluding that no alternative way of conceptualizing it could be probable? How would one know unless one has shown that to be so by considering and refuting an appropriately large sample of the most plausible theisms? It is a bit akin to a political leftist defeating the ideology of G. W. Bush and then inferring that she has cast sufficient doubt on political conservatism to justify leftism. Surely she must realize that some conservatisms in politics are more worthy than others, especially Bush's. Dawkins' is a kind of atheism by default, as he commits precisely the same kind of error in logic that the creationist does in assuming that only God could fill the gaps of evolution (a god*lessness* of the gaps, as it were). Dawkins assumes without independent argument that the only conceptual options worth addressing are traditional Christian theism and atheism, and that if he refutes the former, that he is warranted in adopting atheism. A more careful mind would not have made such a mistake, but rather would have delved into

---

[34]   One author accuses Dawkins of caricaturing theism in the form of fundamentalist Christianity (Jones, *Challenging Richard Dawkins*, p. 1).

more sophisticated theologies that explicitly attempt to accommodate the various concerns raised about traditional theism.

In short, Dawkins commits the errors of atheism discussed in the previous chapter. It involves the committing of a bifurcation fallacy, a straw person fallacy, equivocation and a hasty conclusion. He commits a bifurcation fallacy to the extent that he does not consider arguments for alternatives to traditional Christian theism and atheism, and he is dismissive of agnosticism. Yet in Chapters 5–6, I shall demonstrate that there are more than the two alternatives he suggests. There are alternatives to supernaturalistic theisms, as well as the New Agnosticism, neither of which Dawkins even considers.

Furthermore, Dawkins falls prey to the straw person fallacy in that he is guilty of refuting a theology that is so outmoded and implausible that few competent, non-fideistic scholars would endorse it. Indeed, even Aquinas, hardly a radical Christian theologian, doubted some of the hyperbolic (yet orthodox) divine attributes. Perhaps Dawkins is unaware that entire schools of Christian (or quasi-Christian) theism have been developed over the past half-century or so that attempt to address precisely many of his concerns—and then some! Undoubtedly, his reason for addressing orthodox Christian theism is because of its popularity in the West, and as a public scholar he is diligently attempting to raise consciousness about natural selection and its power to explain various phenomena. This much is perfectly understandable—even laudable. However, for Dawkins to draw the conclusions he draws without at least delving somewhat into such alternative theologies is misleading, if not irresponsible.[35] For it gives readers the impression atheism must be the best answer when in fact Dawkins has not justified this claim.

---

[35] It is, however, unsurprising given his lack of respect for theology as a discipline, as captured by his remark that: "I have yet to see any good reason to suppose that theology (as opposed to biblical history, literature, etc.) is a subject at all" (Dawkins, *The God Delusion*, p. 57). How in the world could this kind of crass assertion be justified? Does Dawkins mean that it is somehow illegitimate to devote reason and even science to the study of the possibility of God's existence? But this presumes that the existence of God has already been disproven, something Dawkins himself denies! Could it be that Dawkins is peddling an atheistic ideology while he commits the very same kinds of excesses of dogmatism that he accuses of traditional theists? Dawkins entertains the possibility that "there are some genuinely profound and meaningful questions that are forever beyond the reach of science" (p. 56). But why then does he rule out the importance of theological investigation?

Moreover, Dawkins, in stipulating atheism in probabilistic terms that amount to agnosticism, commits a fallacy of equivocation. In order to avoid this error, he must define "theism," "atheism," and "agnosticism" in ways that are not arbitrary and that do not render the conceptual boundaries of these categories nonsensical. No party to the debate about God is permitted logically to win by definitional fiat.

Finally, Dawkins commits (by implication) a hasty conclusion insofar as he assumes that his refutation of traditional Christian theism can be generalized as the refutation of all supernaturalistic theisms. For if he did not assume this generalization, he would not in light of his argumentation be able to claim himself to be an atheist.

When carefully combined, certain process and liberation theologies can go a long way toward addressing many of Dawkins' concerns with theism, making theism more of a live option than Dawkins ever considers it to be.[36] And even if in the end they are problematic, they are far more plausible and deserving of our respect and perhaps even our rational assent or consideration than is orthodox Christian theism. This implies that unorthodox theism, and if not this brand of theism, then agnosticism, is more probable than Dawkins leads one to believe. While Dawkins seems to admit that science can lead one to agnosticism,[37] he does not explore this possibility. And while Dawkins' arguments can serve rightly to awaken many traditional Christian theists from their dogmatic slumbers, Dawkins' own thinking, ironically, suffers from a dogmatic and rather limited understanding of theism that prevents him from taking theism as seriously as it deserves to be taken. Indeed, Dawkins' way of thinking about the possibility of God's existence might well be described in George Santayana's description of philosophical heresies, namely, as a "whole plague of little dogmatisms"[38] strung together into one larger one. Perhaps Dawkins ought to take Santayana's advice and not "substitute the pursuit of sincerity for the pursuit of omniscience."[39] In this respect, then, Dawkins' quoted words

---

[36] The project of synthesizing these views in order to address this very problem is found in Chapters 5–6.

[37] Dawkins, *The God Delusion*, p. 71.

[38] Santayana, "Philosophical Heresy," p. 563.

[39] Santayana, "Philosophical Heresy," p. 564. Perhaps, in the midst of his atheistic fervor, Dawkins is "proud to be a radical, [though] he can not imagine that he is a dupe" (p. 566). In reading Dawkins, one forms the unmistaken impression that the following description of the dogmatist applies to him: "He bends all his powers to justify his belief in some particular conception that he has espoused; he is looking, not in general, but for some one explaining

from Peter Medwar's review of Teilhard de Chardin's *The Phenomenon of Man*[40] apply to Dawkins' *The God Delusion*: "its author can be excused of dishonesty only on the grounds that before deceiving others he has taken great pains to deceive himself."[41] Dawkins, as a self-described scientist-activist exhorting the public to adopt a particular scientific ideology[42] (some of which is sound) has deceived himself into drawing an invalid inference perhaps because he is unconcerned with the genuine truth of the matter about God's possible existence. For if Dawkins were truly concerned about whether or not God exists, he would have taken much more seriously the depth of argumentation and analysis that the most respectable nontraditional (some even Christian) theologies proffer. Instead, he ignores or is ignorant of philosophies of religion or theologies that are not so easy prey for his scientific criticisms that work so well against traditional and outmoded theologies. Instead of admitting that his criticisms do not address particular theologies of a more sophisticated nature, such as some that I address in Chapters 5–6, Dawkins gives the impression that he is only addressing supernatural ideas of God,[43] implying that all there is to

---

principle upon which he has set his mind and heart" [W. H. Sheldon, "The Rôle of Dogma in Philosophy," *The Journal of Philosophy*, 24 (1927), p. 393].

40 Teilhard de Chardin, *The Phenomenon of Man*, B. Wall (trans.) (New York: Harper & Row Publishers, 1965). Also see Teilhard de Chardin, *The Future of Man*, N. Denny (trans.) (New York: Harper & Row Publishers, 1964); *The Hymn of the Universe* (New York: Harper & Row Publishers, 1961).

41 Dawkins, *The God Delusion*, p. 154.

42 "If this book works as I intend, religious readers who open it will be atheists when they put it down" (Dawkins, *The God Delusion*, p. 5). Precisely how this exemplifies a spirit of "open-minded" inquiry of free spirits that Dawkins claims he supports (p. 6, and elsewhere) is a bit unclear.

43 "I am calling only *supernatural* gods delusional" (Dawkins, *The God Delusion*, p. 15). Furthermore: "I am not attacking any particular version of God or gods. I am attacking God, all gods, anything and everything supernatural, wherever and whenever they have been or will be invented" (p. 36). Dawkins also loads the term "God" with such preposterous notions that only a traditionalist would accept (p. 18). Moreover, his definition of what counts as atheism seems to rule out some leading and well-respected theological views that attempt to reconcile in legitimate ways good science and plausible theology. For example, Dawkins states:

An atheist in this sense of philosophical naturalist is somebody who believes there is nothing beyond the natural, physical world, no *super*natural creative intelligence lurking behind the observable universe, no soul that outlasts the body and no miracles — except in the sense of natural phenomena that we

reality is that which can be tested and measured by the sciences. But this simplistic worldview is unfair to legitimate science which understands the chasm of methodological differences that lie between science and religion. And no amount of Dawkins' dogmatically presumed logical positivism can bully its way past the logic that prohibits his view from establishing itself unless and until certain conceptual barriers are surpassed. He is correct to ask, "What is so special about religion that we grant it such uniquely privileged status?"[44] Dawkins asks this important question in the context of his discussion of how religion has for centuries gained a privileged

---

don't yet understand. If there is something that appears to lie beyond the natural world as it is now imperfectly understood, we hope eventually to understand and embrace it within the natural. (p. 14)

But this line of reasoning is curious. For if the only theological ideas that are sound are those that can be confirmed by scientific investigation, then Dawkins has from the outset effectively and dogmatically set the terms of investigation in favor of scientific verification (and perhaps even falsification). But this position, reminiscent of logical positivism, suffers from the flaw of question-begging methodology. Even though I concur that what we accept ought to, *as far as methodologically possible*, be verifiable or falsifiable by legitimate scientific means of investigation, it is nonetheless a methodological bias that cannot legitimately be imposed, no matter what dogma or ideology one wished to persuade others of, without exposing itself to proper criticism. But even worse is Dawkins' claim that "if there is something that appears to lie beyond the natural world as it is now imperfectly understood, we hope eventually to understand and embrace it within the natural." This seems to imply that Dawkins' own scientism amounts to a dogma in itself—one that, not entirely unlike the traditional Christian dogma he seeks to dissuade others of, lies beyond the realm of independent verification or falsification! He also attempts, illegitimately of course, to win the argument by definitional fiat. For Dawkins desires to illicitly categorize anything in the future that can be known by scientific means as not theistic. But why not think that it is theistic, properly construed? Again, Dawkins' simple-minded notion of theism prevents him from understanding what several respected theologians have known for some time now, namely, that science is a good means by which the wonders of God can be discovered, a position that Dawkins ironically wonders why theists seem not to want to accept: ". . . if God really did communicate with humans that fact would emphatically not lie outside science" (p. 154). But in spite of Dawkins' incredible theological ignorance, several theists in fact do.

44   Dawkins, *The God Delusion*, p. 27. This is hardly an original idea, however, as many Christian theologians themselves have raised this issue in the name of religious pluralism. Indeed, this point is made with particular regard to the manner in which Christianity is given preferential treatment throughout U.S. history [See Vine Deloria, Jr., *God is Red* (Golden: Fulcrum Publishing, 1994), Chapter 12].

status in various societies, and he is right to do so. But this question can also be raised in the context of scientific investigation, even by those of us who in large part embrace the sciences but simultaneously seek independent evidence for our conclusions wherever evidences for competing views do not easily admit of unbiased investigative methods. Yet Dawkins fails to address this methodological issue as he presumptuously proceeds as if scientific methods are unproblematic in the context of the discussion about God's existence. This is especially curious as he himself explicates that he is only concerned with supernatural notions of God.

One might think that Dawkins' somewhat careful statement that he is only targeting supernatural forms of religion allows him to escape the criticism that there are alternative nontraditional theisms that do not run afoul of his scathing critique. But this depends on what is meant by "supernatural," and whether or not it can be shown whether all that exists can be measured by scientific methodologies. This is surely a question I do not intend to answer as it is beyond my intended purview. But it is reasonable to wonder whether or not good science even claims what Dawkins implies here. And so it is Dawkins, not only the traditional Christian theist, who must defend certain assumptions that are quite controversial. Dawkins' construing "supernatural" and its cognates to mean something like "beyond the natural world and what is observable by the sciences" simply begs the question against supernaturalistic religions. For he attempts by some form of intellectual coercion to win the debate about God's existence by a kind of definitional fiat that is remarkably reminiscent of logical positivism: Only that which the sciences can measure is real; God cannot be measured by the sciences (because God is spirit and beyond the natural world); therefore, God is not real (does not exist). If this is not a classic case of question-begging, then no such example exists! Surely atheism has better arguments on which to rely than some of those set forth by Dawkins.

Dawkins' construal of theism is so extreme that he sees what he refers to as "Einstein's religion" as metaphorical and pantheistic and "light years away from the interventionist, miracle-wreaking, thought-reading, sin-punishing, prayer-answering God of the Bible, of priests, mullahs and rabbis, and of ordinary language."[45] Once again, Dawkins sees things in simplistic and bifurcatively fallacious terms: either God exists as something totally congruent with what most think God is, or God does not exist at all and that this is totally explicable in scientific terms. This, coupled

---

[45]   Dawkins, *The God Delusion*, p. 19.

with his committing the atheist's error of wrongly inferring the superiority of atheism over theism when all he refutes is a popular form of it, means that Dawkins commits a straw person fallacy as well. So we have in Dawkins' reasoning one logical fallacy heaped onto another, a feat that one would think is beyond the reach of serious science, theology, and philosophy. One wonders, then, why Dawkins is so arrogantly confident in his pronouncements against theism. One would think that such confidence ought only to be grounded in sound reasoning and conceptual clarity.

Finally, just as Dawkins accuses some theologians or religious folk of "intellectual high treason" in that they confuse the metaphorical sense of "God" with the more literalist sense, Dawkins himself seems to commit intellectual high treason. To paraphrase what one well-known and respectable religious leader once said: one must be careful not to point out the sliver of wood in someone else's eye lest the beam in one's own eye leave oneself blinded (and, one might add, delusional). This point applies to theists, agnostics, and atheists alike. Apparently, Dawkins has in great measure strayed from one of his own statements: ". . . we on the science side must not be too dogmatically confident."[46]

In the end, I think, we ought to follow Russell's advice: "I cannot believe that mankind can be the better for shrinking from examination of this or that question."[47] And while ". . . complete skepticism would, of course, be totally barren and totally useless,"[48]

> The question is how to arrive at your opinions and not what your opinions are. The thing in which we believe is the supremacy of reason. If reason should lead you to orthodox conclusions, well and good; you are still a Rationalist. To my mind the essential thing is that one should base one's arguments upon the kind of grounds that are acceptable in science, and that one should not regard anything that one accepts as quite certain, but only as

---

[46] Dawkins, *The God Delusion*, p. 124. Perhaps Dawkins means to imply that a certain amount of dogmatic confidence is permissible by those who embrace science in the way that he does. Perhaps he means also that this point applies only to contexts of evolutionary explanations of the world. But not even Dawkins' refutation of the "Argument from Personal Incredulity" and the "Divine Knob-Twiddler Argument" of the crude creationist entitles him to any kind of arrogant dogmatism. For dogmatism simply has no place whatsoever in serious philosophical, theological, or scientific investigation.

[47] Al Seckel, Editor, *Bertrand Russell on God and Religion* (Buffalo: Prometheus Books, 1986), p. 89.

[48] Seckel, Editor, *Bertrand Russell on God and Religion*, p. 86.

probable in a greater or less degree. Not to be absolutely certain is, I think, one of the essential things in rationality.[49]

But Russell admits that "No sensible man, however agnostic, has 'faith in reason alone.'"[50] And it is, on his view, not impossible to reconcile science and religion, if "religion" means something akin to a system of ethics as opposed to some form of dogma.[51] Moreover, agnosticism can be reconciled with a version of Christianity that amounts to a kind of morality.[52] This point is made humorously when Russell states the following in answer to the question: "Can an agnostic be a Christian?"

> If you mean by a "Christian" a man who loves his neighbor, who has wide sympathy for suffering, and who ardently desires a world free from the cruelties and abominations which at present disfigure it, then, certainly, you will be justified in calling me a Christian. And, in this sense, you will find more "Christians" among agnostics than among the orthodox.[53]

Nielsen argues exactly the opposite point, namely, that fideist theists are in a real sense agnostics insofar as they insist in the mysteriousness of God.[54] In any case, Russell asserts:

> We want to stand upon our own feet and look fair and square at the world— its good facts, its bad facts, its beauties, and its ugliness; see the world as it is, and be not afraid of it. Conquer the world by intelligence, and not merely by being slavishly subdued by the terror that comes from it. The whole conception of God is a conception derived from the ancient Oriental despotisms. It is a conception quite unworthy of free men. . . . We ought to stand up and look the world frankly in the face. We ought to make the best we can of the world, and if it is not so good as we wish, after all it will still be better than what these others have made of it in all these ages. A good world . . . It needs a fearless outlook and a free intelligence.[55]

Dawkins' view is stated much more eloquently decades ago by Mackie, whose alleged atheism amounts to a kind of probability claim to the

---

[49] Seckel, Editor, *Bertrand Russell on God and Religion*, p. 84.

[50] Seckel, Editor, *Bertrand Russell on God and Religion*, p. 80.

[51] Seckel, Editor, *Bertrand Russell on God and Religion*, p. 81.

[52] Seckel, Editor, *Bertrand Russell on God and Religion*, pp. 76–77.

[53] Seckel, Editor, *Bertrand Russell on God and Religion*, p. 76.

[54] Kai Nielsen, *Philosophy & Atheism* (Buffalo: Prometheus Books, 1985), pp. 16f.

[55] Seckel, Editor, *Bertrand Russell on God and Religion*, p. 71.

effect that the "balancing of probabilities" favors atheism over the God hypothesis:

> This conclusion can be reached by an examination precisely of the arguments advanced in favour of theism, without even bringing into play what have been regarded as the strongest considerations on the other side, the problem of evil and the various natural histories of religion . . . the extreme difficulty that theism has in reconciling *its own* doctrines with one another in this respect must tell heavily against it. . . . The balance of probabilities . . . comes out strongly against the existence of a god.[56]

However, Mackie commits some of the errors of atheism[57] as he fails to remain within the parameters of what his own argument allows him to conclude. For Mackie's conclusion, as stated probabilistically, can also be held by the agnostic, and like Dawkins' position, does not amount to the claim that it is not the case that God exists. Quite simply and to the point: "It is not the case that God exists" does not have the same informational content as "The balance of probabilities . . . comes out strongly against the existence of a god." So we can trace Dawkins' error in contemporary times to Mackie. The substantive difference between them is that Mackie, unlike Dawkins, at least gives some amount of attention to some alternatives to traditional Christian theism, and Mackie's criticisms of the traditional arguments for God's existence is far more detailed and responsible than Dawkins', though it should be pointed out that Dawkins provides a more detailed scientific assessment of the teleological argument for God's existence.

In Chapters 5–6, I shall explain how certain theologies can begin to make much better sense of the nature and function of God and yet are unaddressed and unacknowledged by Dawkins' activist-motivated jabs at religion and theism (he seems to not know the difference at times). Prior to that, however, I shall set forth an account of the New Agnosticism.

---

[56] J. L. Mackie, *The Miracle of Theism* (Oxford: Oxford University Press, 1982), p. 253.

[57] This cluster of errors is discussed in the previous chapter.

CHAPTER 4

THE NEW AGNOSTICISM

The trouble with so many of our contemporaries is not that they are agnostics but rather that they are misguided theologians.

—E. Gilson[1]

The atheist says that no matter what definition you choose, "God exists" is always false. The theist claims only that there is some definition which will make "God exist" true. In my view, neither the stronger nor the weaker claim has been convincingly established. . . . .

. . . But the true default position is neither theism nor atheism, but agnosticism—that is to say, the position of one who does not know whether or not there is a God. A claim to knowledge needs to be substantiated; ignorance need only be confessed.

—Anthony Kenny[2]

Having described and demonstrated the problematic nature of atheism as it has been articulated by some leading atheistic philosophers, and having provided an even more detailed picture of how and why the atheism of a popular evolutionist goes terribly awry in that, among other things, it exaggerates the conflicts between science and religion, it is important to describe in some detail the New Agnosticism by juxtaposing it to various kinds of atheism, on the one hand, and theism, on the other. And this will be accomplished without providing self-serving categories of these genera that inherently support the New Agnosticism. The taxonomy that has been provided of kinds of atheism, theism, and agnosticism conforms to common sense or "folk" understandings of these categories and seeks to inform us of more nuanced understandings of these notions.

The fact is that "the subject of agnosticism has not received the philosophical attention it merits . . . agnosticism is a perfectly possible position, and it raises a variety of questions that deserve subtle consideration."[3] It is hoped that this chapter will provide agnosticism the philosophical attention it deserves, and that the New Agnosticism will stand as the

---

[1] E. Gilson, *God and Philosophy* (New Haven: Yale University Press, 1941), p. 137.

[2] Anthony Kenny, *What I Believe* (London: Continuum, 2006), p. 21.

[3] Piers Benn, "Some Uncertainties about Agnosticism," *International Journal for Philosophy of Religion*, 46 (1999), p. 172.

most plausible, however tentative, position on the problem of God's existence.

My argument herein will constitute a defense of agnosticism, which has received far less attention in the philosophy of religion literature than either theism or atheism. The "New Agnosticism" (as I shall call it) supports and deepens considerably Bertrand Russell's agnosticism. It is unlike the "new" agnostic humanism or "secularism" of G. J. Holyoake, whose view amounts to a kind of dogmatic or doctrinaire empiricism and humanism.[4] The New Agnosticism seeks to be dogmatic about nothing except, perhaps, the fallibilism that accompanies our need to employ reason as best we can in order to discover the truth about God's possible existence, as it subscribes to no basic beliefs.[5]

While my agreement with atheists that the orthodox Christian notion of the nature and function of God is problematic for many of the same reasons that have already been provided throughout centuries of discussion, my argument is that atheism (even J. L. Mackie's balancing of probabilities type) is untenable unless it is the case that there is *no* plausible notion of God worthy of the name. While this hardly constitutes—nor is it intended to be—an *apologia* for traditional Christian theism, it does serve to soften significantly the threat of atheism for honest, truly devout, Christians and other theists for whom "rational" and "scientific" are not offensive. For the arguments shall demonstrate that the jury is still out on the question of God's existence. However, this hardly supports the inference drawn by Hans Küng that arguments for and against the existence of the orthodox Christian conception of God are equally inconclusive and that this entitles one to "make a free decision" in favor of orthodox Christian theism that is rationally justified.[6] Furthermore, the evidence for "God exists" and the evidence for its denial are to a meaningful extent incomparable such that at the present time a final verdict on the God hypothesis is not possible

---

[4] G. J. Holyoake, *The Origin and Nature of Secularism* (London: Watts, 1896).

[5] Epistemologically speaking, "basic beliefs" are those posited by foundationalists who believe that some beliefs are properly basic and beyond question. They are self-justified and serve as the "foundation" of other nonbasic beliefs in one's doxastic system. Alvin Plantinga is a theistic foundationalist. Problems with foundationalism include its inability to conceptually stop the epistemic regress of justification pertaining to beliefs. Whether fallibilistic or infallibilistic, foundationalism suffers from severe difficulties [Keith Lehrer, *Theory of Knowledge*, 2nd Edition (Boulder: Westview Press, 2000), Chapters 3–4].

[6] Hans Küng, *Does God Exist?* E. Quinn (trans.) (New York: Doubleday and Company, 1980), pp. 540, 544, 568f., 646, etc.

absent reasonable doubt about the existence of God. And this is precisely where a good agnostic ought to find herself. This much is consistent with, if not inspired by, Russell's view as stated in Chapter 2. But the New Agnosticism shall deepen Russell's position on the problem of God, and in interesting ways for both philosophers and theologians alike.

It is helpful to note that the New Agnosticism differs from the agnosticism expressed in David Hume's *Dialogues Concerning Natural Religion* wherein agnosticism amounts to "a total suspense of judgement."[7] Instead, a judgment will be made by the New Agnostic, namely, that of recognizing whatever truth-value there is to the theistic arguments, on the one hand, and also whatever truth-value there is to the atheistic critiques of them, on the other. But it will also insist that due to certain supernaturalistic biases of the theist and certain naturalistic ones of many atheists, that the incomparable nature of such sets of evidence makes it presently too difficult, though not in principle impossible, to make an adequate and final decision between the two opposing positions.

The New Agnosticism is consistent with John Stuart Mill's statement that "From the result of the preceding examination of the evidences of theism . . . it follows that the rational attitude of a thinking mind toward the supernatural, whether in natural or revealed religion, is that of skepticism as distinguished from belief on the one hand, and from atheism on the other."[8] So the New Agnosticism shares with Mill a kind of neutral skepticism that simply cannot reasonably choose, all relevant things considered and at the present time, between theism (properly construed) and atheism (properly understood). The difference between the New Agnosticism and the agnosticism of Mill and Russell lies in the fact that the New Agnosticism refuses to rest assured (as atheists tend to) that the refutation of traditional Christian theism in particular spells the demise of theism more generally, a point left untouched by these (and other) philosophers. Rather, it seeks to delve into modified and more plausible forms of theism that evade concerns about God's hyperbolic qualities in light of certain real-world realities, and it holds atheism to the task of providing a defense of itself. For as noted in a previous chapter of this book, the mere refutation of a position is not in itself an epistemic entitlement to accept its denial. If I lack sufficient reason to accept the claim that X is evil, I am not

---

[7] David Hume, *Dialogues Concerning Natural Religion*, N. K. Smith, Editor (Indianapolis: Bobbs-Merrill, 1947), p. 186.

[8] Quoted in Stephen L. Weber, *Proofs for the Existence of God: A Meta-Investigation* (Ann Arbor: University Microfilms Inc., 1970), p. 217.

entitled to accept that claim that it is not the case that X is evil, though I may, *al la* Mackie, accept a probability judgment that in light of the available evidence it is more likely than not that it is not the case that X is evil. However, this position is not atheistic, but agnostic (recall from Chapters 1–2 that atheism is the view that it is not the case that God exists. It is the logical denial of theism).

If I am correct in my characterization of atheism, there seems to be a rather chronic presumptuousness of atheism. Yet this is no minor error in reasoning, as it points to a dogmatic rejection of theism itself in that some of the atheists are philosophers and scientists and ought to know better than to reason so poorly. If theism is to be genuinely refuted and atheism made plausible, it must be true that the strongest (not the most extreme or hyperbolic) form of theism available must be refuted. It makes no difference that some weak form of theism overloaded with several doctrines of faith is shown to be impoverished—no matter how popular it is.

In the interest of fairness and truth, I address the problematic arguments made by some leading atheists in refuting some of the poor arguments made in defense of the traditional Christian notion of God. And in light of my criticism of atheism, I bear the burden of demonstrating that there is an analysis of the nature and function of God that is plausible and evades the formidable objections to the traditional Christian notion of God.

I shall argue that, while the orthodox Christian notion of God falls prey to the standard objections raised by various philosophers, there is a more plausible process-liberationist conception of God, one of the ideas of which can be mined from the likes of Alfred North Whitehead,[9] Charles Hartshorne,[10] John Cobb, Jr.,[11] David Ray Griffin,[12] and liberationists such

---

[9]   Alfred North Whitehead, *Process and Reality* (New York: The Humanities Press, 1929); *Religion in the Making* (New York: The Macmillan Company, 1957).

[10] Charles Hartshorne, *Anselm's Discovery* (LaSalle: Open Court, 1965); *The Divine Relativity* (New Haven: Yale University Press, 1948); *The Logic of Perfection* (LaSalle: Open Court Publishing Company, 1962); *Man's Vision of God* (Hamden: Archon Books, 1964); *Natural Theology for Our Time* (LaSalle: Open Court, 1950).

[11] John B. Cobb, Jr, *God and the World* (Philadelphia: The Westminster Press, 1969); John B. Cobb, Jr. and David Ray Griffin, *Process Theology* (Philadelphia: The Westminster Press, 1976).

[12] David Ray Griffin, *Evil Revisited* (Albany: SUNY Press, 1991); *God, Power and Evil: A Process Theodicy* (Philadelphia: Westminster Press, 1976).

as James H. Cone,[13] Gustavo Gutiérrez,[14] among others. Moreover, I shall further develop the process notion of God and briefly note how it evades the criticisms of the ontological, cosmological, and teleological arguments. Then I shall explain how some of the essentials of liberation theologies can be made congruent with those of process theologies in constructing a hybrid minimalist theism (a process-liberation theology) that can evade all or most of the problems facing orthodox Christian theism.

It should be borne in mind that Mackie's famous article, "Evil and Omnipotence"[15]—not unlike Russell's critique of traditional Christian theism—is not intended by Mackie to refute all forms of theism, but only the traditional one in which God is construed as being omnipotent, omni-benevolent, omnipresent, and omniscient.[16] In response to Mackie's ingenious argument against orthodox Christian theism, I shall argue that the process-liberationist conception of God provides a plausible answer to the problem of evil, as well as answers to basic religious matters of prayer and respect for self, others, and nature. In the end, while it may be true that traditional Christian theism does not survive rational scrutiny as so many philosophers have argued, atheism fails to demonstrate at this time that it is not the case that God exists or, even more strongly, that the existence of God is impossible. If all available versions of theism fail and atheism worthy of the name is inadequately justified, what is viable *at this time* is agnosticism. I write "at this time" to accentuate the fact that the argumentation about God's existence is predicated on what we know now based on arguments from the past, and we must remain open to the possibility that further argumentation might well provide a good reason for us to be dissuaded. Atheism will remain in doubt so long as some conception of God genuinely worthy of the name is plausible, all relevant things considered.

One benefit of my analysis of the existence of God is that, unlike most philosophical accounts, mine is better-informed theologically. And unlike most theological accounts, mine is well-informed philosophically and places no restrictions on the employment of reason in this context of

---

13 James H. Cone, *God of the Oppressed* (New York: Seabury Press, 1975); *Risks of Faith* (Boston: Beacon Press, 1999).
14 Gustavo Gutiérrez, *A Theology of Liberation* (Maryknoll: Orbis Books, 1973).
15 J. L. Mackie, *The Miracle of Theism* (Oxford: Oxford University Press, 1982), Chapter 9.
16 As pointed out in the previous chapter, however, this caution does not prevent Mackie from committing the errors of atheism.

discourse. My account makes significant use of some of the best works in theology as well as in the philosophy of religion. In so doing, my account evades a rather common error committed by many atheists, namely, part of what I have referred to as the "errors of atheism": That since the traditional notion of the nature of God is highly problematic, there is no God. In arguing that there is a more plausible and religiously viable notion of God available to us, I insist that the atheist bears the burden of demonstrating her position in light of this information. For what the atheist actually refutes is a straw person notion of the nature of God.

So it is not only that, as even some theologians claim, following Friedrich Nietzsche, that the God of traditional Christian theism is "dead,"[17] though, as I argued in the Introduction, it is rather queer, if not nonsensical, to refer to something as "dead" if it never existed in the first place![18] Of course, the "God is dead" movement in Christian theology is a call to relinquish the orthodox notion of God in favor of one that is secularized and meaningful to a scientific world.[19] It is not a denial of the obvious fact that the orthodox notion of God "lives" in hearts and the minds of religious people. Indeed, it has taken up seemingly permanent residency in such quarters!

Thus the debate continues, but now with the way cleared of the debris of unnecessary and hyperbolic religious language about God and religious experience in favor of a conception of God's being that makes better sense of genuine religious experience, absent the nonsense. Thus the atheist now has a new burden to bear, a challenge to refute this more plausible idea of God. It does not follow, however, that traditional Christian theism gains any plausibility in light of these facts. Conceptually speaking, it is not a "live option," to borrow a phrase from William James. For it has long since been defeated in argument, despite the great and noble efforts of some of its most astute minds to defend it.

Earlier I noted that I shall pursue and further develop a process-liberation conception of the nature of God. I shall do this in a rather eclectic manner, however. For I shall borrow ideas from existentialist theologians such as Paul Tillich, Christian *kerygmatic* theologians such as Rudolf

---

17 Thomas J. J. Altizer, *The Gospel of Christian Atheism* (Philadelphia: The Westminster Press, 1966).
18 A similar point is made in Mackie, *The Miracle of Theism*, p. 8.
19 Paul van Buren, *The Secular Meaning of the Gospel* (New York: The Macmillan Company, 1963).

Bultmann, liberation theologians like Cone[20] and Gutiérrez,[21] liberation-theologian activists such as Martin Luther King, Jr., religiously motivated political activists like Malcolm X, and combine them with the basics of process theology outlined in the major works of Whitehead, Cobb, Jr. and Griffin, respectively. Moreover, the immanentism of process theology will be appropriated, one which finds its roots in, among others, American Indian religions wherein the divine is seen in nature, and where humans are part of nature and enjoy no special privilege among natural beings or objects and should strive to always live in harmony with the natural world.[22]

American Indians, taken generally, believe in the "great web of life, the interconnectedness of spirituality and the environment," the mutual relatedness of all things and mutual responsibility among humans.[23] Contemporary environmental ethics, philosophical or religious, are rooted in Indian religious thought and practice, unbeknownst to most in the U.S. who consider themselves ecologically sensitive. And as Winona LaDuke states, ". . . there is only one law. That is the Creator's law, the Breathmaker's law, or natural law."[24] So the very notion of natural law may well have its roots in Indian religions. It is a presumption of grand proportions to think that the ideas of environmentalism and natural law originate with Western thinkers.

Moreover, the very conception of God had by Indians is quite philosophically rich, reminiscent of Anselm and Tillich. As Charlotte Black Elk tells us,

> We have a word, *Wakan*, that is our word for God. In our household language *Wakan* would mean sacred or mystery, and *Takan* would be magnificent, great. So you could get the expression *Wakan Tanka*, "Great Spirit," in the household language. But in the formal language, *Wakakagano*, *Wa-ka* means "that which is that it is." The word "*Ka*" means "that which makes it what it is." And *Ga* means "that with no beginning and no ending." So it is a philosophical concept that contains our word for God, but within that is the word for sacred—"that which is that it is."[25]

---

[20] James H. Cone, *A Black Theology of Liberation* (Maryknoll: Orbis Books, 1990); *God of the Oppressed* (New York: The Seabury Press, 1975).

[21] Gutiérrez, *A Theology of Liberation*.

[22] Vine Deloria, Jr., *God is Red* (Golden: Fulcrum Publishing, 1994).

[23] Phil Cousineau, Editor, *A Seat at the Table* (Berkeley: University of California Press, 2006), p. 40.

[24] Cousineau, Editor, *A Seat at the Table*, p. 46.

[25] Cousineau, Editor, *A Seat at the Table*, p. 61.

While this Indian conception of God sounds quite similar to that of the Christian notion of God, Black Elk notes that the grave dissimilarity lies in the different ideas of nature. According to a literal interpretation of the *Genesis* account of creation, the transgression of humans led to banishment to nature, while in Indian religions nature is our Mother, hardly something to conquer, but that which is to be revered as God Herself and with which to live in harmony. Furthermore, she continues, "All things that live on Earth are children of the Earth, and they are our relatives. I don't have a greater right to live than a tree does. An elk doesn't have a greater right to life than a fish does. We all have equal rights."[26] "We have a responsibility not to change the Earth in ways that we can't repair. Such changes are violations against God."[27] And it is in the very ritual of the Sun Dance that Indians give back to the Earth out of respect to it.[28] Rather than the disunity between humans and nature as depicted in orthodox Christian theology, Indian theology teaches that "when the universe was created, each piece of it was given a song. When we go there and do our ceremonies we bring that whole song into play. When the song of the universe is being sung, then all Creation can rejoice."[29] Note how Black Elk capitalizes "Creation" whereas orthodox Christians capitalize "Creator." This alone signifies by implication the supernaturalism of orthodox Christianity and the immanentism of American Indian religions.

The distinctions between orthodox Christian theology and Indian theologies is further captured in the words of Douglas George-Kenentiio:

> Here is the *fundamental division* between the Iroquois and the Christians. It is that we believe the Creator speaks through all the natural elements. We don't worship the different forms of Creation. We realize that the Creator speaks through those elements of Creation. We realize that life is fundamentally good, that we are given all the blessings to enjoy this Creation, and that we have to act as custodians.[30] We believe in an infinite number of Creators, not just a singular God, that when we return to our spiritual world, it is

---

26   Cousineau, Editor, *A Seat at the Table*, p. 66. Also consult the words of Chief Oren Lyons (pp. 173–174).

27   Cousineau, Editor, *A Seat at the Table*, p. 68. Also consult the words of Douglas George-Kanentiio in Cousineau, Editor, *A Seat at the Table*, p. 83.

28   Cousineau, Editor, *A Seat at the Table*, p. 69.

29   Cousineau, Editor, *A Seat at the Table*, p. 72. Compare this notion with the idea of humans as symbionts having reverence for nature, found in Arthur Peacocke, *Creation and the World of Science* (Oxford: Oxford University Press, 2004), pp. 298–299.

30   This American Indian idea is expounded in terms of humans being "priests of creation," stewards or managers of it, having reverence for creation because

not a time of trauma for us but one of great release. Our primary role on this Earth as human beings is to act as custodians and to extract whatever beauty from this world will enable us to return to the Creator in peace and harmony.[31]

This is hardly the heathenistic view of a savage people that orthodox Christianity sought to persuade the world of in its support of the violent conquest of the Americas from their indigenous peoples. To these can be added the Indian beliefs in peace, an ethic of sharing, justice, and a responsibility to the future,[32] each of which are concepts copied by several Western thinkers usually without the least bit of recognition of their indigenous origins. These are some of the shared beliefs of the myriad of organizations referred to as the "Native American Church."

The importance of this brief discussion of American Indian religion and its contrast with orthodox Christian theology is that it sets the stage for my hybrid minimalist theism that follows in Chapters 5–6. But prior to that analysis it is vital to become clear about some of the desiderata for an adequate theism.

Desiderata for an Adequate Theism

In an attempt to build a more plausible theism in response to atheistic objections to orthodox Christian theism, it is important to outline at least some of the desired features of such a standpoint. What is desired of an adequate theism?

First, an adequate theism should avoid most if not all of the conceptual problems posed by philosophers. Primarily, these include the objections to the natural theological "proofs" which are the ontological, cosmological, and teleological arguments for God's existence, along with the moral and

---

God is in it as interpreter of the natural world and co-sufferer with it (Peacocke, *Creation and the World of Science*, pp. 295–312).

[31] Cousineau, Editor, *A Seat at the Table*, pp. 90–91. Also consult the words of Tonya Gonnella Frichner in Cousineau, Editor, *A Seat at the Table*, p. 137. In particular: "When you violate the natural world, you will pay for it in proportion to your violation" (pp. 137–138). Also consult the words of Chief Leon Shenandoah: "We must live in harmony with the natural world and recognize that excessive exploitation can only lead to our own destruction" (p. 169).

[32] These are discussed by Chief Oren Lyons in Cousineau, Editor, *A Seat at the Table*, pp. 180–182.

religious experience ones. But in doing so, theism cannot run from reason, but rather must utilize reason to the fullest and employ no question-begging or *ad hoc* tactics in the process. In short, an adequate theism must be truly rational, not merely apparently so. "Faith" is not an excuse for irrationality or lack of rational argument. It may not replace sound argument with blind leaps into the dark, backwards. Faith is only permitted after reason-giving justification has been attempted in good faith, and succeeds. This is both a philosophical and theological desideratum. It requires that theism be justi-fied or justifiable to the facts of the world, that it correspond to reality as it is, not merely how it is hoped that reality is. This implies that the epistemic criterion of coherence, while enough for personal justification, is insufficient for robust justification. And as Keith Lehrer argues, complete justification or knowledge requires that the "keystone" principle is satisfied. This requires that what is justified in the robust sense or known match the real world.[33] So insular dogmas, theological or otherwise, will not do here. Arguments and analyses pertaining to the nature and function of God must pass the reality test. I shall refer to this as the "desideratum of rationality."

Second, an adequate theism should be worthy of the name "theism" without being duped into thinking that it must employ hyperbolic and traditional categories to describe the nature and function of God. An ade-quate theism need not, in other words, amount to orthodox Christian theism. In fact, it ought not to do so! For that position is not tenable and has deservedly lost the credibility within philosophical circles of most inquirers, and has simultaneously lost the patience of several of those who are serious about the problem of God. Whatever God is, *if* indeed God is, God is *not* what orthodox Christians say She is. What remains to be seen is whether a more plausible notion of God can both fit the category mean-ingfully, and withstand the barrage of objections that doomed orthodox Christian theism. This is the "desideratum of openness."

Third, an adequate theism should not resort to revelation as the pri-mary argument for God's existence, as that is question-begging. Indeed, if theism is to employ or invoke revelation, it must do so only after it has provided sufficient rational evidence that the use of this or that particular source of putative revelation is justified in and of itself, and also justified relative to competing sources of alleged revelation. In other words, no special pleading is permitted concerning alleged sources of divine inspira-tion. I call this the "desideratum of testimony."

---

[33]   Lehrer, *Theory of Knowledge*, p. 172.

Fourth, no particular religious experience or tradition is *a priori* to be given special status, though it is permissible to make particular use of one or more such traditions in order to construct a viable theism. The key is to do so openly and with the admission that one's employment of categories from this or that particular religious tradition must at some point pass the test of plausibility when compared to and contrasted with the most plausible of other religious faiths. This point is related to the third one, and is the "desideratum of religious experience."

Fifth, a plausible theism should be practical. It must address well the most important concerns facing humankind, and beyond. It must not run afoul of the most common sense and considered judgments of science, philosophy (including ethics), and history. For instance, if it is a fact that the universe is Y years old, no theism is acceptable that contradicts this claim wildly and without sound scientific evidence. Where there are gaps in scientific, philosophical, or historical understandings, then there is room for theistic dispute about those issues. But where considered judgments and strong evidence lead to X, no desirable theism will contradict X too badly. Assumed here is the idea that disagreement is often a matter of degree, and that there is more than one extent to which disagreement can obtain. I refer to this as the "pragmatic desideratum."

Sixth, while recognizing the need for complexity in philosophy and theology, especially concerning the nature and function of God, it is nonetheless desirable that Ockham's Razor guide our deliberations. Other things being equal, a theism is desirable to the extent that it is simplest when simplicity is an option, and a plausible theism ought not to multiply its tenets beyond necessity. Strategically, this is a good idea, as the more extraneous dogmas invoked by theism, the more difficult it is to defend it. This, of course, is the "desideratum of simplicity."

These are desired features of a plausible theism. They are not sufficient conditions. Rather, they are important guidelines in the pursuit of answering atheism's claim to justification. To the extent that these desiderata are satisfied, the atheist has no legitimate complaint that the theist is exceeding the bounds of reason in attempting to establish theism. With these guidelines in mind, we can better attempt to construct a more plausible theism than the one that in Western societies has dominated the discussions thus far—and with impoverished and damaging results.

I now turn to the task of developing my hybrid theism, appropriating some of the least controversial basic features of process and liberation theisms, thereby creating a minimalist theism that can serve as a meaningful challenge to atheism's claim that it is not the case that God exists. But this hybrid minimalist process-liberation theism stands as an insurgency of theological genius against the theology of orthodox Christianity in its attempt to ignore or dismiss unorthodox theologies. As such process and liberation theologies represent a team of allies in the possible attainment of theological truth as they confront the self-appointed orthodox viceroys of the Christian faith and religious faith more generally. Let us see if this version of unorthodox theism is sufficiently plausible to stymie atheism.

Given the current state of affairs in Western philosophy of religion wherein neither atheists nor orthodox Christian theists seek substantially novel and creative paths to ground theism for the aim of arriving at truth and avoiding error, it is the task of the New Agnosticism to lead the way in this regard. And should it turn out that further inquiry into God does not justify theism plausibly construed, and should the arguments for atheism be defeated, only then will agnosticism be a resting place for those who seek with utmost fervor answers to the problem of God's existence.

PART II

GROUNDING GOD

If people become so blinded to their observations that their beliefs override their actual experiences, would it not seem possible that the whole method of interpreting events needs drastic revision?

—*Vine Deloria, Jr.*

. . . in order to ask the proper questions, one must believe that reality is a bit different from what we have been taught to believe . . ..

—*Vine Deloria, Jr.*

CHAPTER 5

NATURALIZING THEISM

The most reliable context for God will be that which, avoiding clashes with other well-established discourse about the universe, leads to articulations which are subsequently verified . . . and is thus a context which in its totality is offered as the simplest, most consistent, most comprehensive, and most coherent map of the universe.

—*Ian Ramsey*[1]

. . . if God is in fact the all-encompassing Reality that Christian faith proclaims, then that Reality is to be experienced in and through our actual lives as biological organisms who are persons, part of nature and living in society. So knowledge of nature and society can never be irrelevant, . . . to our experience of God, ...

—*Arthur Peacocke*[2]

While on the one hand agnostics like Bertrand Russell generally deny that traditional Christian dogma can be reconciled with science, and atheists such as Kai Nielsen and Richard Dawkins argue more specifically that a supernatural notion of God cannot be reconciled with evolutionary science, on the other hand E. Gilson and many other theists believe that science is ill-equipped to address the metaphysical questions of God's existence. However, there are those who believe that sound evolutionary science and a more plausible notion of God can be reconciled one with another. And this holds, according to this view, whether or not the evolution in question is continuous or saltational. They are those who, not unlike many American Indians,[3] believe in some cosmogonical and cosmological conception of reality that makes God the initial and continuing creator of the evolutionary process, either subject to the laws of nature and science or creator of those also.[4] For example, Arthur Peacocke adopts the metaphor of the "two

---

[1] Ian Ramsey, *Christian Discourse: Some Logical Explorations* (Oxford: Oxford University Press, 1965), p. 82.

[2] Arthur Peacocke, *Creation and the World of Science* (Oxford: Oxford University Press, 2004), p. 17.

[3] Vine Deloria, Jr., *God is Red* (Golden: Fulcrum Publishing, 1994), Chapter 5.

[4] See Ian G. Barbour, *Issues in Science and Religion* (New York: Harper Torchbooks, 1966), p. 415; S. L. Bonting, *Creation and Double Chaos* (Minneapolis: Fortress Press, 2007); John Cobb, Jr., *God and the World*

books" to convey the idea that God makes Herself known through nature and scripture by way of science and religion.[5] He argues that "Theology should be neither immune from the changing outlook of the sciences of man and nature nor should it be captive to them."[6]

However, there are also those who hold to the "enchantment" of nature. "The process of enchantment," writes Richard Fenn, "thus begins when one takes a particular experience out of the flux of everyday life in order to give it sacred meaning."[7] And it is precisely nature that process theists and other panentheists like Peacocke attempt to "reenchant" with the sacred consonant with Rudolf Bultmann's quest for the demythologization of the *kerygma*.[8] Consistent with these views is the one that holds that "Science may well be able to answer many of our questions about causality, but it is one thing to ask what caused the world, and quite another to ask what it means."[9]

The general theistic hypothesis in question in this chapter is whether or not it is reasonable to accept the idea that God as divine spirit can be gradualistically and even continuously active in the world through persuasion, though perhaps only saltational in Her actual influences due to human free will and action that often vitiates God's active influence. More specifically, I explore the possibility of a kind of reconciliatory position concerning science and religion vis-à-vis evolutionism and theism. In short, I seek to begin to naturalize theism by understanding God in terms of reason and science. While this general approach to philosophy of religion is hardly new, the results of my analysis are original.

My approach is to address those who are open to the convergence of science and theology without assuming or arguing that either field of inquiry has a privileged position, philosophically speaking, in addressing the matter of God's possible existence. This is because "the creative exchange between theology and science is as old as science itself, even if

---

(Philadelphia: The Westminster Press, 1969); John Cobb, Jr. and David Ray Griffin, *Process Theology* (Philadelphia: The Westminster Press, 1976); David Ray Griffin, *Evil Revisited* (Albany: SUNY Press, 1991); *God, Power, and Evil: A process Theodicy* (Philadelphia: The Westminster Press 1976); *Reenchantment without Supernaturalism* (Ithaca: Cornell University Press, 2001); Peacocke, *Creation and the World of Science*; Hugh Rice, *God and Goodness* (Oxford: Oxford University Press, 2000).

[5] Peacocke, *Creation and the World of Science*.
[6] Peacocke, *Creation and the World of Science*, p. 371.
[7] Richard Fenn, *Time Exposure* (Oxford: Oxford University Press, 2001), p. 15.
[8] Griffin, *Reenchantment without Supernaturalism*.
[9] Tina Beattie, *The New Atheists* (Maryknoll: Orbis Books, 2007), p. 12.

religious authorities and scientists have sometimes treated one another with mutual contempt."[10]

I shall assume that those who affirm dogmatically all manner of religious convictions and deny the validity of even the most basic of scientific findings are unworthy of attention for purposes of this discussion. If there is anything that is truly unreasonable, it is an attitude reminiscent of the early Catholic church's refusal to admit even some of the basic facts of science, or a fundamentalist protestant's dogged reliance on such an antiscientific perspective. For if God exists, She endows us (by way of creation and/or evolution) brains and reason to better understand the world and reality around us. It would, then, be an insult beyond measure to God Herself should one deny the most basic scientific knowledge in favor of dogmatic antiscientific beliefs of any kind. However, this is not to insist that whatever is true must conform to the methods of science. Rather, it is to accept that science is one major method by which to test most claims, and that no plausible theology will want to violate scientific knowledge more than in minimal ways, if at all. It is also to understand that "the relationship between science and religion is complex and variegated,"[11] and while questions of empirical reality lie within the legitimate scope of the sciences, questions of meaning lie within the domain of philosophy, theology, and related disciplines.

Moreover, if science is a legitimate manner by which to understand the world, and if God is in the world, then to know the world is in some measure to know God, and science becomes one important means to understanding God—at least in part. Far from seeing science as being a threat to theism, mature theism is willing to embrace science as one of the primary ways by which God might be best understood. I write "one" here because it is, I assume, reason that is our very best method of comprehending the divine. Scientific methodology can take us only so far as it can test and measure that which is empirical by nature. But it is reason that must guide us every step of the way in our discovery of who and/or what God is and whether or not God exists.

Consistent with my description of the nature of God (in previous sections of this book), I further stipulate the following about the nature of

---

[10] Beattie, *The New Atheists*, p. 98. For a discussion of the interactions between theology and science, see John Polkinghorne, *Belief in God in an Age of Science* (New Haven: Yale University Press, 1998).

[11] A. McGrath and J. McGrath, *The Dawkins Delusion?* (Downers Grove: IVP Press, 2007), p. 38.

God, should God exist. At a minimum, the picture I provide of God's nature strives for conceptual coherence, though further argument must demonstrate that there is a matching of such a conception of God to reality. If God exists, God is spirit, as American Indians insist. Although God is in the world, God is still *to some extent* beyond the ability of science to examine in the same way science examines, say, a physical object. Nonetheless, science can serve as a way to understand God's workings in the world, as God inspires and works through that which is in the world to accomplish that which is good or best under the circumstances. Instead of a being who is external to the world and who stands ready and alert to answer the prayers of those who believe that God is always on their side, some forms of prayer become a person's way by which she can hope that she is doing that which would bring goodness into this or that circumstance. In so doing, she obeys God and follows the "will" of God. Indeed, as some existentialist theologians put it, one experiences God when one encounters goodness in the world. One obeys or follows God when, say, one is morally responsible (in the duty sense) and feeds the hungry, or otherwise assists the needy. One experiences God when one comes to understand the truth of a matter, say, through one's own epistemic responsibility. More will be said of this notion of God, below. It is recognizably a synthesis of some of the crucial elements of both process theology, on the one hand, and liberation theology, on the other.

Process theism disavows the several hyperbolic attributes of God in favor of a toned-down understanding of the nature and function of God in the world. It is, then, consistent with the negative theology of Moses Maimonides who argues that God "has no essential attributes" and that to think that God does possess them is a form of idolatry.[12] If we construe Maimonides' point as Hilary Putnam does, namely, that "there are no 'propositions' about God that are adequate to God,"[13] then, strictly speaking, God has no attributes, but only "attributes."[14] This of course implies that every "proof" for the existence of God must equivocate on "exists" (in the case of the ontological argument) or "cause" (in the case of the cosmological argument) and is unsound.[15]

---

[12] Moses Maimonides, *Guide to the Perplexed*, Volume 1, S. Pines (trans.) (Chicago: The University of Chicago Press, 1963), p. 50.
[13] This is what Putnam refers to as the "paradox of negative theology" [Hilary Putnam, "On Negative Theology," *Faith and Philosophy*, 14 (1997), pp. 411–412]. For if it is true that there are no statements about God that are adequate to God, then this includes this very proposition itself, resulting in a paradox.
[14] Putnam, "On Negative Theology," p. 412.
[15] Putnam, "On Negative Theology," p. 412.

But from the supposition that we cannot fully adequately describe God, it hardly follows that we cannot in some minimally adequate manner describe Her. And this leads even Maimonides to argue that we can and must describe God as good. As Putnam states, "Maimonides is not opposed to our using inadequate ideas in speaking of God. What he is opposed to is the *unknowing* use of inadequate ideas. To use inadequate ideas thinking that one is literally describing God is to fall into idolatry."[16] Now it is this notion that opens the door for process theism to abandon the poorly supported notions of orthodox Christian theism in favor of a more refined and plausible conception of the nature and function of God. In effect, it heeds Maimonides' point that the attribution to God of all manner of doctrines that are "paradoxical" is a form of idolatry, or as I term it: an "idolatry of ideology." In the name of "mystery," orthodox Christian theism effectively secures reference absent comprehension. And there can be no virtue, moral, epistemic, or religious, in such linguistic meaninglessness. So process theism can be used to enable us to focus our attention on the very basics of God, ignoring the doctrinal idols of the traditional Christian church such as the trinity, the virgin birth of Jesus, etc. In this way, it seeks to bring some degree of clarity to the imbroglio that is the philosophy of religion.

This "minimalist" notion of God is consistent with Paul Tillich's[17] notion of God as "ultimate concern." For him, God is infinite and as such, is ineffable. Nonetheless, whatever we believe about the nature of God must conform to good scientific outlooks, say, about cosmogony and cosmology, natural development of species, social and personality evolution, and the like. And there is in Tillich an explicit rejection of orthodox Christian dogmas regarding divine omnipotence, divine omniscience, God as Creator *ex nihilo* of the universe, the traditional ideas of heaven and hell as actual places for the afterlife of good and bad people, the *parousia*, etc. However, we must be careful in labeling this Tillichian conception of God as "minimalist" (in a bad sense) in that in doing so, we run the risk of begging important questions against it and in favor of, say, the thick and hyperbolic orthodox Christian conception of God. Yet it is the latter that bears the much greater philosophical and theological burden of argument. And if it should turn out that Tillich and other unorthodox minimalist theists are

---

[16] Putnam, "On Negative Theology," pp. 412–413.
[17] Paul Tillich, *Systematic Theology*, Volumes 1–3 (Chicago: The University of Chicago Press, 1951, 1957, 1963). Also see Robert C. Coburn, "God, Revelation, and Religious Truth: Some Themes and Problems in the Theology of Paul Tillich," *Faith and Philosophy*, 13 (1996), pp. 3–33.

closer to the truth about God than is the orthodox Christian theist, then "minimalist" is somewhat of a misnomer indeed insofar as it is a dismissive term used by traditional Christian theists to refer to those conceptions of divinity that are not exaggerated as is their own. In point of fact, it would be precisely correct to call it "accurate" and the orthodox Christian theistic notion of God "hyperbolic."

What I mean when I refer to Tillich's unorthodox conception of God as "minimalist" is that it is quite a pared-down idea of God relative to the orthodox Christian notion. It is an attempt to detach theism from any supernaturalistic, mythologized or prescientific worldview.[18] In this respect, it is consonant with Bultmann's theology. Indeed, my hybrid minimalist process-liberation theism is also meant to be consistent with the basics of Tillich's theology.

Of course, those enamored with orthodox Christian theism and who think of God in hyperbolic terms might wonder whether such an idea of divinity is sufficiently robust to preserve the traditional notion of God as Creator and Sustainer of the universe.[19] In fact, if one is under the spell of that conception of God, this very question seems ludicrous in light of the informational content of the previous paragraph. Nonetheless, traditional Christian creationism that does not take seriously scientific explanations as being at least partially helpful in explaining evolutionary origins runs afoul of Alfred North Whitehead's point that ". . . God is not to be treated as an exception to all metaphysical principles, invoked to save their collapse."[20] This is because treating the idea of God in this way is essentially *ad hoc*. But it is also question-begging insofar as it presumes that the exaggerated notion of God of traditional Christian theism is accurate. However, if that is what God is supposed to be (hyperbole and all), then there is no God and the atheist is correct.

God is not the Almighty Creator and Sustainer of the universe or reality in the way that traditional Christian theism sometimes supposes with its

---

18 A similar point is made in reference to Christianity in Ramsey, *Christian Discourse: Some Logical Explorations*, pp. 65–66.

19 Here I assume what is argued in B. Carter that there exist an "ensemble of universes" [B. Carter, "Large Number Coincidences and the Anthropic Principle in Cosmology," in M. S. Longair, Editor, *Confrontation and Cosmological Theories with Observational Data* (Dordrecht: D. Reidel Publishing Company, 1974), pp. 291–298, cited in agreement by Peacocke, *Creation and the World of Science*, p. 69].

20 Alfred North Whitehead, *Process and Reality* (New York: Humanities Press, 1929), p. 521.

often antiscientific rhetoric.[21] Instead, we must look to science to see what the options are for theology on this matter. This is not the same as insisting that science is in no epistemological position to adequately address metaphysical questions such as those pertaining to the nature of spiritual substance. But a theism that postulates numerous doctrines that cannot possibly be addressed by science places itself in an unenviable position of having that much more to prove rationally beyond what science can assist it in proving. It is assumed here that a theism that controverts science least is, *ceterus paribus*, the more acceptable one. And as Steve Fuller states, "Science and religion are not mutually exclusive categories. There is no evidence that belief in a deity, even a supernatural one, inhibits one's ability to study the natural world systematically."[22]

As one orthodox Christian theist asserts: "If there is a God, then God ought to be a pretty impressive, unique, and intriguing being, and there ought to be some impressive, unique, and intriguing things to be said about God."[23] One question, of course, is what counts as "impressive, unique and intriguing." If by this is meant indefensible and hyperbolic dogmas that orthodox Christian theists have no serious intention of ever relinquishing subsequent to serious rational and nonquestion-begging examination, then

---

[21] Following theologians such as Rudolf Bultmann in his call to demythologize Christian scripture and theology, Thomas J. J. Altizer argues for the death of the traditional Christian notion of God and in favor of an intellectually tenable one alive in today's world [Thomas J. J. Altizer, *The Gospel of Christian Atheism* (Philadelphia: The Westminster Press, 1966); Thomas J. J. Altizer and William Hamilton, *Radical Theology and the Death of God* (Indianapolis: The Bobbs-Merrill Company, Inc., 1966); Thomas J. J. Altizer, "The Religious Meaning of Myth and Symbol," in Thomas J. J. Altizer, William A. Beardslee, and J. Harvey Young, Editors, *Truth, Myth, and Symbol* (Englewood Cliffs: Prentice-Hall, Inc., 1962), pp. 87–108]. Another theological move along these lines is the one to secularize the nature and function of Christianity in the world. While this position was popularized in Harvey Cox, *The Secular City* (New York: The Macmillan Company, 1965), a more current expression is found in Richard Fenn, *Time Exposure; Beyond Idols* (Oxford: Oxford University Press, 2001). These views promote the idea that at the core of genuine Christianity is a tendency toward radical secularity, rather than the idolatry of doctrine, or even scripture. In the process, the Christian church must become something wholly other than itself in that it must gain authentic faith and shed its religiosity. This point is captured in Fenn's claim that "One can lose one's religion in the course of acquiring faith" (Fenn, *Beyond Idols*, p. 7).

[22] Steve Fuller, *Science vs. Religion* (Cambridge: Polity, 2007), p. 11.

[23] William Hasker, "Can Philosophy Defend Theology?" *Faith and Philosophy*, 11 (1994), p. 277.

this kind of assertion seems to reflect an intellectual dishonesty perhaps beyond measure in philosophical and theological circles. But if by the statement is meant an honest, sincere, and open-minded inquiry into the problem of God, then what is offered in the remainder of this book precisely is an attempt to begin to make the best sense of the nature and function of God as the most "impressive, unique, and intriguing" being, without defense of unreasonable dogmas that are deemed important only by orthodox Christianity.[24]

As Nielsen states in the context of traditional theisms, "A claim that some miracles have really been established to be true or that we have a new perfectly sound argument for the existence of God is more likely to be met with a yawn rather than with philosophical interest."[25] What is needed, then, is to take seriously the more nuanced and philosophically sophisticated theologies in order to give theism an opportunity to provide plausible replies to the several concerns that many atheists have expressed over the centuries.[26] In the end, we will see past traditional Christian theism, and understand that some unorthodox theism is required if theism is to have anything important to recommend it to the epistemically responsible person.[27]

Furthermore, if epistemic responsibility is a precondition for reasonableness, and if it presupposes an honest and open-minded response to the challenge that science poses for certain doctrines of traditional Christian

---

[24] An example of honest theistic inquiry within orthodox or neo-orthodox Christian theism is found, for example, in James A. Keller, "Method in Christian Philosophy: Further Reflections," *Faith and Philosophy*, 5 (1988), p. 166. Referring to principles of interpretation of Christian scriptures, he writes that one ought to be willing "to examine the hermeneutical principles that underlie her own understanding of the Christian faith. I do think that no one should adopt hermeneutical principles or use them in such a way as to make it impossible to discover or admit that they are inadequate."

[25] Kai Nielsen, *Naturalism and Religion* (Buffalo: Prometheus Books, 2001), p. 68.

[26] One such attempt to create dialogue between orthodox Christian theists of the "openness" or free will variety and process theists resulted, I believe, in the latter's asking serious questions of the former, and receiving little but the same warmed-over answers that seek to protect cherished dogma at all costs, while refusing to follow the best arguments wherever they might lead [John Cobb, Jr. and Clark H. Pinnock, Editors, *Searching for an Adequate God* (Grand Rapids: William B. Eerdmans Publishing Company, 2000)].

[27] For an account of epistemic responsibility, see J. Angelo Corlett, *Analyzing Social Knowledge* (Totowa: Rowman & Littlefield Publishers, 1996), Chapter 4; "Epistemic Responsibility," *The International Journal of Philosophical Studies*, 16 (2008), pp. 179–200.

theism, then we cannot concur with Frederick Herzog who, in placing primacy of authority on Judeo-Christian revelation, argues that abstract arguments about the existence of God are irrelevant to the oppression of peoples and their need for liberation.[28] It is reasonable, however, to concur with the claim that religious experience and socioeconomic oppression and liberation from it is perhaps something that abstract analysis and argumentation cannot fully capture and that such experience and liberation from oppression is of deep concern to the religious as well as to others.[29] As we shall see below, I do not understand how these basic and vital points from liberation theologies cannot in principle be incorporated into a viable process theology in order to better understand the nature and function of God. To the extent that this move is conceptually feasible, it will serve as an important step in warding-off various concerns with theism. And it will not do to insist that abstract argument and analysis are impertinent to religious experience. Of what good is it to claim to have a religious experience of this or that kind if it turns out that God does not exist? This fideistic lapse in some of liberation theology's otherwise brilliant and important content places it partly in the category of neo-orthodox Christian theism. But liberation theology need not have this feature. Indeed, in his recent work, James H. Cone expresses a disappointment with the anti-intellectualism of many black Christian folk, whose faith is, in the words of James Baldwin from *The Fire Next Time*, "not fit for an intelligent dog."[30] Thus I shall out of generosity hereby ignore this infelicitous claim of Herzog's about abstract theory, while in the next chapter embracing and centering liberatory themes from Cone and Gustavo Gutiérrez (and some other first wave liberationists) in creating a theological response to atheistic concerns. But

---

[28] Frederick Herzog, *Liberation Theology* (New York: The Seabury Press, 1972). Also see Carl Braaten, *The Future of God* (New York: Harper & Row Publishers, 1969).

[29] Indeed, elsewhere [J. Angelo Corlett, *Race, Racism, and Reparations* (Ithaca: Cornell University Press, 2003)] I argue that oppressed peoples are owed reparations by their oppressors, a point that seems to be lacking from liberation theologies perhaps because of their concern with reconciliation between such parties. But why cannot reparations become one of the vehicles of liberation of the oppressed? Indeed, genuine reconciliation requires forgiveness, which in turn requires a genuine apology a precondition of which precisely is compensatory justice [J. Angelo Corlett, *Responsibility and Punishment*, 3rd Edition (Dordrecht: Springer, 2006), Chapter 5].

[30] Quoted in James H. Cone, *Risks of Faith* (Boston: Beacon Press, 1999), p. xiii. Here Cone speaks of "his own search for a reasoned faith in a complex and ever changing world" that inspired him to pursue seminary studies.

now I shall focus my attention on process theism and how it can answer a number of pressing questions posed by atheists.

Nor is an even less biased (in favor of Christian orthodoxy or neo-orthodoxy) position on the authority of revelation acceptable. It is unacceptable for the Christian theist to hold that the Christian scriptures are the "best guide" to Christian "faith," unless of course this means that the said documents are the most reliable historical guides for those wishing to be informed of how the early Christian church evolved. But it is hardly the case that such writings constitute a reliable guide to the problem of God as they presuppose the existence of God rather than prove it. So it is question-begging for Christian theists to take the scriptures "as our best guide" and the "primary basis for constructing an overall understanding of the God in whom we have faith, . . ."[31] This holds, of course, assuming that they are serious about truth rather than mere dogma.

Is traditional Christian theology correct in insisting that God exists as Creator and Almighty Sustainer of the universe? Is God omnibenevolent, omnipresent, omniscient, perfect love, and eternal? Is God transcendent of the universe? Must a plausible theism embrace certain details of revelation? Must it, even if it is a Christian theism, accept the doctrine of the trinity, the *parousia,* or the physical resurrection of Jesus?[32] Must it also accept the various other miracles that are reported in the Judeo-Christian scriptures to have been performed by, for instance, *Yahweh,* Moses, or Jesus? Must it construe any particular self-described representative institution of God as authentically representative of divine work in the world?

---

[31] James A. Keller, "Accepting the Authority of the Bible: Is it Rationally Justified?" *Faith and Philosophy,* 6 (1989), pp. 393–394.

[32] Note that this question is not the same as the question of whether or not it is rational to believe in the resurrection of Jesus, a problem that has received widespread discussion in Christian theological circles over the centuries. A few relatively recent discussions include Rudolf Bultmann, *Theology of the New Testament* (New York: Scribner's, 1951–1955); Stephen T. Davis, "Doubting the Resurrection," *Faith and Philosophy,* 7 (1990), pp. 99–111; J. F. Jansen, *The Resurrection of Jesus Christ in New Testament Theology* (Philadelphia: The Westminster Press, 1980); James A. Keller, "Is it Possible to Know That Jesus was Raised from the Dead?" *Faith and Philosophy,* 2 (1985), pp. 147–159; "Response to Davis," *Faith and Philosophy,* 7 (1990), pp. 112–116; W. Marxsen, *The Resurrection of Jesus of Nazareth* (Philadelphia: Fortress Press, 1970); T. L. Miethe, Editor, *The Resurrection Debate* (New York: Harper & Row Publishers, 1987); Wolfhart Pannenberg, *Jesus—God and Man* (Philadelphia: The Westminster Press, 1968), pp. 88–106.

These are some of the many questions that concern those who take Western theology seriously.

Instead of traversing the already familiar grounds of the traditional arguments for the existence of the God of traditional Christian theism, I shall instead presuppose that the reader has at least a basic familiarity with those arguments and their astute criticisms. I shall proceed to the reconceptualization of the notion of God itself as I believe that sufficient doubt has been cast on that idea of God that it has been rendered problematic.

Beginning, then, with the challenge of science to theism, I shall follow the lead of growing numbers of those who in recent decades have sought to merge science and theism. Then I shall borrow from process and liberation theologies central themes that serve as conceptual bases for the demythologization of the concept of God. While my analysis of the nature and function of God adopts from these current trends in theology, I seek to synthesize some of their ideas in novel ways in arguing that atheism is epistemically unjustified in the sense of strong justification. And because of this lack of sufficient justification, atheists have more reason to become agnostics than to remain atheists (at least, until the most plausible varieties of theism have been rendered implausible). So unlike the process and liberation theists, I do not take my reconstrual of God's nature and function to count as a defense of theism that wins the day. But unlike atheism, the reconceptualization of God along these lines places atheism in a vulnerable, if not embarrassing, position.

So the need for a clear and fair statement and defense of agnosticism is provided by the New Agnosticism, which I provided in the previous chapter. But in order to establish its plausibility, a case must be made for my hybrid minimalist process-liberationist theism, the process element of which will now become my focus of attention.

Is God the Creator of the Universe?

According to Peacocke, ". . . any affirmations about God's relation to the world, and doctrine of creation, if it is not to become vacuous and sterile, must be about the relation of God to, the creation of God by, the world which the natural sciences describe."[33] Can a theistic cosmogony make sufficiently adequate sense in light of scientific cosmologies and evolution of species? Can the challenge to demythologize theism be met in part by a

---

[33] Peacocke, *Creation and the World of Science*, p. 46.

scientific approach to theistic ideas? Or, must we follow E. Gilson's route of denying a legitimate place for science to investigate the metaphysical question of God's existence as creator?

In asking such questions, we must not engage in cosmogony while presumptuously thinking that the universe had to have a beginning. As Antony Flew argues: " . . . it cannot be taken for granted that the universe had a beginning, any more than it can be taken for granted that it will have an end."[34] But on the assumption that the universe might well have had a starting point, let us examine some explanations for what might have been its coming into existence. Furthermore, a plausible cosmogony would need to explain not only the origin of the universe, but to what extent it is sustained.[35] With these cautionary remarks in mind, let us proceed to approach some of the main issues of cosmology.

There are various cosmologies in the fields of astronomy, physics, and the sciences more generally. Perhaps the most popular among atheists and agnostics is the big bang theory of origins devised by George Gamow,[36] according to which the universe began as a single dense concentration of neutrons which then decayed radioactively and produced atoms. From that matter gradually collected into stars, and so forth. One disappointment of this cosmology is that Gamow postulates no beginning or origin of the collection of initial neutrons. A theist might without conceptual absurdity postulate God as their origin, their Creator.

Frederick Hoyle,[37] among others, devised the steady state theory according to which matter has always been coming into existence uniformly throughout infinite time and space. It was these newly formed isolated atoms that condensed into stars. But this theory seems not to be able to account for the continuous creation of hydrogen atoms that "simply appear" throughout the universe. Although Hoyle and more contemporary steady state theorists have revised the theory in order to provide a more

---

[34] Antony Flew, *Atheistic Humanism* (Buffalo: Prometheus Books, 1993), p. 33. Ironically, Thomas Aquinas concurs with Flew on this point. Aquinas, in arguing against the position of Bonaventure, holds that there is no rational proof that the world has not always existed. As a Christian, Aquinas believes that God created the world, but as a philosopher he can find no rational justification for that belief. I owe this point to Thomas Maloney.

[35] Flew, *Atheistic Humanism*, p. 33.

[36] George Gamow, *The Creation of the Universe* (New York: The Viking Press, 1952). Peacocke refers to it as the "hot big bang" theory (Peacocke, *Creation and the World of Science*, p. 79).

[37] Frederick Hoyle, *The Nature of the Universe* (New York: Harper and Brothers, 1950).

complete explanation of the origin of the universe, the theory remains controversial insofar as it is explanatorily incomplete.

It appears that all such cosmologies arrive at a juncture at which there is an unexplained cause of the initial event of origins. As Gilson writes in criticism of the scientific cosmology of Jean James: "The truth of the case simply is that on the problem of the existence of man modern astronomy has strictly nothing to say."[38] And even if we take into account evolutionary science and append it to big bang or steady state cosmologies, the result is still the inability thus far to explain adequately the origins of whatever such scientists theorize as being the commencement of life from mere matter. While it would constitute a fallacy of reasoning (*ignoratio elenchi*) to infer from such theoretical gaps in such cosmologies that God exists as the creator of all that is, it is not unreasonable to wonder if certain kinds of theisms might be able to provide plausible answers to explain such gaps in human understanding.[39] In either case, there exist gaps pertaining to the origins of the universe, and it appears no more reasonable to accept a scientific explanation than a theological one as regress arguments concerning such origins face either one.

In discussing the nature and plausibility of evolutionary theory, it is important to understand that "evolutionism" is ambiguous. David Ray Griffin has pointed to several versions of evolutionism, some of which are relevant to our discussion given that scientific (social) naturalist philosophers such as Nielsen and biologists like Dawkins subscribe to evolutionism in defense of their self-described atheisms. Yet only some versions of evolutionism rule out the plausibility of theism, and only certain kinds of evolutionism are contrary to yet only certain kinds of theism. In fact, Griffin, hardly an orthodox Christian theist, argues in favor of a Whiteheadian theistic naturalism that embraces theistic evolutionism.[40]

Microevolution is the minor genetic and at times phenotypical changes within a species, or even the changing of one species into a new species.

---

[38] E. Gilson, *God and Philosophy* (New Haven: Yale University Press, 1941), p. 124.

[39] For a discussion of cosmology in terms of wave function law and the indecisiveness thereof, se S. W. Hawking, *A Brief History of Time* (New York: Bantam, 1988); Quentin Smith, "Stephen Hawking's 'Cosmology and Theism'," *Analysis*, 54 (1994), pp. 236–243; N. Markosian, "On the Argument from Quantum Cosmology Against Theism," *Analysis*, 55 (1995), pp. 247–251; Robert J. Deltete and Reed A. Guy, "Hartle-Hawking Cosmology and Unconditional Probabilities," *Analysis*, 57 (1997), pp. 304–315.

[40] David Ray Griffin, *Religion and Scientific Naturalism* (Albany: SUNY Press, 2000), Chapters 4 and 8.

Macroevolutionism is the view that all present species of living things have descended from previous species over millions of years. Neither of these versions of Darwinian evolutionism rule out either divine creationism or theistic evolutionism. For if these views are correct, God could have created the basic components of the universe and all that is in it and left it up to evolution to take its natural course. Or, if there was no beginning of the universe and all that is in it, God could creatively work through evolutionary means to effect changes throughout the world. And this might be the case even though all supernaturalistic or miraculous workings do not exist, that is, if the evolutionary processes are entirely naturalistic.

Thus far Nielsen's social naturalism (discussed in Chapter 1) is accommodated to the extent that supernaturalism in the traditional theistic sense is ruled out. Moreover, uniformitarianism (the idea that only causal aspects of the present can be employed to explain natural evolution) can be taken into account, making Nielsen's naturalism even more plausible. In other words, an evolutionary theistic naturalism can make sense of the aspects of evolutionism thus far enumerated so long as the traditional Christian conception of God's omnipotence and absolute supernatural sovereignty over nature is abandoned. And while there are evolutionary theories that employ materialistic, reductionistic, and deterministic metaphysics, Nielsen's is not burdened by such controversial ideas.

However, Nielsen's atheistic evolutionism and naturalism insists that there is no theistic influence whatsoever in the natural evolutionary process. The theist, Nielsen wants to argue, cannot have it both ways: Either naturalistic evolutionism is plausible, or it is not. If it is, then theistic influences in the natural evolutionary processes are not possible as they violate the laws of nature. And since miracles have been ruled out of this discussion, then such a position is not open to the theist. For Charles Darwin's insistence on natural selection via randomness in nature cannot permit the idea of theistic interventions or influences in nature in any sense of these terms.

Now this dialectical move attributed to Nielsen is not, by the way, an attempt to appeal to Darwin's authority in order to win an argument about evolution. Despite the implications or statements of some philosophers that Darwin was an atheist,[41] it is unclear whether Darwin was an atheist.[42]

---

[41] Daniel Dennett, *Darwin's Dangerous Idea* (New York: Simon & Schuster, 1995), p. 83. But contrast pp. 67, 149–150, 164, and 180 where Dennett seems to depict Darwin as one who accepts some notion of "divine design."
[42] Griffin, *Religion and Scientific Naturalism*, p. 259.

In either case, some have argued that, whether or not Darwin was an atheist, he ought to have been one given the content of his overall theory of natural evolution.[43] Yet the debate in question need not embrace progressivistic or nonprogressivistic, moralistic or nonmoralistic forms of evolutionism as these seem not to be essential to the discussion of the problem of God. For even if any combination of these particular views holds true, it says nothing in particular about whether or not God exists. God may exist or not, regardless of whether these kinds of evolutionism are true.

In any case, Nielsen's brand of social naturalism is not materialistic, as he makes clear. He wisely steers clear of denials of human consciousness and certain other nonmaterial realities in the world.[44] Yet it is on this point where Nielsen and many theists disagree. Where theists want to argue that God exists as a particular form of consciousness and nonmaterial reality, atheists such as Nielsen deny this claim. However, since the atheist and the theist seem to concur on matters of material and certain nonmaterial substances as being real, we can do ourselves a favor in bypassing protracted discussions of whether or not material substance exists. We can also avoid otherwise important discussions regarding the origin of morality. Valuable as they are, they seem not to pose difficulties in discussions of Nielsen's atheistic views. So I set aside discussion of what might be termed "neo-Darwinism" or "neo-evolutionism" of the sort that is materialistic, positivistic, or deterministic, for example.[45] For my task is to focus attention on particular kinds of atheism, especially Nielsen's.

While my minimalist hybrid theism agrees with Nielsen that the problem of God must be settled by way of reason, and where relevant, science, it is quite unclear whether evolutionary science can provide an adequate answer to the question of cosmic origins. And while Flew, as I have quoted him above, is keen to ask why there must be a first cause of the universe, the fact that evolutionary science has not shown that there is an initial cause of original material substances leaves open the possibility that God might have caused them. This is neither meant to be a convincing or finally persuasive argument for God as the Creator of the universe, nor an *ignoratio elenchi*. Rather, it is an argument against the finality of atheism, and one consideration that tends to show that cosmological considerations

---

[43] Griffin, *Religion and Scientific Naturalism*, p. 259.

[44] This assumes, of course, that human consciousness is a nonmaterial reality.

[45] For a discussion of these kinds of Darwinian evolutionism, see Griffin, *Religion and Scientific Naturalism*, pp. 265f.

such as this do not transparently support either theism or atheism. As Michael Denton states:

> The failure to give a plausible evolutionary explanation for the origin of life . . . represents yet another case of a discontinuity where a lack of empirical evidence of intermediates coincides with great difficulty in providing a plausible hypothetical sequence of transitional forms. . . . [T]he seemingly intractable difficulty of explaining how a living system could have gradually arisen as a result of known chemical and physical processes raises the obvious possibility that factors as yet undefined by science may have played some role.[46]

It would appear, then, that scientific cosmologies and evolutionisms which are based on them have reached a similar point as did traditional Christian theism of not being able to adequately explain the ultimate origin of the universe, without, that is, postulating some ultimate first cause of things. As Ian G. Barbour puts it: "Both theories push explanation back to an unexplained situation which is treated as a 'given'—the 'primeval nucleus' in Ganow's case, the 'continual creation' of matter in Hoyle's."[47] And yet neither scientific theory even addresses the concept of time and its possible origin. As we know, traditional theism of the creationist variety posits God as the first cause of all things in the universe (as creator *ex nihilo*) as its grounds for the cosmological argument for God's existence. Gilson offers his own explanation for why scientific cosmologists who are atheists omit the notion of God as creator from their accounts:

> . . . scientists much preferred to introduce into physics the nonmechanical notions of discontinuity and indeterminacy rather than to resort to anything like design . . . because they much prefer a complete absence of intelligibility to the presence of a nonscientific intelligibility. . . . Posited at the beginning of such a chain, or inserted in it where they are needed, they provide the scientist with the very existences which he needs in order to have something to know.[48]
>
> Yet the fact that final causes are scientifically sterile does not entail their disqualification as metaphysical causes, and to reject metaphysical answers to a problem just because they are not scientific is deliberately to maim the knowing power of the human mind. If the only intelligible way to explain the existence or organized bodies is to admit that there is design, purposiveness, at their origin, then let us admit it, if not as scientists, at least

---

[46]   Michael Denton, *Evolution* (London: Burnett Books, 1991), p. 271, cited in Griffin, *Religion and Scientific Naturalism*, p. 288.

[47]   Barbour, *Issues in Science and Religion*, p. 367.

[48]   Gilson, *God and Philosophy*, p. 130.

as metaphysicians . . . to posit the existence of a thought as cause of the purposiveness of organized bodies is also to posit an end of all ends, or an ultimate end, that is, God.[49]

Gilson posits God as the metaphysical answer to the metaphysical question of what lies behind the universe, behind its biological and otherwise empirically observable processes. And it is, moreover, a fallacy for scientists to refuse to consider a plausible metaphysical answer to the problem of God's existence which itself is a distinctively metaphysical question.[50] In sum, he argues, "Science can account for many things in the world; it may someday account for all that which the world of phenomena actually is. But why anything at all is, or exists, science knows not, precisely because it cannot even ask the question."[51] The reason for this, Gilson affirms, is because "God has not to be posited as a *scientific probability* but as a *metaphysical necessity*."[52]

What Gilson accomplishes, philosophically speaking, is the taming of the scientific (indeed scientistic!) attitude that all questions that are worth asking can be answered by the scientific method, as if everything that matters is empirical. While not all scientists hold to such a view, some do. And Gilson's words remind us that it is a fallacy to think that a purely empirical method can answer all metaphysical questions. It would appear, then, that evolutionism and creationism, each most plausibly construed, stand on roughly equal explanatory footing when viewed from a relatively impartial standpoint. This has led some orthodox and neo-orthodox Christian thinkers to argue that the existence of nature serves as a witness to God's existence as the ultimate Creator of all things, and that Christianity may, along with some other religions, be a sound witness to God's existence.[53]

What we appear to have in the discussion about God's possible existence is a confusion, and at various levels. On the one hand, atheists and orthodox Christian theists seem to have fallen prey to the error of thinking that any theism worthy of the name must be supernaturalistic, contrary to the call to demythologize the *kerygma*, and, I take it, theism as a whole. This leads them to think that the only alternative to theism of the supernaturalistic variety is atheism of the naturalistic kind. This set of errors follows

---

49 Gilson, *God and Philosophy*, pp. 132–133.
50 Gilson, *God and Philosophy*, pp. 134–135.
51 Gilson, *God and Philosophy*, p. 139.
52 Gilson, *God and Philosophy*, p. 141.
53 Diogenes Allen, "The Witness of Nature to God's Existence and Goodness," *Faith and Philosophy*, 1 (1984), pp. 27–43.

from the errors of atheism noted in Part I. The problem with that line of thought is that, as process thinkers are not want to point out in creative detail, there are naturalistic versions of theism, and no atheistic denial that naturalistic theisms can qualify as genuine theisms suffices to demonstrate that they are not indeed theistic, or that traditional Christian theists and atheists alike have not committed a series of conceptual blunders.

What is of importance here is that the theist need not worry about which scientific cosmology is correct, as God might not in fact be creator of all things, but rather *related* to all things, as Langdon Gilkey asserts.[54] By this I take it that he means something akin to sustainer and influencer of nature. On this note, Whitehead writes:

> The notion of God as the "unmoved mover" is derived from Aristotle, at least so far as western thought is concerned. The notion of God as "eminently real" is a favourite doctrine of Christian theology. The combination of the two into the doctrine of an aboriginal, eminently real, transcendent creator, at whose fiat the world came into being, and whose imposed will it obeys, is the fallacy which has infused tragedy into the histories of Christianity and of Mahometanism.[55]

The literalist Christian notion of God as creator of all things must be discarded in favor of the idea that what God as creator really means is that God's relation to all there is makes us related to God and requires our obedience to Her. On this view, the creation myth in *Genesis* 1-2 is not a reference to some actual historical origin of things, as "Creation stories may simply be the survivors' memories of reasonably large and destructive events."[56] This theological move is part and parcel of the demythologization of Christian theology. It is not an evasive tactic by the theist to defend a point about God's existence. Rather, it is an exercise of philosophical and theological genius! We do not say of scientists who think plausibly outside the box in order to resolve a puzzle facing them that they are evasive. Instead, we consider them open-minded, clever, and intelligent. Why, then, ought one to accuse theists of evasiveness when they exercise the same intellectual virtues and skills? Furthermore, if science is able to finally resolve the dispute between these and other theories of the origin of the

---

[54] Langdon Gilkey, *Maker of Heaven and Earth* (New York: Doubleday and Company, 1959).

[55] Whitehead, *Process and Reality*, p. 519.

[56] Deloria, Jr. *God is Red*, p. 138. The religious and existential importance of creation myths and religious experiences for American Indians is detailed on pages 144–155.

universe, then the theist can adopt the most plausible scientific theory of origins. For whatever else God is, God is not such that She is responsible for the origins of all things. Implicit in this notion of God as the creator of all things is the idea of omnipotence, which is one of the greatest misattributions to God in human history.[57] The theist, then, has a plausible response to the famed evolutionist objection to supernatural theism, a reply that traditional Christian theism lacks because it is unwilling to take sufficiently seriously whatever good science might contribute to the problem of origins.

Orthodox Christian creationists might respond to this line of reasoning by asking why they ought to concede the matter of divine origins to science when the leading scientific cosmologies admit of incompletion exactly as theism does. But my point is not that the notion of God as the first cause of all things except Herself be discarded, but rather that the basics of evolutionary theories ought to be embraced and melded with an otherwise plausible theistic cosmology. In the end, if the evidence might warrant it, the theist ought to be prepared to accept the most explanatorily powerful scientific theories of origins of evolution as part of the demythologized theistic cosmology. This is precisely what is meant by the locution, "naturalizing theism."

But in case one is tempted to think that the atheistic evolutionist has won her battle with theism and has in turn grounded atheism simply because theism might suffer from some problems requiring it to revise itself in light of certain evidences, it hardly follows logically that atheism is established and it is not the case that God exists. And it is precisely in the conceptual restructuring of theism that God may exist as the most dynamic and powerful being ever understood. Theists should be all too happy to embrace this possibility.

---

[57] Not even progressive liberation theologians such as James H. Cone seem to take this point with sufficient seriousness, as he insists in light of the problem of evil that we ought to consider how certain political and social structures cause evil in the world—and work toward the liberation of the oppressed from the evil. But while one ought to concur with Cone's point about evil, oppression, and the need for humans to liberate the oppressed, this does nothing to rescue traditional Christian dogma from the fact that, in Cone's own words: "The persistence of suffering seems to require us to deny either God's perfect goodness or his unlimited power. . . . God is either unwilling or unable to deliver the oppressed from injustice" [James H. Cone, *God of the Oppressed* (New York: Seabury Press, 1975), p. 163]. Cone is right to think that the liberation of the oppressed ought to be the starting point of addressing evil in the world (Cone, *God of the Oppressed*, p. 163). However, God need not be omnipotent in any strict sense in order for this goal to be achieved.

So theism, naturalistically construed, has new life. Atheism must, if *it* is to be taken seriously, study with care and diligence the theologies of revisionist and unorthodox theologians who endeavor to provide neoteric meaning to the concept of God, whether they are process theologians, liberation theologians, or some other plausible theism by which both God and the world might be understood. Let us continue to explore a Western conception of God that appears to be compatible with evolutionary science.

Is God the Creator of Humans?

While the possible origin of the universe is extremely complicated, the evolution of humans is also complex. Instead of there being a single lineage from apes to humans, both may share a common line of ancestry. There is scientific evidence of the "continuity of man with lower forms" of nature, casting doubt on the idea that we singularly descended from apes.[58] Even the modes of evolution are complex, involving cooperation as well as competition between and within species.[59] Nonetheless, given these and other related complexities,[60] there is an almost undeniable overall direction of evolutionary development within nature. As Michael Polanyi argues, "It is the height of intellectual perversion to renounce, in the name of scientific objectivity, our position as the highest form of life on earth, and our own advent by a process of evolution as the most important problem of evolution."[61] All of this can and should be granted to the evolutionist by the scientifically enlightened theist.[62] This attitude can be traced at least to

---

[58]   Barbour, *Issues in Science and Religion*, pp. 369–372.

[59]   Charles Darwin, *On the Origin of Species* (London: J. Murray, 1859); *The Descent of Man* (New York: D. Appleton, 1883); *Genetics and the Origin of Species* (New York: Columbia University Press, 1937); *Heredity and the Nature of Man* (New York: Harcourt, Brace and World, 1964); T. Dobzhansky, *Genetics and the Evolutionary Process* (New York: Columbia University Press, 1971); *Mankind Evolving* (New York: Bantam Books, 1970).

[60]   Darwin himself refused to provide a clear theory of inheritance, according to Fuller, *Science vs. Religion*, p. 55.

[61]   Michael Polanyi, *The Tacit Dimension* (London: Routledge & Kegan Paul, 1967), p. 47.

[62]   For discussions of naturalistic theistic cosmologies along process theological lines, see Philip Clayton and Jim Schall, Editors, *Practicing Science, Living Faith* (New York: Columbia University Press, 2007); Philip Clayton and Paul Davies, Editors, *The Re-Emergence of Emergence* (Oxford: Oxford University Press, 2006); Philip Clayton, Editor, *The Oxford Handbook of Religion and Science* (Oxford: Oxford University Press, 2006); Philip Clayton and J. Schloss, Editors,

Benjamin Warfield who sought to reconcile Christianity with Darwinism,[63] and to Peacocke who seeks to do the same. However, while Warfield, Peacocke and others have gone to great lengths to attempt this feat, it is not clear that the peculiar orthodox Christian dogmas (the deity status of Jesus, along with other Christological doctrines, for example) with which they seek to reconcile evolution are even remotely plausible. One difficulty with such an attempt is that it typically presumes the historical and theological authority of the Christian scriptures, which is controversial. Instead, why not attempt to reconcile evolutionary science with a more general theism?

In recent decades, a process philosophy of religion has developed out of a process theology which grew out of process philosophy:

> To speak of process philosophy of religion is to refer to process theology insofar as it is a "natural theology" discussing general ideas that could in principle be employed by the theologians of all religions ... because it bases its truth-claims not on the authority of any putative revelation but solely on the general philosophical criteria of adequacy and self-consistency.[64]

As I argued earlier, it is, according to such an approach to the problem of God, reason that above all decides what is appropriate to accept and what ought to be rejected as lacking adequate justification.[65]

But as panentheists[66] Charles Hartshorne, John Cobb, Jr. and Griffin argue, God is not omnipotent in the strict sense of the term. There are limits to God's power. God is the *most* powerful being there is and has been, and most likely ever will be. As Griffin notes of panentheism,

> Like pantheism, it holds that the existence of God necessarily involves the existence of the world. Like traditional theism, it holds that God is distinct

---

Evolution and Ethics (Grand Rapids: Eerdmans, 2004); Philip Clayton and M. Richardson, Editors, *Science and the Spiritual Quest* (London: Routledge, 2002); Philip Clayton, *God and Contemporary Thought* (Edinburgh: Edinburgh University Press, 1997).

63 Fuller, *Science vs. Religion*, p. 55.

64 David Ray Griffin, "Process Philosophy of Religion," *International Journal for Philosophy of Religion*, 50 (2001), p. 131.

65 Griffin, "Process Philosophy of Religion," p. 133.

66 I do not assume that these are the only panentheists. Indeed, panentheism has a lengthy and distinguished history from Plato to B. Spinoza to J. Edwards, to F. Schleiermacher to Shelling and G. W. F. Hegel, to E. Troeltsch to C. S. Pierce and W. James and H. Bergson, among others, as discussed in John W. Cooper, *Panentheism: The Other God of the Philosophers* (Grand Rapids: Baker Academic, 2006).

from the world, able to act in it, and that our particular world . . . exists contingently, being rooted in a free divine decision.[67]

Process theism, by rejecting this supernaturalism, is a form of *naturalistic* theism. God is "all-powerful" in the sense of having all the power that one being could possibly have, but not in the sense of essentially having literally *all* the power, because that is (by hypothesis) impossible.[68]

Thus God is ever-present in the world, even where there is evil. For God is attempting to move us to eradicate it. Thus one of the central points of process theologies is consistent with Anselm's claim, rendering implausible the concern that process thought about God is so idiosyncratic that it cannot possibly reflect plausible thinking about God. Process theologians follow Whitehead in arguing that, contrary to deism, there is an active relationship between God and the world at every moment in what amounts to acts of "continuing creation."[69] Thus God's immanence implies God's activity in the world.[70] "God is not *before* all creation, but *with* all creation,"[71] Whitehead argues. He clarifies these points thusly:

> But God, . . . is the beginning and the end. He is not the beginning in the sense of being in the past of all members. He is the presupposed actuality of conceptual operation, in unison of becoming with every other creative act. Thus by reason of the relativity of all things, there is a reaction of the world on God. . . . He shares with every new creation its actual world; . . . God's conceptual nature is unchanged, by reason of its final completeness. But his derivative nature is consequent upon the creative advance of the world.[72]

---

[67] Griffin, "Process Philosophy of Religion," p. 134. William Rowe notes that "*Pantheism* is the view that God is wholly within the universe and the universe is wholly within God, so that God and the universe are coextensive, but not identical. . . . *Panentheism*, agrees with pantheism that the universe is within God, but denies that God is limited to the universe . . . . the universe is finite and within God, but God is truly infinite and so cannot be totally within or otherwise limited to the finite universe" [William Rowe, "Does Panentheism Reduce to Pantheism? A Response to Craig," *International Journal for Philosophy of Religion*, 61 (2007), p. 65; also see pp. 65–67]. For those who conflate the two views, Rowe offers the following reasoning: "The fact that God is distinct from the world in that God is not identical to the world, does not in any way preclude the world from being included in God" (p. 67).

[68] Griffin, "Process Philosophy of Religion," p. 135.

[69] This is what Peacocke refers to as God being "*simper Creator*" (Peacocke, *Creation and the World of Science*, p. 105).

[70] Alfred North Whitehead, *Religion in the Making* (London: The Macmillan Company, 1957), pp. 111–120.

[71] Whitehead, *Process and Reality*, p. 521.

[72] Whitehead, *Process and Reality*, pp. 523–524.

> One side of God's nature is constituted by his conceptual experience. . . . This side of his nature is free, complete, primordial, eternal, actually deficient, and unconscious. The other side originates with physical experience derived from the temporal world, . . . It is determined, incomplete, consequent, "everlasting," fully actual, and conscious. . . .[73]
>
> . . . He does not create the world, he saves it: . . . with tender patience leading it by his vision of truth, beauty, and goodness.[74]

This Whiteheadian panentheism is elaborated more recently by Peacocke, who states that:

> The world is still being made and, . . . man has emerged from biological life and his history is still developing. Any static conception of the way in which God sustains and holds the cosmos in being is therefore precluded, for the cosmos is in a dynamic state and, . . . it has evolved conscious and self-conscious minds, who shape their environment and choose between ends.
>
> It is this understanding of God which underpins and develops with the Christian conception of God the Holy Spirit, God as active and personally immanent in creation, in man and in the Christian community."[75]

Thus as Peacocke claims, God must at least in some meaningful sense exist actually in time and space, contrary to the orthodox notion of God as being transcendent of nature.[76] Moreover, Whitehead states: "It is as true to say that God creates the World, as that the World creates God."[77] Or, as Umberto Eco states, ". . . God reconstitutes himself and in a manner of speaking educates and enriches himself."[78] Thus God is not the possessor of the hyperbolic attributes (such as omnipotence and omniscience) traditionally ascribed to him. Rather, God is in the process of becoming, and is in the world, working with and through it toward the aims of truth, beauty, and I would add: justice. "Thus each temporal occasion embodies God, and is embodied in God."[79]

---

[73] Whitehead, *Process and Reality*, p. 524.

[74] Whitehead, *Process and Reality*, p. 526.

[75] Peacocke, *Creation and the World of Science*, pp. 80–81.

[76] Peacocke concurs with process theologies on many other points, as indicated in Peacocke, *Creation and the World of Science*, pp. 140–146.

[77] Whitehead, *Process and Reality*, p. 528.

[78] Umberto Eco and Carlo Maria Martini, *Belief of Nonbelief?* M. Proctor (trans.) (New York: Arcade Publishing, 1997), p. 24.

[79] Whitehead, *Process and Reality*, p. 529. That "God programmed the universe with stochastic variables, the values of which are supplied by free human acts, thereby rendering God the source of all power without exerting total control" is argued by Charles Babbage (Fuller, *Science vs. Religion*, p. 55), or

That Whitehead's notion of God is an attempt to naturalize the traditional Christian idea of God as transcendent vis-à-vis the world is captured
in his statement that "God is the infinite ground of all mentality . . . Neither
God, nor the World, reaches static completion. . . . Either of them, God and
the World, is the instrument of novelty for the other."[80] And contrary to
traditional Christian doctrine concerning the otherworldliness of God and
the multistoried universe of orthodox Christian myth and heaven as a
reward to believers in the by and by, Whitehead offers a different theology:
". . . the kingdom of heaven is with us today" and this is experienced in the
acts of the love of God in and for the world in particular circumstances:
"What is done in the world is transformed into a reality in heaven, and the
reality in heaven passes back into the world. . . . In this sense, God is the
great companion—the fellow sufferer who understands."[81] The relevance
of his theology to our world is not lost on Whitehead when he ends *Process
and Reality* with the following inspiring words:

> Throughout the perishing occasions in the life of each temporal Creature, the
> inward source of distaste or of refreshment, the judge arising out of the very
> nature of things, redeemer or goddess of mischief, is the transformation of
> Itself, everlasting in the Being of God. In this way, the insistent craving is
> justified—the insistent craving that zest for existence be refreshed by the
> ever-present, unfading importance of our immediate actions, which perish
> and yet live for evermore.[82]

For Whitehead, God influences the world by way of creative persuasion.
For Hartshorne, it is by divine sympathetic participation in the world as it
evolves into its eventual fullness. Moreover, God is not sovereign over the
world, but influences it nonetheless. As Cobb, Jr. puts it: "Whitehead attributes to God the all-decisive role in the creation of each new occasion."[83]

For Hartshorne, God is not immutable as traditional Christian theism
holds. Nor is She omniscient or omnipotent, strictly speaking. God is

---

what John Stuart Mill refers to as the "limited liability God" (Fuller, *Science vs.
Religion*, p. 56), thereby excusing or mitigating God's responsibility for harmful wrongdoing of a blameworthy variety. Of course, Spinoza holds that we
actually inhabit the realm of the divine in nature, as God does not reside supernaturalistically beyond nature.

80   Whitehead, *Process and Reality*, p. 529.
81   Whitehead, *Process and Reality*, p. 532. Or, as Peacocke states: ". . . transcend-
      ence is manifest in immanence" (Peacocke, *Creation and the World of Science*,
      p. 146).
82   Whitehead, *Process and Reality*, p. 533.
83   John Cobb, Jr., *A Christian Natural Theology* (Philadelphia: The Westminster
      Press, 1965), p. 205.

changing in the content of Her experience yet *eternal* in Her character and purpose, not contingent on anything for Her essential nature; God is perfect in love, goodness, and wisdom. She is omniscient in knowing all reality, though not the future which is undecided and hence inherently unknowable.[84] Strictly speaking, then, divine omnipotence and omniscience are myths mostly likely intended to capture the vastness and depth of God's power and knowledge. But this hardly implies that it is not the case that God exists.

So here we have an encapsulation of some of the basics of process philosophy of religion,[85] especially pertaining to the nature of God. It is this kind of notion of God that, I believe, is not taken seriously by atheists. Until it is, atheists are not ultimately justified in reaching their conclusion that it is not the case that God exists. This is especially true to the extent that process theology can furnish plausible answers to some of the major concerns raised about the orthodox theistic "proofs" for God's existence. Just as it is generally thought that the cumulative effect of the criticisms of these proofs, on balance, renders belief in God's existence dubious, one might begin to see the ideas of process theology as providing new hope in the cumulative effect of its power to reply plausibly to those criticisms.

Consider, for instance, the teleological argument. If big bang and steady state cosmologies are unable to account adequately for the ultimate origin of the universe, and if theism can embrace via process thought those theories insofar as they explain most of the universe's beginnings, does this not set theism in its naturalized condition roughly on par with atheism in terms of being able to explain ultimate origins? After all, after the scientific explanations are given, if the ultimate explanation for everything or first things is essentially indeterminate (as far as we know), then might not the existence of a divine designer make some meaningful sense? And is the same true regarding naturalized theism and ultimate human origins in terms of the evolution of species? It would appear that process theism can

---

[84] Barbour, *Issues in Science and Religion*, p. 445.

[85] For an alternative account of the core doctrines of process theology, see David Ray Griffin, "Process Theology and the Christian Good News: A Response to Classical Free Will Theism," in J. Cobb, Jr. and C. H. Pinnock, Editors, *Searching for an Adequate God* (Grand Rapids: William B. Eerdmans Publishing Company, 2000), pp. 1–38. Other recent discussions of the essentials of process theology include John Cobb, Jr., *The Process Perspective*, J. B. Slettom, Editor (Atlanta: Chalice Press, 2008); Jay McDaniel and Donna Bowman, Editors, *Handbook of Process Theology* (Atlanta: Chalice Press, 2006); Robert C. Mesle, *Process Theology* (Atlanta: Chalice Press, 2008).

stand on all fours in addressing the questions challenging the teleological argument. There seems to be nothing barring theism from accepting the basic findings or theories of science on these matters.

Regarding the cosmological argument, process theism renounces the orthodox theistic idea of divine *creatio ex nihilo* in favor of the natural creative process of God in the world, as described above. Insofar as scientific theories and evidence are unable to prove precisely the ultimate origin of all things, theism can provide at least a tentative answer to the question in terms of a coherently naturalized God as the first cause of things consonant with big bang and steady state theories, yet not necessarily reducible to a kind of deism. Thus it seems that process theism's readiness to jettison *creation ex nihilo* in favor of either big bang or steady state cosmologies can go some distance in muting the challenge to the cosmological argument. Nonetheless, one must be mindful to not run afoul of Whitehead's caution, above, about attributing to God all manner of things that seem to have no other good explanation.

As far as the ontological argument is concerned, process theology can argue that the common charge of theistic circularity can be softened insofar as circularity is not necessarily a dead end for arguments that are more virtuous than vicious,[86] that is, explanatorily powerful. In light of this, then, the ontological argument might gain significant support from process theology in addressing the problem of nonnatural evil.

Process Theism and the Problem of Evil

Thomas Nagel writes that "We have always known that the world is a bad place. It appears that it may be an evil place as well."[87] But precisely what explains the existence and persistence of evil in the world? Is God its cause or origin? Or is there some other explanation? Perhaps the first

---

[86] This point about virtuous circularity is made, following William P. Alston, in A. I. Goldman, *Knowledge in a Social World* (Oxford: Oxford University Press, 1999), p. 84. It bears noting that this reply concerning the ontological argument is also open to orthodox Christian theism in its reply to certain atheistic challenges.

[87] Thomas Nagel, *Mortal Questions* (Cambridge: Cambridge University Press, 1979), p. 74. For philosophical analyses of the nature of evil, see Joel Feinberg, *Problems at the Roots of Law* (Oxford: Oxford University Press, 2003), Chapter 6; J. Angelo Corlett, "Evil," *Analysis*, 64 (2004), pp. 81–84.

philosophical statement of the problem of evil in the Western world is found in Epicurus:

> God either wishes to take away evils, and is unable; or He is able, and is unwilling; or He is neither willing nor able, or He is both willing and able. If He is willing and is unable, He is feeble, which is not in accordance with the character of God; if He is able and unwilling, He is envious which is equally at variance with God; if He is neither willing nor able, He is both envious and feeble, and therefore not God; if He is both willing and able, which alone is suitable to God, from what source then are evils? Or why does He not remove them?[88]

Another formulation of the problem of evil is found in Nelson Pike:

> If God exists, how can evils be explained? For an omnipotent being would have the power to prevent any and all evils if it wanted to; an omniscient being would know all about them; and a perfectly good being would want to prevent/eliminate all the evils it could. Thus, it seems, if God existed, and were omnipotent, omniscient, and perfectly good, there would be no evils.[89]

From David Hume to J. L. Mackie, this basic argument has been restated to challenge the coherence of the traditional Christian (seemingly unrestricted) notions of the omnipotence, omniscience, and omnibenevolence of God. While orthodox Christian theologians and Christian philosophers such as Alvin Plantinga and Richard Swinburne seek to provide *apologia* to rebut the concern, their efforts have been unpersuasive.[90] Something conceptual must be sacrificed here. God cannot be both omnipotent and omnibenevolent at the same time in light of the complexities of evil in the world. And the attempt by some to actually deny the reality of evil seems to perversely insult both God and those who experience evil. Such replies seem to explicitly or implicitly deny the reality of evil in its fullness, or

---

[88] Cited in Lactantius, "On the Anger of God," in W. Fletcher (trans.), *The Writings of the Ante-Nicean Fathers* (Grand Rapids: W. B. Eerdmans, 1951), Volume 7, p. 271. Cited in Cone, *God of the Oppressed*, p. 178.

[89] Cited in Marilyn McCord Adams, *Horrendous Evils and the Goodness of God* (Ithaca: Cornell University Press, 1999), p. 7.

[90] For a critique of Plantinga's free will defense, see Graham Oppy, "Arguments from Moral Evil," *International Journal for Philosophy of Religion*, 56 (2004), pp. 59–87. For an exposure of Plantinga and Swinburne as supporting a rather conservative version of orthodox Christian theism, see Michael P. Levine, "Contemporary Christian Analytic Philosophy of Religion: Biblical Fundamentalism, Terrible Solutions to a Horrible Problem, and Hearing God," *International Journal for Philosophy of Religion*, 48 (2000), pp. 89–119.

otherwise not take it sufficiently seriously. Yet denying the reality of evil only worsens the problem for theism. Plantinga's "free will defense" is set forth in order to justify the existence of nonnatural evil such as oppression. It is hardly the first attempt to cite free will as an explanation of evil in the world in defense of the traditional idea of God.[91]

Of course, one ought to consider whether or not traditional Christian theism has the conceptual wherewithal to adequately answer the problem of evil as have Plantinga and Swinburne. While several other philosophers[92] and theologians have attempted this feat, a more recent attempt to do this is found in some recent work by Marilyn McCord Adams. She asserts not only that God's traditionally ascribed attributes are coherent, but that the various traditional Christian doctrines such as the trinity, immortality of the soul, divine miracles, and so forth can be brought to bear in order to answer the problem of evil. Adams believes that the philosophical discussion of the problem of evil has been carried out at too high a level of abstraction and that "atheologians" such as Mackie have equivocated in their "value-theory imperialism"-based objections to traditional Christian theism. More precisely, she cautions, "I warn Mackie's heirs against 'short way' inconsistency proofs that fail to pay detailed attention to subtlety and nuance in the belief system under attack."[93] She attempts this feat by "drawing on the wider resources of our religion to explain how an omnipotent, omniscient, and perfectly good God could both permit and defeat even horrendous evils."[94] By "wider resources," she means an array of Christian dogmas extracted from orthodox Christian scriptures, ones explicitly rejected by others because of their lack of "faith" in those dogmas.

However, Adams' orthodox Christian theistic reply to Mackie's critique is only as plausible as the orthodox dogmas of the divine trinity, the

---

[91]   Boethius argued that in light of human free will, it is divine providence that explains the reality of evil but nonetheless, he argues, does not indict God as its author or responsible party [Boethius, *The Consolation of Philosophy*, Richard Green (trans.) (Indianapolis: The Bobs-Merrill Company, Inc., 1962), Books Four and Five].

[92]   One set of discussions is found in P. J. McGrath, "Evil and the Existence of a Finite God," *Analysis*, 46 (1986), pp. 63–64; Roger Crisp, "The Avoidance of the Problem of Evil: A Reply to McGrath," *Analysis*, 46 (1986), p. 160; Michael B. Burke, "Theodicy with a God of Limited Power: A Reply to McGrath," *Analysis*, 47 (1987), pp. 57–58.

[93]   Marilyn McCord Adams, *Horrendous Evils and the Goodness of God* (Ithaca: Cornell University Press, 1999), p. 4.

[94]   Adams, *Horrendous Evils and the Goodness of God*, p. 4.

immortality of the human soul, and divine miracles that she invokes to save orthodox Christian theism from philosophical disrepute in light of the reality of evil in the world. Now the charge here is not one of mere circularity, as the overall theistic account Adams tries to give is meant to provide adequacy based on the overall preponderance of plausibility of the entire account. Instead, the point I am making is that, given that she indeed appeals to rationally unsubstantiated beliefs in order to construct a theodicy, her theodicy is no stronger than the beliefs to which she appeals. And unless and until she is willing to face up to an objective and fair-minded assessment of those beliefs against the rules of reason, absent Christian revelation, hers is no impressive theodicy. The fact is that without Christian revelation and the doctrines (taken as basic or foundational beliefs) extracted from it by orthodox Christian theists, the dogmas mentioned stand no reasonable chance of adequate rational support.[95] Thus Adams' reply to Mackie is based on question-begging rhetoric that one expects from orthodox Christian theology masquerading as philosophy. If God exists, then the reason with which She endows us is sufficient for us to be able to explain Her existence without poor reasoning. No breaches of reason are necessary to know whether or not God exists. This makes appeals to revelation otiose as well as rationally suspect.

While orthodox Christian approaches to the problem of evil (*tout court*) and the problem of God more generally find themselves in a myriad of difficulties, less dogmatic thinkers, in focusing on the depth of the problem of evil, argue that "the problem of evil, . . . favors minimal over maximal conceptions of deity . . ."[96] For those who prefer to follow the arguments wherever they lead, this becomes a more promising solution to a problem that has plagued theism in general for centuries.

A less orthodox and perhaps more promising approach to the problem of evil is found in John Hick. While admitting that the problem of evil is

---

95 Indeed, given the wide range of standpoints in scholarship of the Christian scriptures, it is by no means obvious—except to orthodox Christians like Adams herself—that the doctrines to which she appeals so confidently are justifiably grounded in a responsible study of those very documents.

96 David P. Hunt, "Evil and Theistic Minimalism," *International Journal for Philosophy of Religion*, 49 (2001), p. 133. It is noteworthy that the objections to theistic minimalism that Hunt discusses (pp. 133–154) do not pose themselves for my hybrid minimalist process-liberationist theism. That the notion of a finite God has received far less attention than it deserves is also noted in Frank Dilley, "A Finite God Reconsidered," *International Journal for Philosophy of Religion*, 47 (2000), pp. 29–41. Even so, Dilley chooses not to discuss, though he does mention, process philosophy of religion.

when all is said and done mysterious, significant (though perhaps not total) sense can be made of it in light of the idea of an afterlife where "soul-making" on earth is completed in the thereafter according to a divine plan.[97] Perhaps the personalism of E. G. Brightman best explains the underlying rationale for this theistic answer to the problem of evil:

> Personalism makes purpose the fundamental category of personality, human or divine. The purpose of God as revealed in experience is not that the universe shall be eternally and simultaneously perfect, but rather that the persons shall have an opportunity to grow. Not static completeness, but development; not a block-universe, but a universe of suffering and growing love—this is the picture that theism presents. The possibility of achievement is as contingent on effort in a personalistic world as it is in a world of neutral entities, the possibility of failure is as real; on the other hand, the incentive for achievement is greater, the tragedy of failure more poignant.[98]

The difficulty with this approach, as Hick understands quite well, is that it links theism to an extraneous belief in an afterlife, which many find rather controversial.[99] One major problem with the soul-making theory is that it seems to presuppose precisely what is in question: the existence of God as the Soul-Maker. If the problem of evil serves as a major objection to the existence of God, it hardly warrants an appeal to God as the Soul-Maker to explain why there is evil in the world. Moreover, even absent this difficulty, there is the additional one of seemingly addressing the said objection in an *ad hoc* manner. Finally, whether Hick's or Brightman's version of this defense, neither one seems to justify the existence of evil in the lives of persons wherein no "lessons" or "soul-making" seems to occur: the starvation of very young children, the massacre of children, the sexual molestation of children (even by some catholic priests, among others!), etc. What sense can possibly be made of incentives to learn life's lessons or soul-making in these and related kinds of cases? Is the young child supposed to learn that the priest is not a person of God or is a sexually perverted felon, or that the pope and cardinals do not care enough about this crime to have priests guilty of it punished? Or is the lesson that life is not worth living in the cases where their lives are cut short by disease in a few years, months,

---

[97] John Hick, *Evil and the God of Love*, Revised Edition (New York: Harper & Row Publishers, 1978); *Philosophy of Religion*, 4th Edition (Englewood Cliffs: Prentice-Hall, 1990), pp. 46–47.

[98] E. G. Brightman, *An Introduction to Philosophy* (New York: Henry Holt and Company, 1925), pp. 334–335.

[99] Robert F. Almeder, *Beyond Death* (Springfield: Thomas, 1987).

or hours? And what are we to make of the cases of child massacres? What possible lesson or soul-making is there to be had for those victimized by those violent and evil acts? Or, is it that such children are killed so that *others* may learn some lesson, wherein the child is used as a mere means to an end of others' education? That life's evils are aimed at soul-making seems a bit morally insulting to those undergoing the horrors of evil. While it may be true that some will find lessons to be learned in the midst of experienced evils, this does nothing to justify them. God is still left holding the bag of moral blame, and Her omnibenevolence is less than certain. Yet divine goodness is precisely one attribute of God that seems most obvious—if anything is obvious about God's nature. Many a theodicy has become morally repugnant in its attempt to save a particular orthodox notion of God while making a mockery of God.

While the extremely problematic ethical theory of act-utilitarianism can make some sense of evil in the world (in spite of its disregard of human rights and justice, for example), and while it might be appended to orthodox Christian theism (indeed, perhaps even presupposed by it!), it is not the case that the principles of an enlightened moral conscience could make sense of such a reply to the problem of evil. We must be careful to not do all we can to explain God's existence while simultaneously making a mockery of God.

The process conception of God assists in explaining why there is evil in the world by providing its own theodicy. The process aspect of hybrid minimalist theism construes God as being most powerful, but not omni-potent. Thus God seeks to persuade humans to do the right things. But they have sufficient freedom to do other than good, and hence humans are often to blame for their own harmful wrongdoings, that is, absent excusing conditions present in their actions, inactions, or attempted actions, as the case may be.

One question that remains is whether or not God is sufficiently power-ful to be rightly held accountable and blameworthy for natural evils that result in human and nonhuman suffering. This problem seems to stand in the path of a hybrid minimalist theism's winning the day for theism. For the free will of humans cannot seem to explain the existence of natural evil, which appears to challenge the goodness of God to the point wherein God is not even powerful enough to prevent natural evils.

There is, however, a reply to this concern. It is that the concern itself appears to assume a particular notion of God's power that is itself prob-lematic. For just as "God could *not* have created beings like us in every way except guaranteed by God always to be and to do good," and just as "*Any beings in any possible world capable of the kinds of values we can enjoy would also necessarily have the kind of freedom we have,* including the freedom to act contrary to the will of God,"[100] God does not possess the attribute of omnipotence such that She could have created us in ways that we would always choose the good. But neither does God possess the power to create a world that would be free of even natural evil.

This naturalized conception of God without omnipotence resolves the problem of evil as a whole, placing the emphasis of the problem of non-natural evil squarely on humans. It is consistent with the second element of my hybrid minimalist theism, which holds that justice is where God is, and that those who are genuinely friends of God behave justly in this world. So God lacks the ability to do away with all evil. But God does have the will and unwavering capacity to attempt to incessantly influence us to do what is right and good. Much more than the doctrines of orthodox Christian theism, this theism makes reasonable sense, placing the burden on humans to do the right things. That which we sow is what we shall reap, as the Christian writ states. Those societies that are uncaring about who they allow into political power get what they deserve. And when those in power declare unjust military invasions and wreak evil in the world, terrorism often results, and folk often get what they deserve. And when they do not get what they deserve, humans ought to make sure that they do what is right and good. For God is "the ground of hope for the ultimate victory of good over evil."[101] In general terms, this is the meaning of process theism's thesis that there is a reign of God on earth in which the problems of war, human rights violations, ecological destruction, and economic injustice will be overcome by God's influence on humans in doing the right things.[102] I take this point of process theism to be central to my hybrid minimalist theism as it conjoins certain aspects of process and liberation theisms into a unified whole.

Since I am interested in exploring the plausibility of a minimalist theism in order to challenge the errors of atheism, I take it that the problem of an afterlife is a feature of some theisms that make it less plausible—certainly less probable—than theisms without it.[103] And some major world religions such as certain Judaistic theisms, among others, do not entail such doctrine. Out of respect for Ockham's Razor I shall follow their lead in not adopting such a view. For my overall task is to determine whether or not

---

[100]   Griffin, *Reenchantment without Supernaturalism*, p. 227.

[101]   Griffin, *Reenchantment without Supernaturalism*, p. 231.

[102]   Griffin, *Reenchantment without Supernaturalism*, p. 246.

[103]   For a process theistic account of parapsychological phenomena and the afterlife, see Griffin, *Religion and Scientific Naturalism*, Chapters 6–7; *Reenchantment without Supernaturalism*, Chapter 3.

atheism is right in proclaiming that it is not the case that God exists. On the assumption that extraneous doctrines of the parapsychological and the afterlife are inessential to any plausible theism, I shall accept only those theistic beliefs that are indeed most essential to theism.

The most epistemically responsible avenue here seems to be one of acknowledging the dilemma concerning evil posed by Epicurus and many other philosophers. But in fairness to the theist, it would seem to be unnecessary to renounce both divine omnipotence and omnibenevolence at this juncture. For there appears to be nothing about the dilemma about God and evil that requires such a drastic move. And it is unclear that divine omniscience, strictly speaking, is plausible anyway when one considers a divine Being who is Herself in the process of becoming, as process theology argues. Does it not make good sense to retain the idea of omnibenevolence, while recanting divine omnipotence, relieving God from being responsible for evil in any direct way?

While this move is superior to the orthodox one of essentially denying that the problem of evil is a serious problem or minimizing the problem of evil, it too falls short. For even if it is true that God is not directly responsible for the evil in the world, She appears to be indirectly responsible for it insofar as She could have, if she wanted to, made a world that lacked evil at all. As Mackie states, God could have made a world in which humans always freely chose good actions rather than bad ones. This means that God is not sufficiently powerful to create a world in which natural or non-natural evil fails to exist. And this seems to imply that God's goodness is in question, if only indirectly, as God is somewhat responsible (causally) for such evil. Thus it appears that no version of the free will defense vindicates God concerning the reality of evil.

Nonetheless, the theist could reply that God is the most powerful and most benevolent being in the sense that God cannot do the logically impossible, and God cannot stop evil from happening absolutely. Furthermore, this implies that God is somewhat to blame for the evil in the world, consonant with Job's complaint to God about the evil Job suffers in *Job*. Why would a theist interested in retaining as much of theism as possible consider this path? Because she might believe that God is that power in the universe that precisely seeks to persuade us to promote goodness for our fellow humans and liberate the oppressed, as Whitehead, Hartshorne, Cobb, Jr., Griffin, Cone, and Gutiérrez argue, respectively.[104] As one

---

[104] Although not normally considered to fall under the category of liberation theology, liberatory themes are also found in William Temple, *Christianity & the Social Order* (New York: The Seabury Press, 1977).

interpreter of *Matthew*, 15:21-28 says: "Those who have a hungry heart and broken spirit are the favorites of God."[105] This pericope of Christian scripture is representative of several other scriptures that support what is basic to the liberationist theistic perspective. In the end, this reply seems weak in that it posits a God who may be the most powerful being there is and ever was and ever will be, but it is unclear whether this account serves as a *reductio ad absurdum* of theism in that the reduction of evil in the world appears to be in our hands, or in no one's hands at all.

Moreover, I shall not spend much time on the moral argument for the existence of God, as Russell and so many others[106] have pointed out how absurd that argument is in light of both the Christian church's perpetration of evils throughout its history, many of which, I would add, have gone unrectified, demonstrating an unwillingness of traditional Christianity to own up to the facts that those atrocities were evil and deserve rectification where rectification is possible. To some meaningful extent, this is due to the Christian church's idolatry of icons and its failure to secularize itself, as Richard Fenn argues.[107] It alone speaks volumes about traditional Christianity's inability to serve as a moral guide to God—ironic as this may be.

Can there be a good morality without God? As Russell pointed out, it depends what we mean by "God." And consonant with *James*, those who are really of God will surely demonstrate such by the way they live. But one thing is clear: Whatever inspired the evils of history in the name of religion was not of God. For God, if She does exist, is good, and would never inspire such madness.[108] As the free will defense implies, God ought not to be blamed for harmful wrongdoings that are properly construed as the responsibility of humans. And as I argued in a previous chapter, whether or not God exists is not contingent on how well humans obey what is good. For God might exist even though no human ever does the right thing.

In general, the moral argument for God's existence posits God as the ultimate source of "true" morality. One would think that the moral argument for the existence of God would find its origin in the ideologies of

---

[105] Helmut Thielicke, *The Silence of God*, G. W. Bromily (trans.) (Grand Rapids: W. B. Eerdmans Publishing Company, 1962), p. 17.

[106] Deloria, Jr., *God is Red*, p. 189.

[107] Fenn, *Beyond Idols* (Oxford: Oxford University Press, 2001).

[108] Of course, there is yet a third possibility, but one that I do not endorse, which is Stesichorus' (640–555 BCE) idea that "the immortal gods did not for all time alike establish over the holy earth strife unending for mortals, nor friendship either, but the gods establish within each day a different mind."

"infidels" rather than in orthodox Christian theology. For while it might suggest the reality of a divine source of human morality, the Christian church is hardly in a moral position to claim to represent it. On balance, it has done more harm that it could ever rectify even in light of its many good works. Fenn puts it quite mildly when he states that the church is "in the precarious position of attacking idols while functioning as an idol in its own institutional policies of repression, censorship, and control over the interpretation of personal experience."[109] Unfortunately, matters are far worse, morally speaking, for the Christian church than Fenn surmises when its behavior during the crusades in Europe and its co-responsibility for genocidal acculturation in the Americas is considered. While the church may preach forgiveness, it surely will never (nor should it) receive it from a truly just authority. For forgiveness requires genuine apology which in turn requires, among other things, compensation.[110] And judging by the orthodox Christian church's behavioral history, no such apology is forthcoming; and we must not presuppose that forgiveness entails mercy. For this reason alone, then, orthodox Christian theists ought—however ironically—to pray that there is no God. For the millions of unpunished evils throughout history will have to be set straight, as the Christian scriptures themselves testify.[111]

However, the moral argument for God's existence involves meta-ethical problems as well.[112] Griffin revives the moral argument for God's existence when he argues for the reality of a holy moral "ought" that grounds ethics objectively. But his argument is one of silence in that just because ethics fails to defeat moral skepticism in some absolute sense, it hardly follows that God is the ground of our moral being. His argument is set forth as follows:

(1) The Holy Reality wants us to X;
(2) We want to be in harmony with the Holy Reality (because it is that which is good in an ultimate, nonderivative way);

---

[109] Fenn, *Beyond Idols*, p. 54.

[110] J. Angelo Corlett, *Responsibility and Punishment*, 3rd Edition (Dordrecht: Springer, 2006), Library of Ethics and Applied Philosophy, Volume 9, Chapter 5; "Forgiveness, Apology, and Retributive Punishment," *American Philosophical Quarterly*, 43 (2006), pp. 25–42.

[111] For more on the problem of evil, see Richard Otte, "Evidential Arguments from Evil," *International Journal for Philosophy of Religion*, 48 (2000), pp. 1–10, among several others in recent decades.

[112] David Ray Griffin, "Theism and the Crisis in Moral Theory: Rethinking Modern Autonomy," in George Allan and Merle Allshouse, Editors, *Nature, Truth, and Value: Exploring the Thought of Frederick Ferré* (Lanham: Lexington Books, 2005), pp. 199–220.

(3) To be in harmony with the Holy Reality requires that we X;

(4) Therefore we ought to X.

This argument presupposes the existence of God. Lacking an independent argument for God's existence, the "holy reality argument for objective ethics" is dubious. Griffin's argument for God as the ground of ethics seeks to defeat ultimate moral skepticism from a moral foundationalist perspective. Yet foundationalism in all its epistemological forms is highly problematic in that it faces the insoluble problem of an infinite regress of justification. Moreover, Griffin's argument mistakenly targets absolute moral skepticism, which is logically self-defeating. (How can a strong moral skeptic claim even her own position when she cannot in principle claim the truth of any moral proposition?) But what Griffin's discussion fails to see is that contemporary moral realism is grounded in arguments against moderate moral skepticism, a skepticism that construed moral knowledge in less than absolutist terms, and where moral knowledge is understood in more coherentist terms.

The more coherent the moral argument, then other relevant things being equal, the more acceptable the moral proposition. And one need not postulate the existence of God to ground such morality, but instead one ought to rely on reason, properly utilized. While Griffin seeks to defeat moral antirealism with theistic ethics and God as the ground of moral being, the defeat of moral antirealism need not entail such a move. Whereas Griffin seeks to replace moral antirealism with theistic moral realism, moral realism seeks to replace moral antirealism with a moral realism grounded in reason. Thus Griffin's approach would seem to owe us an explanation as to why the existence of God is needed above and beyond what reason can provide us in moral reasoning. If Griffin seeks to identify God with reason, then I see no serious problem with this move as God would be both the source and means by which we discover and develop and live the moral life. But if by "God" Griffin means something other than this, he must provide a separate argument for God's existence as it is controversial.

As already noted, God's essential nature according to traditional Christian theism is that God is, at the very least, omnibenevolent, omnipresent, omniscient, and omnipotent. But to what do these attributes amount? While throughout the history of ideas different nuanced varieties of these properties have been defended, I shall further stipulate (along with some leading traditional Christian theistic philosophers) that God's omnipotence means that She has the power to create, conserve, or destroy anything, and that she is not limited by the laws of nature. Quite simply: God can do anything (except the logically impossible).[113] But we have seen that the problem of evil poses serious difficulties for the idea of divine omnipotence.

Moreover, according to orthodox Christian theism, God is omniscient in that God knows everything; whatever is true, God knows it is true, and whatever is false, God knows it is false.[114] Furthermore, God is infallible. She is never wrong about the truth value of a proposition. So it is not simply, as Swinburne argues, that "All God's beliefs are true, and God believes everything that is true,"[115] it is that none of God's beliefs are false, and God cannot believe a falsehood insofar as belief entails sincerity of the acceptance of a proposition. God's omniscience also means that God knows at time t_n all that is logically possible to know at t_n, excluding knowledge of the future. For while God, being omnipotent, might have the best inductive knowledge regarding future events, She will lack certainty about them.[116] Even in orthodox Christian theistic terms, divine omniscience is not really what it seems to be, strictly speaking. The doctrine of divine omniscience, then, must be discarded.

Furthermore, God is spirit or *pnuema*, or bodiless in any physical sense. And this makes it possible that God is omnipresent. This poses a special difficulty for traditional Christians who ascribe to Jesus the exclusive status of divinity among humans and physical objects (within the material world). But just as one can be a theist, perhaps even a Christian, and disbelieve in immortality and the resurrection of Jesus, one can also disbelieve that Jesus is God and be a theist worthy of the name.[117]

If God is spirit and omnipresent, it makes sense to think that She is in the world, rather than God's being part of some dualistic multitiered mythological world wherein God is absent until God decides to intervene in it. As noted in the Introduction, Rudolf Bultmann was one of the first Christian theologians of the modern era to argue that we ought to abandon

---

[113] Richard Swinburne, *Is There a God?* (Oxford: Oxford University Press, 1996), pp. 5–7, where Swinburne argues that "God cannot do what is logically impossible."

[114] Richard Swinburne, *Is There a God?* p. 6.

[115] Swinburne, *Is There a God?* pp. 5–7.

[116] This refinement of divine knowledge is found in Swinburne, *Is There a God?* p. 8, though he notes that it is derived from Aquinas. It bears noting, however, that process theologians such as Hartshorne, Cobb, Jr., and Griffin have been discussing such a conception of God for decades.

[117] And this despite orthodox Christian protestations! Orthodox Christianity holds no special keys to the membership of the theistic community. Nor does any other version of Christianity.

the multitiered mythology of the Christian scriptures in favor of a scientific one.[118] His claim was that one ought to "demythologize" the informational content of the message of the Christian scriptures, as it was formulated in a multitiered world of natural and supernatural beings and needs to have the dualistic mythology extracted from it in order to speak to contemporary people.

So there is an increasing number of sophisticated and well-respected theologians within Christianity alone who believe that the most important aspects of Christian theology can be reconciled with the fundamental knowledge of science. One challenge, then, is to make sense of God as the greatest spiritual presence in the world in light of scientific knowledge. But this ought not to be impossible, as good scientists know the limits of their own method, just as good philosophers and theologians know the limits of ours. And it is outside the realm of science to investigate matters of spiritual reality. So the task is to develop a coherent notion of God as the divine spiritual presence in the world (as opposed to Her being external to it) in light of scientific knowledge of the world. I believe that this possibility cannot be ruled out *a priori*, though apparently many atheists seem to think otherwise. I write "many" in that I am aware of no research by an atheist that actually investigates philosophically and theologically numerous theologies that might attempt to do precisely this. And until this is done, the atheist is not entitled by reason to accept her most basic claim, namely, that it is not the case that God exists. Until this is done, the atheist cannot escape at least one of the errors of atheism as described in Chapter 2, namely, that of hasty conclusion.

Not only is God spirit and the most powerful and knowledgeable being, but God is also omnibenevolent (perfectly good). Swinburne thinks of God that

> His being perfectly good follows from his being perfectly free and omniscient. A perfectly free person will inevitably do what he believes to be (overall) the best action and never do what he believes to be an (overall) bad action . . . . a person free from desires who formed his purposes solely on the basis of rational considerations would inevitably do the action which he believed (overall) the best one to do, or . . . one of the equal best actions.[119]

---

[118] Rudolf Bultmann, *Jesus Christ and Mythology* (New York: Scribners, 1958); *Theology of the New Testament*, K. Grobel (trans.) (New York: Scribners, 1951–1955).

[119] Swinburne, *Is There a God?* pp. 12–13.

Apparently, with the use of "(overall)" Swinburne makes God out to be the divine act-utilitarian. But act-utilitarianism suffers deeply from the flaws that it cannot make good sense of justice, rights, backward-looking reasons and promise-keeping. And if it is morally problematic that utilitarianism be employed by humans, then reason tells us that it is also morally problematic for God to use utilitarian calculations in Her dealings with the world. According to a utilitarian calculus for action, God would be justified in having a minority of persons tortured for the sake of bettering social utility, could have the rights of minorities violated for the sake of most (other) persons in the world, could break Her promises to humans and could ignore the past injustices in favor of a smoother life for most (other) persons in the world. And in case one is tempted to argue that Swinburne's point can be salvaged in terms of a rule-utilitarian theory of divine ethics, one ought to bear in mind that that is hardly an uncontroversial move in ethical theory, as demonstrated by John Rawls and some others subsequent to his "Two Concepts of Rules."[120] Even if we took this move seriously, Swinburne would then owe us an explanation as to which rules God would follow in this or that circumstance in order for God not to be unjust or unfair, e.g., not "perfectly good." The point here is that Swinburne's notion of God's omnibenevolence is severely limited because it says nothing of God's justice. Surely if God is perfectly good, She must be just and fair. If this is so, then God is no divine utilitarian. For the sake of justice and fairness, God will sometimes need to punish the ruling majority for what they have done wrongly. And God may work through members of the oppressed minority to accomplish this aim. To deny this theological point would be to deny that God would ever work to assist the oppressed minorities of the world by way of political violence, for example.[121]

Returning to the point about atheism's challenges to the traditional notion of God, another point is in order. In the spirit of Russell's claim that he is not an atheist because he cannot disprove the existence of God, I argued that to point out that the traditional idea of God's nature is self-contradictory is insufficient to disprove theism and thereby prove atheism. The reason for this can be illustrated thusly. Consider the claim that martians or space aliens exist, a claim that many of us remember when such claims were popular several decades ago. Some popular motion pictures depicted what were believed to be space aliens. Now if someone were to

---

[120] John Rawls, *Collected Papers*, S. Freeman, Editor (Cambridge: Harvard University Press, 1999), Chapter 2.

[121] It would deny the wisdom found, for example, in Cone, *God of the Oppressed*; Gustavo Gutiérrez, *A Theology of Liberation* (Maryknoll: Orbis Books, 1973).

claim that such space aliens exist (as they were and are depicted even today in popular movies and science fiction novels), it would not suffice to disprove their claim by asking them to bear their burden of proof and note that they have not done so and then conclude that there is no life form aside from those on Earth, as many concluded. The reason for this is because it may be true that martians and other space aliens as they were depicted in popular movies and science fiction novels quite clearly do not exist. After all, the most powerful telescopes, it might be argued, have yet to discover them. Not even space exploration has confirmed the existence of such alleged entities. However, it hardly follows from this that no plant or animal life forms exist outside of the planet Earth, or that they cannot exist. (After all, if either the big bang theory or steady state theory of the origin of biological evolution can occur here on Earth, why cannot it also occur at least on some other planets in this or another solar system or universe?) In fact, some leading scientists believe precisely this claim.

This account tells us something important, I believe, about the debate concerning the existence of God. For centuries the orthodox Christian church has persuaded millions of folk into believing that the God of traditional Christian theism exists, and that they ought to worship "Him." But as I argued in previous chapters, on the assumption that *that* "God" has been shown to not exist (indeed, never has existed except as an idea in the minds of orthodox Christians and their atheist interlocutors!), it does not follow that there is no God whatsoever, or that it is not the case that God exists.

As I have stated in Part I, what counts as a being worthy of the name "God" ought not to be dictated to us by those theists and atheists who have been lulled into thinking that only an overly thick notion of God is worthy of the name "God," if anything or anyone is. We must not, that is, allow the discourse about the problem of God to continue to be controlled by the minds of those who have (collectively) dominated the discussion for centuries, only to have led us down a conceptual cul-de-sac. This implies that one of the most central tasks of a philosophy of religion is to explore with honesty and rigor all *prima facie* plausible avenues of thought in order to resolve this philosophical quandary. Although the work on religious pluralism has explored this matter to some extent, those discussions have usually revolved around the issue of what orthodox Christian theism ought to hold about competing theologies, rather than focusing on the particulars of whether or not a particular theistic stance can evade the telling objections to orthodox Christian theism, as well as most or all other concerns.

But what if, as in the present case, theists and atheists have fundamentally different ways by which to ground their respective positions?

One, but certainly not the only manner, by which to state this position is that to the extent that religious experience is one legitimate way (in addition to others) by which to argue for the existence of God, the problem then arises as to how to handle this kind of evidence when various pur- ported religious experiences have as their subject of experience conflicting—even contradictory—ideas of God. So traditional Christian theism also faces this difficulty head-on,[122] and must resolve it without self-serving or question-begging argumentation insofar as it supports the "only-one-true-religion" view.[123]

As noted, the atheist tends to base her views on scientific method, while theists tend not to limit the defense of their view thusly. I say "tend not to limit" here because some theists are quite amenable to scientific method and knowledge and see, for instance, evolutionary theory as rather compatible with theistic belief, properly construed. But setting aside creationist-evolutionist accounts for the time being, it is important to understand that theism might or might not ground itself in scientific method and what it discovers,[124] while the typical atheist will surely do so. Nonetheless, each opposing position might be constructed coherently.

Moreover, while it may be true that any such theory will be to some extent circular, such circularity need not be vicious or unacceptable. For as I mentioned above, some circles are more virtuous than others. Here I assume that the more virtuous circles are the ones that do not involve

---

[122] For examples of attempts to do precisely this, see David Basinger, "Plantinga, Pluralism, and Justified Religious Belief," *Faith and Philosophy*, 8 (1991), pp. 67–80; "Hick's Religious Pluralism and 'Reformed Epistemology'," *Faith and Philosophy*, 5 (1988), pp. 421–432; "Pluralism and Justified Religious Belief," *Faith and Philosophy*, 13 (1996), pp. 260–265; Jerome Gellman, "Religious Diversity and the Epistemic Justification of Religious Belief," *Faith and Philosophy*, 10 (1993), pp. 345–364; "Epistemic Peer Conflict and Religious Belief," *Faith and Philosophy*, 15 (1998), pp. 229–235.

[123] This point is made in John Hick, "Religious Pluralism and the Rationality of Religious Belief," *Faith and Philosophy*, 10 (1993), pp. 242–249; "Religious Pluralism and Salvation," *Faith and Philosophy*, 5 (1988), pp. 365–377.

[124] In fact, there is a parallel discussion among some Christian theists about the proper role of technologies. While Cox embraces them [Cox, *The Secular City*; Frederick Ferré, *Shaping the Future* (New York: Harper & Row, 1976); *Philosophy of Technology* (Englewood Cliffs: Prentice-Hall, 1988)], others, including Jacques Ellul, find technologies contrary to authentic Christian ideals [Carl Mitcham and Jim Grote, Editors, *Theology and Technology* (Lanham: University Press of America, 1984), p. 129, and elsewhere].

uninformative ideas, but rather ones that give us the most informative account of the world, all things considered. On the face of it, then, theists can provide a coherent theory of reality, but so can atheists. Yet each side bears a burden to prove itself. And yet scientific method is not suited for a complete explanation of the nature of God, as God is not a material body and so escapes comprehensive empirical inquiry. "Since it is neither obviously true that [God] exists, nor obviously true that he does not, we need to examine what *reasons* there are to think that he exists, what *reasons* there are to think that he does not, to weigh them against each other, and thereby come to *the most reasonable view* we can."[125]

At this juncture of the dialectic it falls upon the serious thinker to examine the arguments for the existence of God, along with their objections. The overall plausibility of theism must be assessed in light of this evidence. Should the test fail, so does theism. But it must be borne in mind that it is the most viable version of theism that we are after, one that evades all or most of the objections that theism might encounter. The end result of this part of the inquiry must be weighed against the arguments for atheism. Now this is a delicate matter, but for different reasons than why the assessment of theism is complicated. For how is one to prove that there is no God, especially when God is not a material body? If one simply assumes that the scientific method is adequate to answer all metaphysical questions, then one is guilty of a kind of philosophical prejudice. Whitehead refers to this kind of perspective as one that commits the "fallacy of misplaced concreteness" in that scientific findings are seen as being exhaustive explanations of reality. This fallacy can be found in logical positivism,[126] which provides no independent argument for its "fact-value" distinction that was part and parcel of its scientific bias against matters of value.

Trading religious dogma for scientific dogma is no answer to the question of God's existence. And if no common ground of investigation exists between theism and atheism, then the overall weight of their respective and independently coherent positions must be considered. Only then can a reasonable assessment of the positions be made.

---

[125] Nicholas Everitt, *The Non-Existence of God* (London: Routledge, 2004), p. 2.

[126] A. J. Ayer, *Language, Truth, and Logic* (London: Victor Gollancz LTD, 1948); *The Problem of Knowledge* (Harmondsworth: Penguin Books Ltd, 1980); "The Vienna Circle," in A. J. Ayer, W. C. Kneale, G. A. Paul, D. F. Pears, P. F. Strawson, G. J. Warnock, and Richard Wollheim, *The Revolution in Philosophy* (London: Macmillan & CO LTD, 1963), pp. 70–87.

On the other hand, one ought not, as Adams does in her attempt to rebut Mackie's rendition of the problem of evil, to commit the fallacy of "biblical" revelation, insisting that the most viable theology is one that adapts itself to the "expression of the biblical message" in an effort to contemporize the spiritual messages of revelation.[127] This approach involves an unacceptable degree of question-begging in favor of theism, and is hardly worthy of serious attention, philosophically speaking. Note that this is different than the call for demythologizing the *kerygma* of Christian faith. In that case, scientific knowledge is brought to bear to most plausibly interpret the essentials of Christian faith.

Furthermore, evolutionary theory faces various problems, including the charge that evolutionary science equivocates between alleged observed instances of macroevolution and microevolution.[128] Of course, intelligent design theorists such as Michael Behe[129] and William Dembski[130] challenge the very idea of macroevolution. None of this is to say that science ought not to play a role in our inquiry about God's existence. Rather, it is that science has a more limited role than reason given that reason can, and science cannot, guide our inquiry without legitimate concerns of appropriateness and question-begging concerning the content of the inquiry and nature of the referent, God. On the other hand, we are beginning to see that unorthodox theism can embrace the findings of science, in particular evolutionary science, in order to explain changes in the world within and between species. This ought not to threaten an informed and plausible theism. In fact, it ought to suggest how science can inform religion and assist it in discarding its ideology in favor of a less mysterious and more naturalized notion of God.

It is of vital interest to note that the traditional Christian idea that God created the world *ex nihilo* is part of the mythology that some early Christians created to refute Gnosticism's notion that material reality was inferior to the spiritual realm. The two-fold account of divine creation in *Genesis* 1–2, however, suggests that the material world originated at the

---

[127] Barbour, *Issues in Science and Religion*, p. 460.

[128] Fuller, *Science vs. Religion*, p. 132. Moreover, Fuller argues, "neo-Darwinian science assumes that the Earth can be treated as 'the privileged planet,' a relatively closed system housing such unique developments as intelligence and even life itself not expected elsewhere in the universe" (p. 133).

[129] Michael Behe, *Darwin's Black Box* (New York: Simon & Schuster, 1996).

[130] William Dembski, *The Design Inference* (Cambridge: Cambridge University Press, 1998); *No Free Lunch* (Lanham: Rowman & Littlefield Publishers, 2001).

doing of God Herself. However, scholars do not possess the original document(s) from which our fragmented copies of Jewish scriptures were copied. Even if we assume for the sake of argument that the *ex nihilo* account of divine creation we find in *Genesis* 1–2 is original word for word, it must be ascertained whether or not: (a) creation *ex nihilo* is a doctrine that is essential to theistic belief; and (b) it is true. It would appear that theism need not hold that God created the world, as "modernist" theologians interpret the creation myth in symbolic or otherwise nonliteral terms. To deny that modernist theologians are genuine theists would be a feat of dogmatic religiosity that perhaps only Christian fundamentalists could muster. Yet they are not serious interlocutors in this or any other informed and mature theological debate.

The more important question is whether or not the idea of divine creation (of the universe and of humans) *ex nihilo* is true. But even if it is false, the nontraditional theist can accept the idea of God as continual Creator of things, whether or not She is the origin of all things other than Herself (She is eternal and is thus without beginning or end). And just as science holds that the universe is dynamic and incomplete and in the process of evolving, cannot the theist accept this and add that God Herself is in some sense the same? God continually evolves and creates throughout time, whether or not God created the universe *ex nihilo*. Or, God creates throughout time, and whether or not She created the universe *ex nihilo* is a matter still unresolved.[131]

While orthodox Christian theists insist that divine *creation ex nihilo* is true and is essential to not only Christian theism, but to theism itself, Griffin has it right when he points out that this kind of thinking "provides a classic example of the way in which undue reverence for secondary and even tertiary doctrines can endanger the primary doctrines of the faith they

---

[131] This idea is consistent with the notion of divine "emergence" found in Christopher Knight, *The God of Nature* (Minneapolis: Fortress Press, 2007), p. 9: ". . . it means we can envisage God as creating in a way that is based on the interplay of chance and physical law. The character of the universe is . . . consonant with the reality of a creator who has 'designed' it with the particular aim that there should arise within it, through naturalistic processes, beings who can come to know God as their creator and redeemer." Again, "The new theology of nature is based . . . on a picture of the process of creation that involves a naturalistic interplay between chance and the physical law that has been designed by God with a providential aim" (p. 10). Thus according to a most plausible theology of science, the existence of God, properly construed, is hardly a logical impossibility, as Bertrand Russell recognized.

were meant to safeguard."[132] I would add that Griffin's point about what counts as essential Christian doctrine applies to what counts as essentially theistic. It is hardly essential to theism properly construed (thinly or thickly) that God created the world out of nothing. Indeed, it is not even essential to theism properly construed that God created the world.

The theist, then, need not and ought not to disregard or reject the scientific cosmology of evolutionism in order to cling to the creation myth found in documents she perceives to be divine revelation. Instead, she can and ought to embrace the best science has to offer along these and other related lines, as God is by hypothesis "in charge" of the evolutionary processes in nature. So once again we face a bifurcation in the debate between fideist Christian theologians (on the one hand) and atheistic scientific evolutionists (on the other). One need not be forced to deny scientific cosmology or evolutionary science.[133] The theist can, and should, embrace evolution and the creativity within natural selection as God's means by which to effect creative change in the world in which we live. So it is not conceptually or logically absurd to reason that God is the ultimate creator within the world, as it remains an open question at this point of time whether or not God created the universe itself.

No argument any scientist has given of which I am aware can either prove or disprove the claim that God created the big bang or steady state. The theist might appease scientifically minded atheists by adopting such a belief about divine creation, and discard the myth that has for centuries stood in the way of significant theistic conceptual advancement. But as noted above, there is no scientifically satisfactory explanation for the ultimate origin of the universe, whether by way of big bang or steady state cosmogonies. So as far as the origin of nature is concerned, theistic creationism is still a viable option. That is to say, it is roughly just as reasonable to accept the proposition that God created the cosmos as it is to accept the denial of that claim. And this is particularly true if the theist is a naturalistic one who accepts the best of evolutionary science in order to explain the continual creation and influence of God in nature, cosmologically speaking. Indeed, it might be argued, contrary to many evolutionary scientists, that

---

[132] David Ray Griffin, "In Response to William Hasker," in John B. Cobb, Jr. and Clark Pinnock, Editors, *Searching for an Adequate God* (Grand Rapids: W. B. Eerdmans Publishing Company, 2000), p. 260.

[133] For an argument in favor of the interventionist argument that God brought into existence physical life, see Hugh Chandler, "Divine Intervention and the Origin of Life," *Faith and Philosophy*, 10 (1993), pp. 170–180.

evolutionary science reveals progressively the reality of God in the world much as William Paley and other proponents of the teleological argument insist! While this might not, as Fuller suggests, render theism a scientific theory, it does make it a theology of science as it seeks to turn on its head the "blind watchmaker" argument of many atheists.

Science need not confound the savvy and honest theist. Instead, it ought to create a sense of wonderment and awe that the closer one investigates scientifically the facts of nature, there is still no conclusive evidence that God does not exist. But as Christopher Knight[134] cautions, this attitude might require a sacrifice on behalf of orthodox Christian theists who are devoted to their cherished dogmas based on largely literal interpretations of "sacred" writ. In such cases, dogmatism must give way to demythologization with the truth that the best of science increasingly reveals the truth about God's providential workings in Her creation.[135]

Once again, the defeat of traditional Christian theism is not tantamount to refuting theism. While it may be true that the doctrine of the immortality of the soul and the resurrection of Jesus are part and parcel of traditional Christian faith, it is hardly true that one must accept these ideas in order to be a theist. Thus theism (in some nontraditional and non-Christian form) might survive the offensive of atheistic criticism. My intent, however, is to defend theism from unfair criticism, seeking to salvage the fundamentals of a nontraditional version of theism in the process.

Even if the analysis of how process theology answers some crucial questions about God's nature and function in the universe provided above is taken as a plausible joint reply to some of the most important objections to orthodox Christian theism, it might be asked if I am playing fast and loose with "God" so much so that I have equivocated on the term in a way

---

[134] Knight, *The God of Nature*, pp. 18–19.

[135] My hybrid minimalist theism makes no theological commitment to the idea of divine special providence. I leave this question open as the result does not effect my posing this version of theism as a challenge to atheism. Whichever notion of divine providence ends up being the most plausible can be adopted by my hybrid minimalist theism without incoherency. Briefly, the spirit of God is not absent from the world as deism asserts. But neither is it obvious that a notion of special divine providence is needed to make sense of intercessory prayer and divine workings within the nature world, contrary to Knight's arguments (Knight, *The God of Nature*, Chapters 4–6, 15). Unlike his "theology of nature" which he refers to as "pansacramental naturalism," my hybrid minimalist theism makes no commitment to the warrant of revelation that requires, it seems, a further commitment to the concept of miracles and special divine intervention into nature.

that renders its meaning essentially ambiguous. The alleged equivocation might be said to be that the nature of God that is set forth in process theology is so distinct from that of orthodox Christian theology that is constitutes a switching of the meanings of "God."

In reply to this concern, it must be borne in mind that my argument assumes that atheism has defeated the orthodox Christian idea of God's nature. However, I argue that most atheists—even the most sophisticated among them like Mackie—have at best only defeated a straw person version of the possible conceptions of God available to us, not to mention the future conceptions that might be developed plausibly.

Moreover, it is the atheist, not me, who is confused about the denotation of "God." In Part I, I explained how atheists and theists alike are often confused about the nature of God, so much so that they do not seem willing or capable of taking seriously much more conceptually viable ideas of God in order to further the discussion about God's possible existence more fruitfully. That my hybrid minimalist theism might be accused of playing fast and loose with "God" is symptomatic of the current state of the debate about God, wherein most of the interlocutors do not, for whatever reasons, think outside the current norms of discourse. For many theists, this might be the result of not taking the possibility of God sufficiently seriously such that novel ways of thinking about God go unexplored, while for many theists, it is perhaps a sign that the possibility of God's existence is taken too seriously in that one is unwilling to abandon one's presuppositions about God, come what may.

One of the ironies of the New Agnosticism is that its explication and defense of process and liberation theologies serve to further theism's plausibility in the joint quest for a total solution to the problem of God. Yet it also serves as a confirmation of atheism's rejection of orthodox Christian theology. The New Agnosticism seeks to renew the philosophical attitude that has been missing for some time now concerning matters of God. And it will be "back to the drawing board" for atheism. It must face the question of whether it constitutes an ideology or dogma in its own right, or whether it will take the problem of God sufficiently seriously to investigate with an open mind alternative ways of understanding the concept of God in its effort to place atheism on a proper philosophical foundation.

But there is more to a plausible theism that atheism must address in order to properly and adequately ground itself. It must do more than align itself with sound science. And it is to this feature of radical theology that I now turn in order to discover more of the possible nature and function of God.

CHAPTER 6

LIBERATING THEISM

The problem of violence and nonviolence is an illusory problem. There is only the question of the justified and unjustified use of force and the question of whether the means are proportionate to the ends . . . if disproportionate means are employed, then the goals of the revolution are betrayed. . . . Any world-transforming act of justice, where it succeeds, corresponds to God's justice on earth.

—Jürgen Moltmann[1]

If the gospel is a gospel of liberation for the oppressed, then Jesus is where the oppressed are . . . The real Church of Christ is that grouping that identifies with the suffering of the poor by becoming one with them.

—James H. Cone[2]

It is a dangerous presumption to suppose that theological propositions are to be understood chiefly as "purely" theological, having no political presuppositions, content, or consequences.

—Dorothee Soelle[3]

Throughout this book I have appealed to the call for the demythologization and naturalization of theism in order to emphasize the importance of trading the mythology of the Christian scriptures for a theology that respects the best findings of good science. But much more is needed of an adequate theology than this. Translating the language of myth in the ancient scriptures into the language of science, or at least the kind of talk that does not offend responsible science, might well leave one with a sense of what the early Christian church believed about this or that. But it might not address adequately the spiritual needs of contemporary Christians (or, I might add, theists more generally). This point is made by Dorothee Soelle in her critique of Rudolf Bultmann. She continues to state that Jesus, Paul, John, and certain others were indeed prophets. However, they are not

---

[1] Jürgen Moltmann, *Religion, Revolution, and the Future* (New York: Charles Scribner's Sons, 1969), pp. 143, 146.
[2] James H. Cone, *Risks of Faith* (Boston: Beacon Press, 1999), pp. 9–12.
[3] Dorothee Soelle, *Political Theology*, John Shelley (trans.) (Philadelphia: Fortress Press, 1974), p. 34.

such absolutely. Contemporary Christians must be guided by God through various other authorities as well.

Soelle's position has the consequence of removing the centrality of Christianity from the teachings of Jesus to whatever divine inspiration we can derive in our day and in our time and circumstance.[4] She writes:

> . . . it is meaningless to ask: Was Jesus a revolutionary? Where did he stand on violence, on landed property? Instead, we as his friends who affirm the intention of his decision must attempt for our part to declare where we stand today on revolution, property, and violence. This function of his on behalf (his *beneficia*) is more important than the words and deeds discoverable by the historian, which lead only to imitation, not to discipleship.[5]

To this it might be objected that Soelle's basic theological commitment is not a Christian one. But we must recall, Socratically, that it is not whether an argument belongs to a certain dogmatic ideology or not, but rather whether or not it is sound. Or, in the words of Johann Baptist Metz, "Any given theological position must strive to appropriate precisely those elements which other positions see as lacking or neglected in it."[6]

It is helpful to understand that the theology of demythology needs to be supplemented by a political theology. And liberation theists provide precisely such a perspective. Indeed, as Soelle points out: "More and more it appears to me that the move from existentialist theology to political theology is itself a consequence of the Bultmanian position."[7] Indeed, "the question raised for Bultmann's theology concerns its openness to a political theology,"[8] and that "a political interpretation of the gospel is not antithetical to the essential intentions of Bultmann's theology."[9] In fact, she goes on to state of theology in general, "As long as liberation and emancipation remain the goal, enlightened criticism is not merely optional but a necessary method."[10]

But what must an adequate political theology do? Metz argues that its primary task is the deprivatization of theology, which is the determination

---

4   Soelle, *Political Theology*, p. 65.
5   Soelle, *Political Theology*, p. 64.
6   Johann Baptist Metz, *Faith in History and Society* (New York: Seabury Press, 1980), p. 119.
7   Soelle, *Political Theology*, p. 2.
8   Soelle, *Political Theology*, p. 6.
9   Soelle, *Political Theology*, p. 55.
10 Soelle, *Political Theology*, p. 4.

anew of the relationship between religion and society.[11] This calls for the
secularization of religious experience rather than the private transcend-
ental experiences of individuals. The Christian church, Metz insists, should
be in the world and shaped by it, bringing the gospel to it in order to trans-
form it. One function of the church is to criticize society where society
needs critical awakening. It is also to criticize religion and itself.[12] Indeed,
a plausible theology must become political.

But what precisely does it mean for theism to become political? I shall
explore an answer to this question in terms of some key components of the
first wave of liberation theisms of Latin and black America, respectively.
What I shall not do is explore political philosophy of religion or theology
that addresses matters of religious freedom, religious diversity in liberal
democratic regimes, separation of church, synagogue or mosque, and the
liberal democratic state.[13] Nor shall I discuss the detailed distinctions
between the variants of liberation theologies. While addressing these
matters would appear to be a desired feature of a comprehensive philosophy of religion, they are beyond the scope of this more focused project.[14]

Having in the previous chapter explained how some of the basics of
process theism can provide plausible answers to questions about God's
nature and functioning in the world and in largely scientific terms that are
quite amenable to scientific cosmologies and evolutionary science, here
I turn to an elaboration of the nature and function of God in more social
and political terms. It is at this juncture that I delve into some of the depths
of liberation theology.[15] In so doing, it is important to note that this

---

[11] Metz, *Theology of the World*, William Glen-Doepel (trans.) (New York: Herder
      and Herder, 1969), pp. 110–111.

[12] Metz, *Theology of the World*, p. 120.

[13] A few of the recent sources on these and related issues are Robert Audi, *Reli-
      gious Commitment and Secular Reason* (Cambridge: Cambridge University
      Press, 2000); Phil Cousineau, Editor, *A Seat at the Table* (Berkeley: University
      of California Press, 2006); Christopher J. Eberle, *Religious Conviction in
      Liberal Politics* (Cambridge: Cambridge University Press, 2002); Jürgen
      Habermas, *Between Naturalism and Religion*, C. Cronin (trans.) (Cambridge:
      Polity, 2008); Jeffrey Stout, *Democracy & Tradition* (Princeton: Princeton Uni-
      versity Press, 2004); *Ethics After Babel* (Princeton: Princeton University Press,
      1988).

[14] A more comprehensive account would include a crucial assessment of the
      theologies of Cecil Cone, Cain Hope Felder, Dwight N. Hopkins, Diana Hayes,
      Ivan Petrella, Gayraud S. Wilmore, and Delores S. Williams, among others.

[15] More specifically, I focus on some of the first wave of Christian liberation
      theology. For discussions of the newer wave, see Mario Aguilar, *The History
      and Politics of Latin American Theology*, Volumes 1–2 (SCM Press, 2007–
      2008); Miguel A. De La Torre, Editor, *Handbook of U.S. Theologies of*

theistic move is meant to liberate God from the confines of traditional Christian theistic dogma in order to focus on the justice of God in the world through the actions of humans in concerted effort to obey the will of God. In this way, liberation theisms begin to fulfill Metz's claim that one task of a political theology is to criticize religion itself.

While there are various kinds of liberation theisms, I shall focus my attention on ones that pertain primarily to ethnicity rather than gender. Gender, feminist or womanist liberationist theists represent a particular category of liberation theism quite worthy of attention in its own right. However, I shall not address them herein, though I have elsewhere addressed feminism from a philosophical and ethical standpoint.[16] Thus I deal specifically with what I shall refer to as "liberation race theisms." While such liberation theisms have certain implications for gender- and class-related issues such as the awarding of compensatory damages (reparations) to the oppressed by their oppressors insofar as oppressed women of certain groups receiving more reparations and other forms of justice than their male counterparts is concerned, I shall emphasize more general matters of liberation theisms in an attempt to provide a portrait of theism that stands as a viable answer to the problem of nonnatural evil.

The first major component of my hybrid minimalist theism is process theism, as covered in the previous chapter. The second main element is its liberation (race) theism. My liberation theism might well be referred to as "Third World theism"[17] in that its primary focus is on the manner in which

---

Liberation (Atlanta: Chalice Press, 2008); Miguel A. De La Torre and Edwin David Aponte, Editors, *Handbook of Latina/o Theologies* (Atlanta: Chalice Press, 2006); Ivan Petrella, *The Future of Liberation Theology* (Burlington: Ashgate, 2004). Others see themselves as comprising an element of this new wave of liberation theologies, calling themselves "postcolonial theologies" [C. Keller, M. Nausner, and M. Rivera, Editors, *Postcolonial Theologies* (St. Louis: Chalice Press, 2004)]. Yet a careful study of these works exemplifies a kind of chauvinistic Christianity masquerading as liberation theology. It neither avoids the charge of Eurocentrism, nor adds little if anything new and worthwhile to the first wave of quite considerable theological insights gleaned from Christian liberation theologies from both the Latin American and black quarters.

[16] J. Angelo Corlett, *Race, Racism, and Reparations* (Ithaca: Cornell University Press, 2003), Chapter 7; "Race, Racism, and Reparations," *Journal of Social Philosophy*, XXXVI (2005), pp. 568–585; "Race, Ethnicity, and Public Policy," in Jorge Gracia, Editor, *Race or Ethnicity?* (Ithaca: Cornell University Press, 2007), pp. 225–247.

[17] Schubert Ogden refers to liberation theologies as "Third World theology" in Schubert Ogden, *Faith and Freedom* (Nashville: Abingdon Press, 1989), p. 23. We clearly mean different things by our different labels.

God addresses the needs and experiences of the oppressed: ". . . liberation theology is articulated in Latin America . . . Yet it is also an important mode of thought in southern Africa, parts of Asia, and amongst the minority and feminist movements of North American society."[18] Like the process element of my hybrid minimalist theism, the liberationist aspect need not be Christian in content, though the liberation theologies on which I shall focus are distinctively Christian, but hardly orthodox. They are Christian in that they hold, among other things, that the Christian scriptures are a primary but not the sole source of divine revelation if there is such a thing as divine revelation, and that its teachings in part support a theology of divine support for the oppressed of the world. It need not, as some insist, hold that theisms that do not employ praxis to address oppression are "guilty of ideology" in assisting the oppressing classes.[19] For it can simply hold the more modest thesis without falling prey to that further charge. But my liberation theism is distinctively philosophical, though it employs liberation theologies in its attempt to build a larger challenge to atheism's implied claim that no theism worthy of the name is plausible.

This liberation theism, I suggest, differs from Soelle's insofar as she believes that "the gospel has to do with freedom for all . . . its essence is the *liberation* of all."[20] Without casting all persons into simplistic moral categories of "good" or "bad," it is a moral fact about the world that some persons are to some extent oppressors. As such, they are hardly in need of liberation from themselves, as Soelle suggests. As she herself points out, Jesus expressed a "partiality against the rich"[21] (Cf. *Matthew*, 19:24).

Moreover, Jesus reportedly said that the first will be last, and the last first, seemingly giving reason to think that on judgment day there will be no equality of treatment: there will be rewards for those who obey God, and punishments for those who do not. All will not be liberated as not all are oppressed. Some are oppressors, and must get what they deserve because God is just. This applies to the many Christians in U.S. history who engaged in or otherwise supported genocidal acts: "Many of the

---

18   James E. Will, "Dialectical Panentheism: Towards Relating Liberation and Process Theologies," in John Cobb, Jr. and W. W. Schroeder, Editors, *Process Philosophy and Social Thought* (Chicago: Center for the Scientific Study of Religion, 1981), p. 243.

19   David Ray Griffin, "Value, Evil, and Liberation Theology," in John Cobb, Jr. and W. W. Schroeder, Editors, *Process Philosophy and Social Thought* (Chicago: Center for the Scientific Study of Religion, 1981), p. 183.

20   Soelle, *Political Theology*, p. 67.

21   Soelle, *Political Theology*, p. 36.

genocidal acts the Westerners committed against the Indians can be laid directly on the doorstep of religious fanatics who saw conversion or death as the only viable solution to the Indian problem."[22] And while Soelle is correct to argue that there is a deeply social and political "undertow of sin,"[23] that the orthodox conceptions of sin cannot seem to capture or do justice to [as Paul states: "For all have sinned and come short of the glory of God" (*Romans*, 3:23)], it hardly follows from this supposition that all are deserving of liberation and that all shall be liberated. In fact, the morally right thing to do in some cases is to punish the oppressors, not reward them with liberation by way of salvation because somehow they are simultaneously oppressing themselves as Soelle claims. Her notion of universal liberation makes God unjust—precisely one who would be co-responsible and ultimately responsible for nonnatural evil. Rather, God is not responsible for such evil, but certain humans are, and they are hardly in need of or deserving of—nor will they receive—liberation from the fruits of their own harmful wrongdoings. Far from holding humans responsible for their horrible misdeeds, Soelle's theology ends up committing the very same error that she cautions against, namely, of "depoliticizing the gospel"[24] insofar as she fails to see the dividing lines between oppressors and the truly oppressed, and as such her theology functions to some meaningful extent "as a medium of social accommodation"[25] insofar as it does not hold those most responsible for evils accountable for what they do. Indeed, the oppressors can, for all Soelle argues, simply continue to do evil to others and all the while expect no punishment because God will in the end liberate all. If this is not an opiate of the people, as Karl Marx termed religion, then there is none. And it is here, in the end, for all the incisiveness of her theology on other matters, where Soelle's notion of forgiveness goes terribly wrong. Lacking an account of repentance or apology by wrong-doers to their victims, Soelle articulates a doctrine of universal and unqualified forgiveness[26] that can hardly serve as a basis for justice for the oppressed. It is not simply that such universal forgiveness ignores or slights

---

[22] Vine Deloria. Jr., *God is Red* (Golden: Fulcrum Publishing, 1994), p. 170. Of course, "religious fanaticism is not the only 'clear and present danger' in our world. The greatest dangers confronting humankind are still those ancient enemies of war, poverty, ignorance and disease" [Tina Beattie, *The New Atheists* (Maryknoll: Orbis Books, 2007), p. 38].

[23] Soelle, *Political Theology*, p. 94.

[24] Soelle, *Political Theology*, p. 33.

[25] Soelle, *Political Theology*, p. 34.

[26] Soelle, *Political Theology*, Chapter 8.

that harmful wrongdoings wrought on the oppressed. It is that it fails to hold responsible the oppressors, making it hard to understand precisely how in the end Soelle's political theology which is so averse to violence can achieve genuine liberation in the real world. Contrary to Soelle, then, it is not the case that "Liberation is possible only as the liberation of all."[27]

If to know God is to do justice, Soelle's political theology does not provide justice for the oppressed, nor does it do so for the oppressors. It provides justice to no one, though it might succeed in providing a delusional sense of peace for those who in their aversion to justice cannot garner the moral fortitude to sometimes liberate through violence, when justified on ethical grounds.[28] Soelle's reply might take the tack of averring that "Jesus wants us all to be friends because humans constitute a common humanity." On her view, this means that we establish a community in which genuine "repentance" and "conversion" occur.[29] This reply is astounding in that it fails to reflect the real world *sitz-im-leben* of evil and badness freely inflicted by some persons on others. And no amount of Soelle's attempting to diminish the fact of degrees of responsibility for degrees of evil and badness in the world by her notion that we are all participants in the badness existentially will defeat the fact that to the extent that we do bad things and are truly responsible for them, we deserve to be punished and forced to compensate those whom we harm unduly.[30] This is the sense of justice lacking in Soelle's political theology of universal liberation. And her calls for forgiveness and mercy hardly serve as solace for the truly oppressed. Indeed, they serve as a stark reminder of how, if liberation theology is to truly liberate, it must be grounded in a genuine sense of justice, not an ideology having an aversion to justice.[31] As Metz argues,

> If love is actualized as the unconditional determination to freedom and justice for the others, there might be circumstances where love itself could demand actions of a *revolutionary character*. If the status quo of a society

---

[27] Soelle, *Political Theology*, p. 102.
[28] For discussions of conditions under which violence is morally justified, see J. Angelo Corlett, *Terrorism: A Philosophical Analysis* (Dordrecht: Kluwer Academic Publishers, 2003) Philosophical Studies Series, Volume 101, Chapters 4–5; Michael Walzer, *Just and Unjust Wars*, 2nd Edition (New York: Basic Books, 2000).
[29] Soelle, *Political Theology*, p. 104.
[30] For accounts of desert and responsibility, see Corlett, *Responsibility and Punishment*, Chapters 2, 4.
[31] For an analysis of forgiveness, see Corlett, *Responsibility and Punishment*, Chapter 6.

contains as much injustice as would probably be caused by a revolutionary upheaval, a revolution in favor of freedom and justice for the sake of "the least of our brothers" would be permissible even in the name of love.[32]

So it makes little sense, even in light of the notion of divine and sisterly love, to deny that some folk will and should receive their just deserts even by way of violence as they are enemies of justice, truth, and the good.

Oppression is not always able to be eliminated by way of nonviolence. There are times when violence not only deserves a response of violence, but warrants it in the name of lovingly liberating the oppressed from the evildoers oppressing them. As Vine Deloria, Jr. states of the American Indian view of retribution in the here and now: "It was not contemplated that the soul would have to account for misdeeds and lapses from a previously established ethical norm. All of the concern was expressed while the individual was alive."[33] This view of religion sees the spirit of God working for justice in this life, retributively as well as distributively. I shall explore the matter of violence as a means of social change in my discussion of the liberation theology of Malcolm X, below.

Influenced by the political and social Christian theologies of Paul Tillich, Wolfhart Pannenberg, and Jürgen Moltmann, Carl Braaten writes of the importance of the workings of God in history to effect liberatory change. Indeed, *this* is the *Basileu tou Theou*:

> It is the power of the future manifesting itself in political and social terms, in the struggle for peace with justice, for solidarity with personal freedom. The Kingdom of God struggles in history to break the tyranny of the strong over the weak, to liberate men from authoritarian systems of power, and to rescue individuals from depersonalizing mechanisms. The Kingdom of God scores a victory when community is built between nations and when the unity of mankind is advanced, when higher unities are built without war and when peace on earth makes mutual fulfillment of individuals and nations possible.[34]

These words suggest the necessity of a liberation theology that will speak on behalf of, indeed, by way of, the truly oppressed. It is an acknowledgment of the life and teachings of Jesus. And "it will seem extremist

---

[32] Metz, *Theology of the World*, pp. 119–120.
[33] Deloria, Jr., *God is Red*, pp. 170–171.
[34] Carl Braaten, *The Future of God* (New York: Harper & Row Publishers, 1969), p. 158.

only to those who hope that problems will be solved without changing anything."[35]

Christian liberation theology calls for deep change within the Christian church and individual and social life itself. In fact, liberatory theologies tend to view the "Lord's Prayer" as an actualization of God's will in the world through human involvement, which is quite consistent with the process theological view that God is in the process of working in and through the world for positive purposes: "Thy Kingdom come, thy will be done, on earth as it is in heaven," though the demythologized understanding of this prayer does not see liberation in terms of some distant place in the by and by.[36] Indeed, Charlotte Black Elk reminds us that on the American Indian account of the religious life, "To simply sit and pray without doing all those things that God tells you to do is not to pray at all. It is what we call 'howling in the wind'."[37] Thus the praxis element of liberation theisms is foreshadowed by American Indian religion and theology.

In short, liberation theologies seek to awaken orthodox Christian theism from its dogmatic slumbers to the actual message of Jesus and his disciples as revolutionary preaching and activity in the world. In this light, then, it is neither difficult nor surprising that Jesus was mistreated in the way that he was in his "trial" and crucifixion.[38] While of course there was no orthodox Christian church during Jesus' lifetime, he was certainly perceived as a threat to the religious powers that be within Jerusalem, whether or not his preaching and other activities were merely perceived or actual threats to the Roman Empire. Morally speaking, it is clear that Jesus did nothing morally wrong according to the extant records, and even if he did something wrong according to the then prevailing religious mores, he certainly did not deserve to be put to death, especially by torture and lynching. In the end, what Jesus experienced in his final days was what John Rawls refers to as "telishment," or unjust punishment.[39] And those who truly concern themselves with the fullness of justice must hope that there is a time

---

[35] Braaten, *The Future of God*, p. 162.
[36] Michael H. Crosby, *Thy Will be Done: Praying the Our Father as Subversive Activity* (Maryknoll: Orbis Books, 1977).
[37] Cited in Cousineau, Editor, *A Seat at the Table*, p. 72.
[38] For an ethical and demythologized account of the trial and death of Jesus, see J. Angelo Corlett, "Is the *Passion of the Christ* Racist? Due Process, Responsibility, and Punishment," in Jorge Gracia, Editor, *Mel Gibson's Passion and Philosophy* (LaSalle: Open Court, 2004), pp. 101–110.
[39] John Rawls, *Collected Papers*, Samuel Freeman (ed.) (Cambridge: Harvard University Press, 1999), Chapter 2.

and "place" where those most responsible for this evil event get what they deserve.[40]

It is God who will provide true justice for the oppressed, at least on the liberation theology of Gustavo Gutiérrez according to which the oppressed are God's preferred peoples as there is no salvation for the oppressor, who in the end shall get what she deserves (*Matthew*, 13:42, 50; 22:13; 25:30, 41, 46). And those, unlike Soelle and Marilyn McCord Adams,[41] who prefer a theology according to which there is no universal salvation—especially for evildoers!—to one with far more orthodox biases about God might wonder whether the embracing of Christian orthodoxy "is an act of North American (and bourgeois) condescension to dismiss liberation theology."[42] I argue that the essentials of Latin American liberation theology provide at least a partial answer to what a plausible theism requires, and concur with Robert McAfee Brown's claim of liberationists that "[t]he presuppositions of bourgeois mentality must be unmasked and denounced."[43] And this pertains to utopian and pacifistic aversions to violence when violence is morally justified.

If one truly believes that God is just, then one must begin to at least seriously question the self-serving presumption made by so many Christian thinkers that even the most horrible evils shall be forgiven, rather than punished, by God. Indeed, contrary to orthodox Christian theists like Adams whose notion of divine deliverance from horrendous evils lacks a robustly liberatory feature[44] or that of Dietrich Bonhoeffer who, in attempting to consider the events of world history "from below," from the standpoint of the "outcast," "maltreated," "powerless," "reviled" and "oppressed" nonetheless states that "[t]his perspective from below must not become the partisan possession of those who are eternally dissatisfied; rather, we must do justice to life in all its dimensions from a higher satisfaction, whose foundation is beyond any talk of 'from below' or 'from above',"[45] it is God's working in the world through the genuinely faithful to liberate the

---

[40] Corlett, "Is the *Passion of the Christ* Racist? Due Process, Responsibility, and Punishment."

[41] Marilyn McCord Adams, *Horrendous Evils and the Goodness of God* (Ithaca: Cornell University Press, 1999), p. 201.

[42] Robert McAfee Brown, *Theology in a New Key* (Philadelphia: The Westminster Press, 1978), p. 11.

[43] Brown, *Theology in a New Key*, p. 58.

[44] Adams, *Horrendous Evils and the Goodness of God*, pp. 82–83.

[45] Dietrich Bonhoeffer, *Letters and Papers from Prison*, E. Bethge, Editor (New York: The Macmillan Company, 1971), p. 17.

oppressed which includes punishing the oppressors that realizes divine justice in the world. And if it is true that there is no afterlife, then those who do not engage in the punishment of evil and other forms of badness in this world can hardly be members of the community of faith. Rather, they are part and parcel of the communities that are *de facto* opposed to God, because they are opposed to an essential aspect of justice.

Furthermore, it might be argued that many orthodox Christian theists do not know God as much as they claim to, as they are, along with their conception of an unjustly and unconditionally forgiving God, not on the side of justice. Their pre-theoretical, dogmatic, and pacifistic commitment to distributive justice stands in their way of seeing another side of divine justice: retributive justice. To repeat: I agree wholeheartedly with liberationists that to know God is to do justice. And it is precisely here where theories of responsibility and punishment enter into the discussion,[46] though it is beyond the purview of the present project to examine them.

The class struggle in the world between the oppressed and their oppressors does not reveal some notion that God loves everyone, including the oppressors. For to love God *is* to love the oppressed. And to oppress others is to be an enemy of God. So the oppressors are enemies of God, whether or not an uncritical consciousness allows one to see this. As enemies of God, oppressors are to be punished, not rewarded with some doctrine of universal salvation and unconditional forgiveness. Caiphas, Andrew Jackson, Adolph Hitler, Benito Mussolini, and many others[47] cannot plausibly be seen as those who are not evil oppressors and, if they were alive today, deserving of the harshest of punishments. And history is loaded with thousands, if not millions, of others who, though perhaps not quite as evil,[48] are evil nonetheless.[49] As such, they are not in moral positions to enjoy the protection of being "on God's side" and participating in the bringing about of the *Basiliou tou Theou*.

There is no neutrality here. One is to some extent for and/or to some extent against God as one acts in this or that circumstance. And while

---

[46] For an account of such theories, see Corlett, *Responsibility and Punishment*, Chapter 2.

[47] We must remember that there are several others who advise these persons and thus serve as significant contributory causes of evils, and there is collective and shared responsibility for evil. Hence the actual group of evildoers is far greater than one might think.

[48] The concept of evil, like many other moral concepts, admits of degrees.

[49] For analyses of the concept of evil, see Joel Feinberg, *Problems at the Roots of Law* (Oxford: Oxford University Press, 2003), Chapter 6; J. Angelo Corlett, "Evil," *Analysis*, 64 (2004), pp. 81–84.

simply being bad hardly qualifies one as being evil, there is far more evil in the world than most folk are willing to admit. And this fact manifests itself in the ways in which persons treat one another, including how one acts within the class struggles of societies. As *James* states: "By their works you shall know them." For genuine commitment to God is true commitment to the world, and it is precisely here where spirituality and liberation meet.[50] To know and love God is to do justice, both distributively and (I would add) retributively. Evil must be brought to justice in the here and now. Failure to do so is to fail to do God's will.

As Brown states, "[t]he rude reality is that my joys and fulfillments are frequently purchased at the cost of misery and denial to others, and freedoms my country extends to me are freedoms it denies to small minorities at home and vast majorities abroad."[51] I would add that orthodox Christian theology is a theology of oppression in denying the proper standing within the church for the voice of the oppressed—the very folk for whom Jesus, the alleged founder of the orthodox Christian church, stood and faced an unjust torturous death. So to deny the essentially distributive and retributivist justice-centered conception of God and the world that is brought to the discussion by liberation theologians is to once again deny the voice of truth, justice, and God Herself. Christian orthodoxy seeks to maintain the status quo socially, economically, politically, and theologically.

Furthermore, one version of orthodox Christian theism teaches that God causes everything that happens—even natural and unnatural evil and that in some sense God wills or approves of it as a means of "soul-making" or such. As liberationists, "we must be suspicious of such theologies; instead of being true understandings of God and the world, they may be contrivances to ensure that the world is not basically challenged, so that those with privileges can enjoy them untroubled by uneasy consciences."[52]

The focus of a genuinely plausible theology must not only be on the nature of the spirit of God, but on the spirit of God as it manifests itself in justice for *los pobres*. In the end, God's faithful will be identified and identifiable as those who side with *los pobres*, the struggling masses.[53] And this is, incidentally, supported by various passages from the Jewish and

---

[50] Robert McAfee Brown, *Spirituality and Liberation* (Philadelphia: The Westminster Press, 1988).

[51] Brown, *Theology in a New Key*, p. 13.

[52] Brown, *Theology in a New Key*, p. 62.

[53] Robert McAfee Brown, *Religion and Violence* (Philadelphia: The Westminster Press, 1973).

Christian scriptures (*Exodus*, 1:8–14; 2:23–25; 3:7f.; *Matthew*, 25:31f.). This implies, or could without conceptual or theological absurdity be thought to imply, that God sides with the oppressed (including the poor) and that those who fail to do so are not part of God's faithful and deserve punishment to the extent that they are significantly responsible for their disobedience to God's will in their direct or indirect oppression of others. *Life is not a question of whether or not we will take sides, but of which side we take.* For we select sides, politically speaking, even in omitting to choose sides. And it is a *kairos* moment of decision for persons each day to side with or against *los pobres*, and with God. In light of these aspects of its perspective, then, it is no wonder why some refer to Latin American liberation theology as "the militant Gospel."[54] It is no wonder, moreover, why even those such as Moltmann[55] who seek to embrace at least some meaningful degree of what liberationists have to offer, are chided for not embracing it enough.[56]

To be sure, to know and love God—to obey God—is to do justice. But again, by this is meant not merely justice in distributive terms, but also retributively. What theism sometimes requires in times of evil is not mere reform as Immanuel Kant would have it, but revolution. For in many cases, reform by and large strengthens the oppressive status quo rather than realizing true revolutionary change for the oppressed. The Kantian moral permission to reform must at times be replaced with the Marxian call for revolt!

It may come somewhat as a surprise to many to know that even some Christians centuries ago living in colonial America were liberationists (albeit of a reformist sort). John Woolman (1720–1772), the New Jersey Quaker minister and tailor who traveled throughout that region meeting Indians and attempting to convert many of his fellow Quakers from their slave-holding ways, wrote and preached much about equal freedom for "negroes" and the wrongness ("evil") of the institution of slavery as it was against his conscience and "inconsistent with the Christian religion." For him, slavery should be abolished because it was an abomination to God. Moreover, for Woolman, it was God's love that was to be used as an instrument of social reform.[57]

---

54   Alfredo Fierro, *The Militant Gospel* (Maryknoll: Orbis Books, 1977).
55   Jürgen Moltmann, *Theology of Hope*, J. W. Leitch (trans.) (New York: Harper & Row Publishers, 1967).
56   José Miguez Bonino, *Doing Theology in a Revolutionary Situation* (Philadelphia: Fortress Press, 1975), pp. 144–150.
57   John Woolman, *The Journal of John Woolman* and *a Plea for the Poor* (Gloucester: Peter Smith, 1971).

But before one jumps to the hasty conclusion that Woolman was a full-blown liberationist, it should be borne in mind that he also believed that it was God who provided the bounties of North America to European whites and that this was a "right" that whites had to the land in concert with Indians. Moreover, though Woolman recounts some of his encounters with Indians, he never seems to do so with blacks or slaves. So no matter how reformist he is in his version of slavery abolitionism, Woolman is a white among whites in colonial America. In light of his musings about slavery, moreover, Woolman never seems to express anything beyond the idea that slavery was against Christian principles. But he falls short of arguing that blacks were equal to whites as humans, or that they ought to be accorded the very same rights as whites in civil society, or that blacks deserve freedom and equality. In light of this, it would be misleading to refer to Woolman, as well-intentioned as he was, as a revolutionary-liberationist. Rather, I refer to him as a liberationist-reformer within Quakerdom who was somewhat ahead of his peers, who in turn were alienated from godliness when it came to such fundamental matters of basic humanity. Like most Christianity at that time, the enslavement of Africans was accepted as part and parcel of what "God" intended for both whites and blacks. To be sure, orthodox Christianity at that time, as in many others, was hardly of God in any robust sense. And as if this were not bad enough, there are orthodox Christian theists who actually deny that God is just.

Orthodox Christian theists like Adams deny that God is just. More precisely, on this view, God is neither just nor unjust because of the tremendous ontological gap between God and us. Thus the language of justice and injustice cannot possibly capture the fullness of the meaning of divine providence, omniscience, and omnibenevolence.[58] What is referred to as "divine antinomianism" entails the view that the realities of God and humans are incommensurable such that human conceptions of justice, for example, do not apply to God. Moreover, Adams' argument seems to be that God is neither just nor unjust, but beyond justice-talk in that justice-talk wrongly assumes rights-talk between the relations of God and humans:

> Created persons have *no rights* against God, because God has *no obligations* to creatures: in particular, God has no obligations to be good to us; no obligations not to ruin us whether depriving our lives of positive meaning, by

---

[58] Marilyn McCord Adams, "The Problem of Hell: A Problem of Evil for Christians," in E. Stump, Editor, *Reasoned Faith* (Ithaca: Cornell University Press, 1993), pp. 301–327.

producing or allowing the deterioration or disintegration of our personalities, by destroying our bodies, or by annihilating us.[59]

Furthermore, on this view, it is logically impossible for God to bind Herself to humans. For "God is not the kind of thing that could be obligated to creatures in any way . . . ," but "God will not be unjust to created persons no matter what He does." Besides, God's love for humans infinitely transcends duties and obligations that are part of the language of justice.

But there are a number of difficulties with this position that denies that God is just. First, if the human conception of justice does not apply to God in that God is far beyond our experience and ability to describe in language, then by parity of reasoning, so too are our conceptions of God's goodness, love, patience, forgiveness, and such. Does Adams' assertion here amount to the Wittgensteinian suggestion that we remain silent about that of which we cannot speak? If so, then why do orthodox Christian theologians speak and write of God at all? Why do they seek to go out into "all the world" to preach the *kerygma* until the very *parousia* itself? According to this conception of God and Her attributes, communication about God is impossible, if not inadequate anyway. Were Jesus, Paul, and the *kerygma* writers too impudent or intellectually indolent to understand the alleged truth of Adams' point here? Thus this view denying that God is just (or unjust) seems to make a mockery of the *kerygma* itself. Its implications are impossible to reconcile with common-sense intuitions about the *kerygma*.

Second, that divine love (whatever that is) infinitely transcends the realms of justice begs the question of the nature and function of God in the world. Is God incapable of creating us such that She cannot even adequately communicate with us regarding Her nature and function in the world? If so, does this not make God a bit unakin to omniscient in that She knows not how to do so, and less than omnipotent in that She simply cannot do so even if She knew how? Yet it is precisely orthodox Christian thinkers like Adams who boldly affirm, against all manner of objections from Aquinas until today, namely, God's omniscience and omnipotence. Moreover, we ought not to blindly assume that divine love runs counter to justice. Again, if liberation theologies are correct, then to know God is to do justice. And this seems to imply that love and compassion for the oppressed and distributive and retributive justice are inextricably linked to one another. Thus we ought not to assume that divine love and justice are not part of the same plan of salvation, of ushering in the *Basileia tou Theou*.

---

[59] Adams, "The Problem of Hell: A Problem of Evil for Christians," p. 308.

Furthermore, Adams' way of thinking about God makes God less than omnipotent in that God cannot even freely choose to enter into obligations "in any way" with those She creates! It is one thing for God to be unable to do the logically impossible, such as to make a stone so heavy that She cannot lift it. But to be unable to voluntarily restrict Her own freedom in order to bind Herself in obligation to us *in some way* is surely a kind of power that, if anyone has, God does. Process theists, in their delimiting of God's powers beyond what is normal in Western theological circles, would not conceive of such *ad hoc* restrictions on God.

Moreover, the quoted passage above from Adams reveals a kind of "horrendous" insensitivity to the problem of evil, implying that God's creating humans fails to bind God to certain limits as to how She treats us. Adams assertion that "God will not be unjust to created persons no matter what He does" hardly guarantees against divinely capricious and unjust behavior. All Adams provides is the lame promise of orthodox Christian dogma here. But she also implies that divine justice, and justice more generally, is necessarily bound to the notion of obligation.

But God can be just, perfectly just, without entering into any obligatory relationship with humans. In other words, God might not owe us a thing, as Adams states, but nonetheless treats us and other "creatures" with perfect justice and fairness as she states. Thus there is a logical flaw in Adams' position on divine justice as she fails to understand that divine justice (and justice more generally) is not tied to obligations. Ironically, this point is implied in her own words: "God will not be *unjust* to created persons no matter what He does." But this point needs to be strengthened, of course, to read that God *cannot* be unjust in any way.[60] Why not? Contrary to Adams, it is because if She exists, God is not capricious. She is not morally arbitrary. She is bound to the principles of truth, justice, and goodness, properly construed. To deny this property of God is to deny part of the very essence of God Herself!

What makes God just, then, is that God never acts arbitrarily or unfairly. And this is no more a restriction on God's power than to say that God is bound to the laws and objectively true principles of reason. In fact, it is in light of this construal of divine justice that divine love can be properly understood.

---

[60] "It is one thing to say that God will not break Her promises; it is another to say that She cannot make them" [Timothy P. Jackson, *The Priority of Love* (Princeton: Princeton University Press, 2003), p. 74].

This latter point implies the falsity of Adams' assertion that "Created persons have *no rights* against God." Perhaps what Adams means here is that there are no valid legal or institutional rules that would ground a legal or institutional right against God, or that there are no valid religious rules that would ground a religious right against God. But what she cannot mean with plausibility is that there is no valid *moral* rule that would ground a *moral* right against God. For if there are human rights, and if, as most human rights theorists argue, human rights are species of moral rights, and if moral rights are noninstitutional ones that are grounded in the principles of an enlightened moral conscience,[61] then "creatures" surely have human and moral rights not to be treated arbitrarily, to due process, to freedom of expression, among others, even if these are in the end *prima facie* moral rights.[62] Thus it is dubious to claim that "Created persons have *no rights* against God," especially if it is true that "the language of rights is the only current candidate for a universal moral discourse,"[63] and, furthermore,

> One might attempt to appropriate rights language while stressing its limitations and the need to root it in some substantial moral theory . . . the language of human rights is the only plausible candidate for a global moral language. . . . To abandon it because of its inadequacies is to make the perfect the enemy of the good. The language of rights has an important function in articulating moral consensus against some of the most flagrant abuses in our time. . . . Rights language can specify some of the general demands of social justice.[64]

Assumed here is that a universal moral discourse is a desirable thing whether orthodox Christian theists think so or not. So if God exists, God is just because the language of rights implies as much. And no amount of

---

[61] Joel Feinberg, *Freedom and Fulfillment* (Princeton: Princeton University Press, 1992), Chapters 8–10.

[62] J. Angelo Corlett, "Analyzing Human Rights," in *Human Rights After 9/11* (Philadelphia: University of Pennsylvania Press, in press). Also see J. Angelo Corlett, *Race, Rights, and Justice* (Dordrecht: Springer, 2009), Law and Philosophy Library, Volume 85, Chapter 5.

[63] David Fergusson, *Community, Liberalism, & Christian Ethics* (Cambridge: Cambridge University Press, 1998), p. 9.

[64] Fergusson, *Community, Liberalism, & Christian Ethics*, pp. 168–169. These points, however crucial, have been made decades ago by the likes of Joel Feinberg, Ronald Dworkin, Carl Wellman, and other rights theorists.

orthodox Christian dogma can minimize the extent to which God is bound not only to laws of logic, but to the principles of an enlightened moral conscience.[65] After all, if there are human rights, then God has an obliga-tion to humans to not violate them.

Hence the challenge to the idea of divine justice is unpersuasive, even unhealthy for those who attach a great deal of merit to the authority of orthodox Christian canonical writings. If God exists, God is, among other things, just. But thus far we have not explicitly recognized the ambiguity of this claim. For, as I mentioned above, there are multifarious ways in which God is just. Two general ways include distributively and retributively, respectively. Liberation theologians have done well to argue for the dis-tributive justice notion. But it is noteworthy that for all that is contained in Christian scriptures about turning the other cheek and forgiveness, not one such statement occurs in the context of the state's treatment of crim-inals. There is no explicit denial in the Christian scriptures of the right of the state to punish legal offenders. And the contexts of forgiveness and related concepts each occur in discussion of communities of the religious faithful.[66]

So long as retributive justice is carried out fairly, there is in all of the Christian scriptures no denial of its moral legitimacy (and if there were such a denial, so much the worse for the Christian scriptures!). Not only, then, is God Herself just, but there is no clear revelatory denial of the state's right to inflict retributive punishment on those who deserve it. Turn-ing the other cheek, forgiveness, and mercy are part of Jesus' life and teach-ings. But they play a limited role in life outside of the Christian communities of faith. There is, then, no good reason for the non-Christian to pay part-icular attention to these in-group religious mores. This is especially true to the extent that God is just and will make certain that everyone gets what they deserve, according to the complexities of their lives. But for this to occur, *we* must carefully carry out the justice that is deserved. For to fail to do so is to disobey God's desire for justice.

Having made the point that God is just in order to ground one of the fundamental assertions of liberation theisms, it is important to continue the discussion of what they argue about God and persons in the world.

---

[65] Assumed here is the moral goodness of God, as well as a Feinbergian concep-tion of rights as articulated in Feinberg, *Freedom and Fulfillment*, Chapters 8–10.

[66] J. Angelo Corlett, *Responsibility and Punishment* (Dordrecht: Kluwer Aca-demic Publishers, 2001), Library of Ethics and Applied Philosophy, Volume 9, pp. 77–79.

While it may concern some that my description of Latin American liberation theology is incomplete, my purpose here is not to provide a comprehensive account of it, but rather to state some of its basic elements that
I shall weave into a synthesis of liberatory themes along with some first
wave black Christian theology, and the liberation theology of Malcolm X.

While recognizing that there exist theological differences between some
first wave Latin American liberationists, my aim is to borrow what I deem
most important for my purposes in order to set forth and defend what
I take to be a plausible theism from a Western perspective, and to see if it
can withstand some of the queries concerning Christian orthodoxy. In
this manner, philosophy of religion shall be advanced importantly, as a
plausible theism emerges that might well cause atheists to pause.

As is widely known, "institutionalized Christianity, like all established
religions, has functioned mainly as a conservative force throughout history.
It has as effectively suppressed or domesticated its own internal rebellions
and uprisings as it has resisted and survived those from the outside."[67]
Moreover, Tina Beattie points out:

> In the late 1960s, the emergence of liberation theology in Latin America
> represented an attempt at a synthesis between Catholic theology and
> Marxism. Although the Vatican has tried to repress liberation theology, it
> continues to influence much religious thought and practice, and has spread
> far beyond the bounds of Latin American Catholicism to different religious
> and political cultures.[68]

Broadly within the Christian tradition, the most influential theologies of
liberation (in the West) are of at least two kinds. One is the Latin American
variety whose founding spokespersons include Hugo Assmann, Rubem
Alves, José Miguez Bonino, Giulio Girardi, and Gustavo Gutiérrez. Another
is that of black liberation theology, founded in part by James H. Cone,
and includes figures such as Martin Luther King, Jr., and Malcolm X,
representing Christian and Islamic religious faiths, respectively. In looking
at some of the main features of these theologies of liberation, I hope to
provide an even deeper picture—especially for atheists who do not seem to
demonstrate an awareness and appreciation for them—of how live an
option theism might be as the nature and function of God is plumbed
beyond the depths of process theology.

---

[67]   Beattie, *The New Atheists*, p. 30.
[68]   Beattie, *The New Atheists*, p. 31.

Latin American Liberation Theology and the Existence of God

The basic theme of Latin American liberation theologies is summed up in the words of Bonino: "There are not two histories: one sacred and one profane or secular. The one history in which God acts is the history of men; it is in this history where we find God."[69] And this strand of theism finds its roots in Marxist humanism. By this it is meant that particular attention is paid to the *Basileia tou Theou* being realized in this world as God works through persons to effect justice and fairness and to combat oppression. For some such theologians, "truth is at the level of history, not in the realm of ideas." This is what is meant by liberation theology's praxis element.[70] As Assmann argues, God can only be found through human faith and action,[71] and as Gutiérrez notes, "This theological process becomes truth when it is embodied into the process of liberation."[72] To this Alves adds that liberation is freedom itself, an act of persons of faith who do the will of God in the world; it is the divine freedom intervening in history to subvert the status quo of oppression and disunity among persons. Thus faith in God provides a future of hope for the oppressed as God is working through those of faith to emancipate the downtrodden. To the extent that the church is genuinely faithful to God's will, it will align itself in solidarity with those who work for the liberation of the oppressed and the oppressed themselves.[73] Indeed, Latin American liberation theology is a militant one, and accepts no substitute for partisanism in doing the will of God. From the perspective of many orthodox Christian theists, it might be construed as a kind of "profane theism."

Generally speaking, Latin American liberation theologians would not be correctly termed "abstract thinkers," as for them, theology

> . . . is not an effort to give a correct understanding of God's attributes or actions but an effort to articulate the action of faith, the shape of praxis

---

69   Bonino, *Doing Theology in a Revolutionary Situation*, pp. 70–71.
70   Bonino, *Doing Theology in a Revolutionary Situation*, p. 72.
71   Hugo Assmann, *Opresión-Liberación: Desafío a los Christianos* (Montevideo: Editorial Tierra Nueva, 1972), p. 112.
72   Gustavo Gutiérrez, "Freedom and Salvation," in Gustavo Gutiérrez and Richard Shaull, *Liberation and Change* (Atlanta: John Knox Press, 1977), p. 82. He argues that faith in God does not consist merely in asserting his existence but rather in acting for God to liberate the poor. For "to believe is to practice," as *James*, 2:14–25 states (Gutiérrez, "Freedom and Salvation," p. 89).
73   Rubem Alves, *A Theology of Human Hope* (Washington, D.C.: Corpus Books, 1969).

conceived and realized in obedience . . . theology has to stop explaining the world and to start transforming it. *Orthopraxis*,[74] rather than orthodoxy, becomes the criterion for theology.[75]

I take this claim to be hyberbolic, though partly accurate, as it is of crucial importance that faith be based on reason's attempt to ever grasp the realities of God in the world. Our conception of God must be grounded, that is, rescued from the otherworldliness of much of abstract theology. Theology must at its best be grounded in God's workings in the world, in the here and now. And how might one know the workings of God in the world without reason's attempt to know the difference between God's will and the will of those inspired by badness or evil? Understanding the nature of God assists those of faith in knowing what can be inspired by God. And while praxis is essential to the life of faith in God, so is the examined life of reasoned faith, including reasoning about God in order to better comprehend God's nature and function in the world. It is for this reason that I prefer the description of the essential task of theology provided by Gutiérrez: ". . . theology is of necessity both spirituality and rational knowledge. These are permanent and indispensable functions of all theological thinking. However, both functions must be salvaged, at least partially, from the division and deformations they have suffered throughout history."[76]

While process thought tends to emphasize the congruence of religion and science and the importance of ecological preservation, liberation theologies tend to stress the importance of addressing and resolving matters of human injustice. In both cases, I might add, the notion of God is secularized in terms of nature, society, and politics. Indeed, whereas process theism grounds God by way of naturalizing the theological conception of Her, liberation theism grounds God by liberating God from the conceptual shackles of abstract debates about what is logically possible for God to do in order to answer equally abstract questions about God's preconceived supernaturalistic nature. And Gutiérrez' statement that "rather than define the world in relation to the religious phenomenon, it would seem that

---

[74] This term is found in other liberationists, such as Gustavo Gutiérrez, *A Theology of Liberation*, Caridad Inda and John Eagleson (trans.) (Maryknoll: Orbis Books, 1973), p. 10. For a few of the numerous reviews of this momentous book, see *Critic* (1973), p. 84; *Commonweal* (1973), pp. 314–316; *The Journal of Religion* (1973), pp. 108–110.

[75] Bonino, *Doing Theology in a Revolutionary Situation*, p. 81.

[76] Gutiérrez, *A Theology of Liberation*, p. 6.

religion should be redefined in relation to the profane,"[77] a theme implied in the demythologization of theology and the secularization of the concept of God, is rather apt. For neither God, nor faith, nor salvation, nor divine grace are other-worldly. They are in the here and now as the faithful act according to the spirit of God. Moreover, in both cases, God and the world, respectively, are in the process of becoming. God is theologically liberated from the confines of abstract theological debates and grounded in the real world. The very idea of divine creation is conceived by process and liberation theologies similarly, as Gutiérrez notes: "It is the work of a God who saves and acts in history; since man is the center of creation, it is integrated into the history which is being built by man's efforts."[78] Of course, it is quite consistent with some of the ideas of each approach to see the environment as not only the context for human life, but deserving of our respect such that, as American Indian religions generally hold, the well-being of humans is linked to the well-being of nature more broadly.[79] Hence the American Indians' indelible respect for the Earth as "our Mother." This point must be borne in mind unless theism repeat the same mistake as traditional Christian theism in thinking, as did Rene Descartes and Kant, in terms of an anthropocentric universe, thereby not condemning or allowing conceptual room for the wholesale exploitation of natural resources to the detriment of both humans and nonhumans alike. So theism must adopt an ecological theology, one which unites the scientific emphasis of process theology and the humanitarian concerns of liberation thought. It is to the latter that I now turn a bit more deeply.

Such theism, it seems, might be partly constructed on a metaphysic of Whiteheadian panentheism. But it must also entail a liberationist element that sees God as working in the world through the faithful to liberate persons from oppression. Oppression, on this account, is a severe harmful wrongdoing. The more harmful the wrongdoing, the greater the oppression, generally speaking. As such, oppression must be eradicated. In fact, it is the liberation of oppressed peoples everywhere that exactly is part of what is the *Basileia tou Theou*. As Gutiérrez argues: "An unjust situation

---

[77] Gutiérrez, *A Theology of Liberation*, p. 67.

[78] Gutiérrez, *A Theology of Liberation*, p. 154.

[79] For more on the Indian conception of God as the "Big Holy," the "Great Spirit," the "Bringer of Law," etc., see Cousineau, Editor, *A Seat at the Table*. This notion is the basis of the ecological view that ". . . all life is interdependent—indeed many creatures can only live in concert with, and often literally on, particularly other organisms (symbiosis)" [Arthur Peacocke, *Creation and the World of Science* (Oxford: Oxford University Press, 2004), pp. 258–260].

does not happen by chance; it is not something branded by a fatal destiny: there is human responsibility behind it."[80] Whatever else God is, God is just. And if *Jeremiah*, 22:13–16 is correct, then "to know God is to do justice"[81]; "To know him is to work for justice. There is no other path to reach him."[82] This not only includes concerns of distributive justice wherein the workings of God in the world are concerned with fairness among persons,[83] but it also involves retributive justice in terms of holding harmful wrong-doers accountable and punishing them for their actions, omissions, or attempted actions that eventuate in oppression and for which culpability is unmitigated.[84] This idea stands in sharp contrast to the unsubstantiated process theological assertion that "The idea of justice continues to be bound up in too many minds with the notion that life will deal us what we deserve and that suffering must be brought about by sin. The expectation of justice in this sense leads repeatedly to disappointment. It leads also to teachings that are truly harmful."[85]

To save the world is to bring justice to it in the midst of the injustice that is in it. It is to bring the power of justice to bear in conquering injustice of all kinds. Put in theological terms, "Sin demands a radical liberation, which in turn necessarily implies a political liberation."[86] And such liberation is necessary in order to realize the *Basileia tou Theou*.[87] Thus the workings of God are within human history. *Heilsgeschichte* precisely is our history insofar as God works through persons to save and to liberate and to bring justice to injustice. And it is by way of this divine process that new persons are created wherein the "Word is *made* man"[88] and in turn every person becomes the temple of God and there is a universalization of God's presence,[89] as held in process theology.

Thus we meet God in our encounters with others, all the more reason to treat one another justly. As Gutiérrez writes: ". . . every human act which

---

[80] Gutiérrez, *A Theology of Liberation*, p. 175.

[81] Gutiérrez, *A Theology of Liberation*, p. 199.

[82] Gutiérrez, *A Theology of Liberation*, p. 272.

[83] John Rawls, *A Theory of Justice* (Cambridge: Harvard University Press, 1971); *Political Liberalism* (New York: Columbia University Press, 1993); *The Law of Peoples* (Cambridge: Harvard University Press, 1999).

[84] Corlett, *Responsibility and Punishment*.

[85] John Cobb, Jr., *The Process Perspective* (St. Louis: Chalice Press, 2003), p. 11.

[86] Gutiérrez, *A Theology of Liberation*, p. 176.

[87] Gutiérrez, *A Theology of Liberation*, p. 177.

[88] Gutiérrez, *A Theology of Liberation*, p. 189. Or, as the Christian scripture states: "The Word is made flesh."

[89] Gutiérrez, *A Theology of Liberation*, pp. 193–194.

is oriented towards the construction of a more just society has value in terms of communion with God—in terms of salvation."[90] Thus to know and love God is to do justice to all, especially the poor and oppressed of the world. In reality, then, to know and love God precisely "*is* to establish just relationships among men, it *is* to recognize the rights of *los pobres.*" The God of biblical revelation is known through inter-human justice. "When justice does not exist, God is not known; he is absent."[91]

For Paulo Freire, the liberation which humanizes the dehumanized involves not only the oppressed, but the oppressors themselves. Or in the words of Gutiérrez, "Universal love is that which in solidarity with the oppressed seeks also to liberate the oppressors from their own power, from their ambition, and from their selfishness."[92] In this way, liberation realizes the humanization of dehumanization as God's act in the world. One must, then, avoid presuming that one acts on behalf of God in the act of liberation. For all are children of God and as such must be delivered from the dehumanization of oppression, whether oppressed or oppressors.[93]

While this attitude certainly finds its roots in Christian and otherwise religious notions of forgiveness and reconciliation, it need not play a role in a liberation theology, or a theism of any kind whatsoever. Plausible theism, whether Christian or otherwise, can get along perfectly well, even in its deepest religious aspects of spirituality, without such ideas and practices as they presume a particular idea of justice that tends to thwart responsibility and punishment, among other things, as noted above. A plausible theism must incorporate meaningful degrees and kinds of both distributive and retributive justice, not simply the former. Or, it must at least provide independent argumentative support for the rejection of retributive justice as a genuine concern or duty.

While Latin American liberation theologians tend to draw their inspiration from both Christian revelation and the political writings of Marx, there is another branch of Christian liberation theology that draws its primary inspiration from either Christian or Islamic revelation. Here

---

[90] Gutiérrez, *A Theology of Liberation*, p. 238.
[91] Gutiérrez, *A Theology of Liberation*, p. 195.
[92] Gutiérrez, *A Theology of Liberation*, p. 275.
[93] Paulo Freire, *Pedagogy of the Oppressed*, M. B. Ramos (trans.) (New York: The Seabury Press, 1968); *Education for Critical Consciousness* (New York: Continuum, 1980). For a recent account of how racism ought to be overcome through "positive social transformation," excluding acts of compensatory reparations by oppressors to the oppressed, see Rubén R. Rodríguez, *Racism and God-Talk* (New York: New York University Press, 2008), pp. 212–250.

I refer to the Christian liberationist King, Jr. and Islamic liberationist, Malcolm X, respectively. It is vital to discuss this branch of liberation theism in that it pertains to the very means by which divine justice might be achieved.

Black Liberation Theology and the Existence of God

There are few issues more important to most U.S. blacks[94] than under-standing the respective views of King, Jr. (Martin) and Malcolm X (Malcolm) on matters of positive social change: the use of political vio-lence versus nonviolence as a means of social change,[95] separation versus integration as possible sub-goals of social change, etc. Yet this is a subject which has received virtually no attention from the community of analytical philosophers. In this section, I shall provide a philosophical description and assessment of Martin's and Malcolm's respective philosophies of social change. The focus will be on Martin's program of nonviolent direct action as a means to ethnic integration as a social aim. However, I make use of Malcolm's views as a critique of Martin's position. But we ought not to forget that Martin and Malcolm were deeply religious persons, and if Cone is correct, "Martin Luther King, Jr., was the most important and influential Christian theologian in America's history."[96] Cone argues that this is true because (a) Martin addressed theologically the most important problem in the U.S.: racism; (b) Martin's courage in addressing racism in such a volatile context; and (c) the scope of his influence throughout the world

---

[94]   For purposes of this discussion, "blacks" refers to those of sub-Saharan African ethnicity whose genealogy traces back to institutionalized U.S. slavery. Also, I follow James H. Cone in referring to Martin Luther King, Jr. and Malcolm X as "Martin" and "Malcolm," respectively [See James H. Cone, *Martin & Malcolm & America* (Maryknoll: Orbis Books, 1991)].

[95]   James Cone points out that Martin sees at least two different kinds of violence: personal and social. Martin does not seem to deny that it is sometimes justified to use violence to defend oneself personally, or to defend one's own family or friends in danger. The kind of violence with which I am concerned is that of social violence. For here violence is employed as a means of social change, not merely as a way of warding-off an intruder or an attack on one's own person. Cone argues that Martin denies the legitimacy of violence when it comes to the matter of social change, not personal self-defense (Conversation with Cone on February 19, 1993, Pacific Lutheran University).

[96]   Cone, *Risks of Faith*, p. xvii.

and on various other movements for social change.[97] I would add that Malcolm was important also and in precisely these ways, not only as a social reformer, but insofar as his political standpoint about racism in the U.S. is greatly informed by his Islamic faith and insofar as he also addressed the "cancer" of racism.[98] Thus it is crucial to include their respective views on God and the world as part and parcel of a plausible theistic perspective. As Cone states, Martin and Malcolm are the ". . . two ministers most responsible for the rise of black liberation theology."[99]

In devoting my discussion in this section primarily to the Black theologies of liberation articulated by Martin, Malcolm, and Cone, I do not wish to in any way deny or ignore the substantial roots of black liberation theology found in Frederick Douglass,[100] or in more contemporary times, William R. Jones,[101] and Gayraud S.Wilmore,[102] among others. Indeed, there is good reason to believe that these thinkers articulated similar views to my own insofar as they are praxis forms of theology, and demythologized, centering on the ways in which humans who obey God's will do God's work in the world, rather than awaiting God's intervention into the affairs of humankind to effect justice for the poor and oppressed. Indeed, "Douglass believed that divine activity came only through human beings because there was no evidence that it acted apart from humans themselves."[103] Moreover, "Jones asserts that . . . God is only accessible in the act of justice on behalf of the oppressed today."[104] These statements imply that humans, not God, are responsible for acts of oppression and nonnatural evil. And it is humans who are responsible for acts of liberation as well. Indeed, the views of Douglass and Jones differ importantly from Cone's in that, while Cone offers a Christocentric theology, Douglass and Jones do not. For Douglass and Jones, it is not God whose sovereignty makes God ultimately responsible for poverty and oppression. But for Cone's neo-orthodox

---

[97]   Cone, *Risks of Faith*, pp. xvii–xviii.

[98]   My point here is inspired by my study of Cone, *Martin & Malcolm & America*; *Risks of Faith*, pp. xx–xxii.

[99]   Cone, *Risks of Faith*, p. xxiv.

[100]   For an incisive discussion of the liberation theology of Frederick Douglass, see Reginald F. Davis, *Frederick Douglass: A Precursor of Liberation Theology* (Macon: Mercer University Press, 2005).

[101]   William R. Jones, *Is God a White Racist?* (New York: Doubleday, 1973).

[102]   Gayraud S. Wilmore, *Black Religion and Black Radicalism*, 2nd Edition (Maryknoll: Orbis Books, 1983).

[103]   Davis, *Frederick Douglass: A Precursor to Liberation Theology*, p. 75.

[104]   Davis, *Frederick Douglass: A Precursor to Liberation Theology*, p. 83.

Christian theology, God must in the end assume responsibility for these evils. As Douglass notes, "It is a ridiculous and absurd notion to expect God to deliver us from bondage. We must elevate ourselves by our own efforts."[105]

Black liberation theology shares with Latin American liberation theology the idea of praxis and it shares with process theology the notion of God's working in the world in order to effect goodness. As Cone states, "The divine liberation of the oppressed from slavery is the central theological concept in the black spirituals."[106] This is the basis of Cone's insight that, contrary to popular opinion, black slaves in the U.S. did not resign themselves to the idea that God wanted them to be subservient to whites,[107] but rather to free themselves from the yoke of bondage. And the content of the lyrics of black spirituals (as well as early blues lyrics) often proclaimed as much. Thus we can see how process and liberation theologies, with their disagreements and variant emphases, concur that God is in the world working through humans to effect positive change. The divine will seeks to work toward justice and fairness in the world by way of influencing human actions to this effect.

The popular image of both Martin and Malcolm is that they are rivals in virtually every respect. Scarcely do people realize exactly how much these two figures have in common.[108] Both of them are black activists who strove to liberate oppressed persons, regardless of ethnicity or gender, from the shackles placed on them by their oppressors. Both were religious leaders, though Martin was a Christian (Baptist) and Malcolm was a minister of the Nation of Islam. This makes their inclusion in this discussion not

---

[105] John W. Blassingame, *The Frederick Douglass Papers,* Volume 2, 1847–1854 (New Haven: Yale University Press, 1979–1985), p. 170.

[106] Cone, *Risks of Faith,* p. 17. Indeed, the black spirituals served as a basis of a black theology of liberation, as the theology of a heaven in the by and by is depicted in them as the standpoint of oppressors who seek to use religion to quell the disappointment of the masses of oppressed (p. 25). Nonetheless, the language of heaven was converted in the black slave communities to provide blacks with a sense of "somebodiness" in the face of the nobodiness of slavery (p. 26). Also see James H. Cone, *The Spirituals and the Blues* (New York: Seabury Press, 1991).

[107] As Solly says in August Wilson's *Gem of the Ocean*: "Ain't nothing worse than slavery!" [August Wilson, *Gem of the Ocean* (New York: Theatre Communications Group, 2006), p. 56].

[108] For an illuminating comparison of the lives and teachings of Martin and Malcolm, see Cone, *Martin & Malcolm & America.*

only relevant, but important in that more than merely the Christian perspective is being discussed. Although at certain points of their respective lives each accused the other of being too narrow insofar as social reform was concerned, each was international in his approach to liberation. For the problems of injustice were global, transcending the social, political, economic, and religious strife throughout the U.S.. To the extreme disappointment of most people, Martin and Malcolm were social reformers both of whom were assassinated at crucial periods of social progress and awakening in the U.S.. Moreover, both Martin and Malcolm were natural law proponents in some important sense. Following Thomas Aquinas, each believed that breaking a morally unjust legal or institutional rule was not wrong. In fact, justice and morality require it.[109] These are but some of the significant points of similarity between Martin and Malcolm. However, I will focus on some philosophical differences between them.

When it comes to the subject of the employment of violence as a means of social change, Martin and Malcolm differ. Black thinkers more generally are divided concerning the moral status of political violence.[110] W. E. B. DuBois, arguably the greatest black philosopher (in a "classical" sense of "philosopher") in the West, altered his view about violence and social change. In 1906, he writes that "we do not believe in violence."[111] However, in 1913, DuBois asks, "Fellow Negroes, is it not time to be men? Is it not time to strike back when we are struck?"[112] Perhaps most blacks in the U.S., and perhaps elsewhere, entertain a creative tension between these two beliefs, given their experiences at the hands of whites and many other nonblacks.

If there is one thing that Martin believes absolutely and religiously, it is that true spirituality demands that violence never be used in human affairs. He writes, "I'm committed to nonviolence absolutely."[113] Although he is

---

[109] Steve Clark, Editor, *Malcolm X Talks to Young People: Speeches in the U.S., Britain, and Africa* (New York: Pathfinder Press, 1991), p. 67.

[110] For an informative account of the subject of social change in the history of African-American thought, see Cone, *Martin & Malcolm & America*, pp. 3f.

[111] W. E. B. DuBois, *An ABC of Color* (New York: International Publishers, 1963), p. 33.

[112] DuBois, *An ABC of Color*, p. 63. Here the context concerns attacks on blacks in general. It does not limit itself merely to individual or collective instances of legal self-defense.

[113] Martin Luther King, Jr., "Showdown for Nonviolence," in James M. Washington, Editor, *A Testament of Hope: The Essential Writings of Martin Luther King, Jr.* (New York: Harper & Row, 1986), p. 69.

aware that most view violence sometimes as a justified means of self-defense, Martin refuses even to explicitly grant that the use of violence is morally justified, noting that violence as a means of self-defense is sometimes permitted by rules of law. He writes,

> In a nonviolent demonstration, . . . one must remember that the cause of the demonstration is some exploitation or form of oppression that has made it necessary for men of courage and good will to demonstrate against the evil. . . . The demonstrator agrees that it is better for him to suffer publicly for a short time to end the crippling evil of school segregation than to have generation after generation of children suffer in ignorance. . . .
>
> It is better to shed a little blood from a blow on the head or a rock thrown by an angry mob than to have children by the thousands grow up reading at a fifth- or sixth-grade level. . . .
>
> Furthermore, it is extremely dangerous to organize a movement around self-defense. The line between defensive violence and aggressive or retaliatory violence is a fine line indeed. When violence is tolerated even as a means of self-defense there is a grave danger that in the fervor of emotion the main fight will be lost over the question of self-defense.[114]

To this Martin adds, in another essay, that the use of violence in the civil rights movement in the U.S. "will not only be impractical but immoral. We are outnumbered; we do not have access to the instruments of violence. Even more than that, not only is violence impractical, but it is immoral."[115] What Martin means by this is that the use of retaliatory violence against oppressors "does nothing but intensify the existence of evil and hate in the universe."[116]

Martin's answer to the use of violence as a means of social change is his program of nonviolent direct action. But precisely what is nonviolent direct action? Many will discover it surprising that nonviolent direct action is not the same as civil disobedience. The primary difference between nonviolent direct action and civil disobedience is that, while it is essential that civil disobedience break a rule of law, there is nothing about nonviolent direct action which requires the breaking of a rule of law.[117] Martin argues that

---

[114] Martin Luther King, Jr., "Nonviolence: The Only Road to Freedom," in James M. Washington, Editor, *A Testament of Hope: The Essential Writings of Martin Luther King, Jr.* (New York: Harper & Row, 1986), pp. 56–57.

[115] Martin Luther King, Jr., "Walk for Freedom," in James M. Washington, Editor, *A Testament of Hope: The Essential Writings of Martin Luther King, Jr.* (New York: Harper & Row, 1986), p. 83.

[116] King, Jr., "Walk for Freedom," p. 83.

[117] For an account of the traditional notion of civil disobedience, see Rawls, *A Theory of Justice*, pp. 365f.; "The Justification of Civil Disobedience," in

nonviolent direct action "is a powerful demand for reason and justice."[118] Nonviolent direct action is the use of "soul force" which is capable of triumph over the physical force of one's oppressor.[119] Far from its being a form of pacifism, nonviolent direct action effectively disarms one's opponent, "exposes his moral defenses, weakens his morale and works on his conscience."[120]

On several occasions, Martin notes the multifarious features of non-violent direct action. First, it is a form of resistance to oppression and injustice.[121] Second, nonviolent direct action does not seek to defeat or humiliate one's opponent, but to win her friendship and understanding.[122] Third, nonviolent direct action is aimed, not at persons or personalities, but against the forces of evil themselves.[123] Fourth, nonviolent direct action avoids the employment of any kind of violence, physical or nonphysical,

Joe P. White, Editor, *Assent/Dissent* (Dubuque: Kendall/Hunt Publishers, 1984), pp. 230f. For a brief sketch of Rawls' position on civil disobedience, see J. Angelo Corlett, "The Right to Civil Disobedience and the Right to Secede," *The Southern Journal of Philosophy*, 30 (1992), pp. 20–21; For a comparison and contrast of civil disobedience with nonviolent direct action, see, Corlett, *Terrorism: A Philosophical Analysis*, Chapter 2.

[118] Martin Luther King, Jr., "Next Stop: the North," in James M. Washington, Editor, *A Testament of Hope: The Essential Writings of Martin Luther King, Jr.* (New York: Harper & Row, 1986), p. 193.

[119] Martin Luther King, Jr., "The Rising Tide of Racial Consciousness," in James M. Washington, Editor, *A Testament of Hope: The Essential Writings of Martin Luther King, Jr.* (New York: Harper & Row, 1986), p. 149.

[120] Martin Luther King, Jr., "An Address before the National Press Club," in James M. Washington, Editor, *A Testament of Hope: The Essential Writings of Martin Luther King, Jr.* (New York: Harper & Row, 1986), p. 102.

[121] Martin Luther King, Jr., "Nonviolence and Racial Justice," in James M. Washington, Editor, *A Testament of Hope: The Essential Writings of Martin Luther King, Jr.* (New York: Harper & Row, 1986), p. 7; "The Current Crisis in Race Relations," in James M. Washington, Editor, *A Testament of Hope: The Essential Writings of Martin Luther King, Jr.* (New York: Harper & Row, 1986), p. 86; "An Experiment in Love," in James M. Washington, Editor, *A Testament of Hope: The Essential Writings of Martin Luther King, Jr.* (New York: Harper & Row, 1986), p. 17.

[122] King, Jr., "Nonviolence and Racial Justice," p. 7; "The Current Crisis in Race Relations," p. 87; Martin Luther King, Jr., "The Most Durable Power," in *A Testament of Hope*, p. 10; "The Power of Nonviolence," in *A Testament of Hope*, p. 12; "An Experiment in Love," pp. 17–18.

[123] King, Jr., "Nonviolence and Racial Justice," p. 8; "The Current Crisis in Race Relations," p. 87; "An Experiment in Love," p. 18.

external or internal (i.e., "violence of the spirit").[124] Finally, nonviolent direct action assumes an optimistic view of the triumph of justice in the world, i.e., that the world is on the side of justice.[125] Thus, the nonviolent resistor accepts suffering without retaliation.[126]

"For practical as well as moral reasons," Martin writes, "nonviolence offers the only road to freedom for my people."[127] Presumably, Martin believes that the practical reasons against the employment of violence as a means of social change are that African-Americans are outnumbered and that violence only begets violence instead of appealing to the conscience of the oppressors. In short, violence accomplishes social annihilation or discord instead of social harmony and progress. Martin is unclear about what the moral reasons against the use of violence as a means of social change amount to. Perhaps he means simply to aver that it is morally wrong, impermissible, or unjustified.

However, there is an ambiguity in Martin's statement about violence. Does he mean that violence (to achieve social change) is never morally justified, permissible, or "right"? Or, does he mean that, if one's goal is social integration, violence will never be successful? If Martin means to affirm the latter point, then he is not providing an absolute moral prohibition against the use of violence, but rather a reason why the use of violence is impractical given the goals of integration, social change, and freedom. But surely Martin's point about the impracticality of the employment of violence does not count as a decisive moral reason against it. For what is "impractical" is often morally permissible, right, or even required. Martin's program of nonviolent direct action as an instrument for the civil rights movement in the U.S. serves as an example. Although it often eventuated in violence against blacks and their supporters, nonviolent direct action was rooted in the principles of an enlightened conscience. Thus it appears that Martin's condemnation of the use of violence as a means of social change is in need of some rationale, philosophically speaking.

Now it might be argued that Martin's position on violence and social change is correct when it is considered contextually. That is, it is the correct view regarding the use of violence for the time and circumstance in which

---

[124] King, Jr., "Nonviolence and Racial Justice," p. 8; "The Current Crisis in Race Relations," p. 87; "An Experiment in Love," p. 18.

[125] King, Jr., "Nonviolence and Racial Justice," p. 9; "The Current Crisis in Race Relations," p. 88; "An Experiment in Love," p. 20.

[126] King, Jr., "An Experiment in Love," p. 18.

[127] King, Jr., "Nonviolence: The Only Road to Freedom," p. 55.

Martin sought to secure justice and freedom, especially for blacks in the U.S. South. For in the South, blacks were for the most part Christians. And Christianity teaches that violence is not a good thing. At least, this is one plausible view of what orthodox Christianity teaches about violence. By engaging, not in violence, but in nonviolent direct action, blacks in the South and their supporters exposed the violence of many whites against blacks so that it might then be dealt with. So it seems that Martin's prohibition against the use of violence for social change has merit when we consider the context in which it is set forth.

However, this construal of Martin's words on political violence will not do. For Martin argues for an absolute moral prohibition against the use of violence in human affairs. Recall that he argues that nonviolence offers the only road to freedom for "his people." This means there is no circumstance in which, for purposes of social change, the use of violence is morally permitted, right, or justified. Contextualizing Martin's claim might enable one to better understand why he argued what he did, but it does nothing in terms of providing a sound philosophical justification for Martin's absolute moral prohibition against the use of violence as a means of social change.

Now that the meaning of Martin's words on political violence are understood, are they correct? Does his absolute moral prohibition against the use of violence as a means of social change stand the test of reason? Let us contrast Martin's view on the moral status of political violence with Malcolm's, asking which of these two views is more plausible in the context of concrete historical experience.

Malcolm's view concerning the use of violence for social change amounts to the thesis that violence is justified in at least some cases of self-defense or defense of others who are endangered. In describing the "new type of black" person, Malcolm says that "he believes in respecting people. He believes in doing unto others as he would have others do to himself. But at the same time, if anybody attacks him, he believes in retaliating if it costs him his life."[128] In the context of political violence and freedom, August Wilson places the following in the mouth of Solly in *Gem of the Ocean*: "Yeah, I burned it down! The people might get mad but freedom got a high price. You got to pay. No matter what it cost. You got to pay."[129] In the Les

---

[128] Malcolm X, "Twenty Million Black People in a Political, Economic, and Mental Prison," speech delivered at Michigan State University, January 23, 1963 [*Malcolm X: The Last Speeches*, Edited by Bruce Perry (New York: Pathfinder Press, 1989), p. 39].

[129] Wilson, *Gem of the Ocean*, p. 75.

Crane Interview of December 2, 1964, Malcolm states that "our people should start doing what is necessary to protect ourselves. This doesn't mean that we should buy rifles and go out and initiate attacks indiscriminately against whites. But it does mean that we should get whatever is necessary to protect ourselves in a country or in an area where the governmental ability to protect us has broken down."[130] On February 15, 1965, days prior to his assassination, Malcolm affirms that "we are for the betterment of the community by any means necessary."[131] In criticism of Martin's program of nonviolent social change, Malcolm states:

> Whenever you, yourself, are attacked you are not supposed to turn the other cheek. Never turn the other cheek until you see the white man turn his cheek, then you turn the cheek. If Martin Luther King was teaching white people to turn the other cheek, then I would say he was justified in teaching Black people to turn the other cheek. That's all I'm against. Make it a two-way street. Make it even steven. If I'm going to be nonviolent, then let them be nonviolent. But as long as they're not nonviolent, don't you let anybody tell you anything about nonviolence. No. Be intelligent.[132]

The very next day, again days before his assassination, Malcolm argues that "We're not for violence. We're for peace. But the people that we're up against are for violence. You can't be peaceful when you're dealing with them."[133] Moreover, though Malcolm does alter some of his views after his second visit to Mecca, he does not appear to alter his position and teachings concerning the use of violence as a means of social change. Furthermore, it would seem that this thesis of Malcolm's (i.e., that the use of violence as a means of social change is sometimes morally justified in self-defense) serves as the basis of a counterexample to Martin's absolute moral prohibition against the use of violence.

However, against Malcolm's view it might be argued that nonviolence alone can serve as a means of social change where social integration is valued as a societal goal. After all, it is said, the use of violence would not foster the kinds of positive attitudes and reconciliation necessary for the rebuilding of the South African regime. How can parties get along with each other after the oppressed group uses violence to gain freedom for itself? Does not social change toward integration require the use of nonviolence in the

---

130 Malcolm X, *Malcolm X: The Last Speeches*, p. 88.
131 Malcolm X, *Malcolm X: The Last Speeches*, p. 133.
132 Malcolm X, *Malcolm X: The Last Speeches*, p. 149.
133 Malcolm X, *Malcolm X: The Last Speeches*, p. 159.

oppressed peoples' attempt to appeal to the sense of justice of the ruling majority?

In reply to this line of thinking, it might be argued that in the case of Apartheid South Africa, the ruling majority in fact had no adequate sense of justice to which the oppressed peoples can appeal. After all, anyone who would support an Apartheid regime has no sense of justice in the first place.[134]

I would argue that the use of violence does not vitiate the dictum that injustice must be met by a sincere appeal to the sense of justice of the ruling class by the wronged parties. Moreover, why is it assumed that social reconciliation is always a good thing? It would seem that the absolutist conciliatory stance is in need of both a supporting and an independent argument in order for Malcolm's view to be defeated. For even if it is true that the use of violence always destroys social unity between opposing parties, what is the goal of preserving such social unity? One basic goal seems to be that of integration. But why is integration a good thing, especially when the parties to be integrated include the oppressors and those they oppressed? What arguments might be brought to bear in favor of the claim that integration is justified, morally speaking?

Many seem to assume that ethnic reconciliation and integration are always good. While social ethnic integration makes sense for many situations, it hardly makes sense in some contexts of severe injustice and oppression. In those cases, the primary moral consideration must be liberation from oppression, followed by rectification and retribution—even by way of violence. To even contemplate reconciliation between parties one of whom has, for instance, attempted genocide against the remaining members of the victimized party, is idealism that smacks of religious dogma—whether it comes from philosophers or theologians. Those believed with strong evidence to be most responsible for the violent oppression must be identified, provided a fair trial, and, if found guilty, must be executed just as in the post-WWII trials of Nazi war criminals. Why? Because retributive justice is a fundamental moral duty as well as a divine value. Truth and

---

[134] In light of recent political developments in South Africa, it might be argued that nonviolence is serving as the correct way to change Apartheid, and that political violence is unnecessary. But my argument is not that political violence is necessary for social change. Rather, it is that in the case of South African Apartheid, political violence is a morally justified means of social change. And the possibility that positive social change can occur without violence does nothing to demonstrate that political violence is morally unjustified.

reconciliation commissions often provide neither truth nor genuine reconciliation. Rather, they often harm the oppressed under the yoke of moral failure to do the right things by way of retributive (including compensatory) justice.

Martin seems to argue that, given the situation in which blacks find themselves, integration is the best way to live without essentially committing mass suicide at the hands of a society whose government and military have consistently demonstrated that it can and will destroy peoples should it be in the interests of those in power. If blacks revolted, the U.S. would have unleashed its military and federal, state and local law enforcement agents to exterminate blacks within days. Martin sees nothing to gain from this. Nor do millions of blacks in the U.S. or elsewhere. Nor do most whites, Latinos, etc. in the U.S. and elsewhere. It would be a tragic loss of grand proportions should such violence occur. And it would constitute one of the most unfortunate acts in history.

However, we can admit this obvious fact and still argue that the integration in question was forced and has never included genuine forgiveness and reconciliation for the evils of black slavery and Jim Crow. For just as reconciliation presumes a healthy relationship to reconcile as well as forgiveness, so too does forgiveness require a genuine apology which in turn requires, among other things, compensation to the victim(s) by the culpable harmful wrongdoer(s). No compensation, no apology; no apology, no forgiveness; no forgiveness, no reconciliation; no reconciliation, no basis for genuine integration.

Moreover, one could still argue that integration with whites by blacks ought to be such that the decision to integrate should be in the hands of blacks, not whites. In any case, one must not simply assume that, normatively speaking, racial integration between oppressed and oppressor groups is always a good thing. Hard paternalism is rooted deeply in the desire and imposition of reconciliation and integration in the U.S.. But it is precisely such paternalism that is so terribly problematic.[135] Ethnic integration in contexts of oppressive ethnic conflict must never be presumed. Instead, it must be construed as the moral prerogative of the oppressed (or formerly oppressed) group.

---

[135] Gerald Dworkin, "Paternalism," and "Paternalism: Some Second Thoughts," in Joel Feinberg and Hyman Gross, Editors, *Philosophy of Law*, 5th Edition (Belmont: Wadsworth Publishing Company, 1995), pp. 209–218; 219–223; Joel Feinberg, *Harm to Self* (Oxford: Oxford University Press, 1986).

Cone presents that idea of reconciliation between blacks and whites in the U.S. in the following theological terms:

> Because God has set us free, we are now commanded to go and be reconciled with our neighbors, and particularly our white neighbors. *But this does not mean letting whites define the terms of reconciliation.* It means participating in God's revolutionizing activity in the world, changing the political, economic, and social structures so that distinctions between rich and poor, oppressed and oppressors, are no longer a reality. To be reconciled with white people means destroying their oppressive power, reducing them to the human level and thereby putting them on equal footing with other humans. There can be no reconciliation with masters as long as they are masters, as long as men are in prison. There can be no communication between masters and slaves until masters no longer exist, are no longer present as masters. The Christian task is to rebel against all masters, destroying their pretensions to authority and ridiculing the symbols of power.[136]

Authentic reconciliation requires true forgiveness of oppressors for their oppression. But this right (not duty) to forgive belongs only to the oppressed, correlated with the duty of oppressors to apologize for their oppression. It is impossible for forgiveness (as opposed to mere forgiving) to occur insofar as adequate and genuine apology is made by the oppressors. Yet a genuine apology requires, among other things, adequate rectification of the wrongs wrought on the oppressed by the oppressors, without which it is impossible even for God Herself to effect forgiveness and reconciliation. For it is impossible even for God to do what is logically impossible, and this assumes that God, should She exist, would even desire to effect forgiveness under such circumstances of pseudo-forgiveness and reconciliation, each of which is predicated on the realization of peace between reconciled parties. No justice, no peace.

The reason why black integration in the U.S. constitutes a form of coercion is, historically speaking, so transparent that it would insult readers to more than note that blacks' being here was coerced. But the injustice remains today in light of the fact that genuine reconciliation does not exist between blacks and the U.S. government and the bulk of its nonblack citizens. There cannot be genuine reconciliation between blacks and others in the U.S. unless and until there is authentic forgiveness of the U.S. by blacks as groups. And this cannot occur unless and until the U.S. truly apologizes to blacks as a group for what it did to them in the form of slavery, Jim Crow, and the incessant refusal to make good on the apology. By "make

---

[136] Cone, *Risks of Faith*, p. 39. Emphasis provided.

good on the apology," I mean to offer a true apology,[137] including compensatory reparations for the lost wages from unpaid labor of their ancestors who were unable to live decently because many whites refused to pay their wages and this meant that blacks were unable to bequeath assets to their children and grandchildren. This situation created a circumstance of continued poverty for most blacks, as one would expect where the bequeathal of wealth is essentially impossible because what should have been earned wages were effectively stolen from them by an institution that effectively gave what should have been that wealth to many white folk who instead bequeathed it to their heirs. To wonder why many of today's blacks suffer from poverty is to ignore this fact of history and economics, as well as the sociological fact of racism in the U.S., a socially—inflicted disease that the U.S. has flaunted especially against blacks ever since its inception.[138]

We cannot simply assume that integration is always a good in itself; this would beg the question against the selective and morally justified use of violence that might oppose integration, or make it very difficult to achieve peacefully. As Malcolm demands, Martin bears the burden of providing an argument in support of the claims that social integration is a good thing and that anything, such as violence, which destroys the social unity needed for integration is morally wrong.[139] Along these lines, Cone's words are instructive: "Violence is not only what black people do to white people as victims seek to change the structure of their existence; violence is what white people *did* when they created a society for white people only, and what they *do* in order to maintain it."[140] Citing Moltmann, Cone writes: "'The problem of violence and nonviolence is an illusory problem. There is only the question of the justified and unjustified use of force and the question of whether the means are proportional to the ends'; and the only people who can answer that problem are the victims of the injustice."[141] It is in this context that Cone exclaims that "God's revolution is found in black liberation."[142] And by this Cone means to include other oppressed peoples such as American Indians.

---

[137] For analyses of forgiveness and apology, see Corlett, *Responsibility and Punishment*, Chapter 5; J. Angelo Corlett, "Forgiveness, Apology, and Retributive Punishment," *American Philosophical Quarterly*, 43 (2006), pp. 25–42.

[138] For arguments for these claims, see Corlett, *Race, Racism, and Reparations*, Chapter 9; *Heirs of Oppression* (forthcoming).

[139] This is not to say, however, that Martin himself subscribes to the view that political violence is morally unjustified on the grounds that it does not make for good integration.

[140] Cone, *Risks of Faith*, p. 35.

[141] Cone, *Risks of Faith*, p. 36. Also see the second epigraph of this chapter.

[142] Cone, *Risks of Faith*, pp. 37–38.

It is God who works through Her people in this world to liberate oppressed peoples everywhere. For freedom is one of the "risks of faith" of God's people. "It is a risk derived from the conviction that death is preferable to life in servitude."[143] Or, as Emiliano Zapata famously said: "*Prefiero morir de pie, que vivir de rodillas*" ("I would prefer to die on my feet, than to live on my knees"). This is what it means (in part) to say that "God is just," referring to the divine retributive aim of justice.

Now there is an argument which states that society as a whole benefits in a maximal way if nonviolence is used as a means for social change, and when integration is a social goal. But this sort of reasoning simply restates the question-begging case against the employment of violence and social separation where there is a strong history of oppressive injustice. Why is social integration always a good thing, especially when the preservation of it in at least some cases serves to hold down certain peoples, politically, economically, socially, etc.? Are there not cases when ethnic and social integration simply preserves the oppressive status quo? If so, would not the judicious and morally justified use of violence sometimes be justified in order to combat and correct such injustices?

Furthermore, even if social integration is a good thing (and for whatever reason), might not Malcolm be correct in arguing that the use of violence is morally justified in at least some cases of self-defense? After all, the social disintegration that typically occurs when violence is used for social change might result in peace for future generations. This line of reasoning attempts to turn on its head Martin's statement (quoted above) that it is better to endure a blow on the head for the sake of educating future generations of children. Why not argue that the use of violence can sometimes achieve a similar end? The morally justified political revolutions of the world are testaments to this very idea.

Surely we do not want to hold the view that violence always begets only violence. For there are plenty of politically violent actions or states of affairs which have led to measures of peace. Is it always better to endure a blow on the head for the sake of school integration than to turn the tides of significant injustice against those who clearly deserve to be violated? Is not Malcolm, instead of Martin, our wiser teacher on this matter?

Even if one agrees with Malcolm that political violence is sometimes morally justified as a means toward positive social change, it is incumbent on Malcolm to explain under what conditions the employment of such violence is morally justified. What are the conditions jointly necessary

---

[143] Cone, *Risks of Faith*, p. 129.

and sufficient for morally justified political violence? First, political violence must be a response to a circumstance of significant injustice. Instances of significant injustice include those such as the denial of voting rights to and enslavement of blacks in the U.S., the denial of an even broader spectrum of human rights of black South Africans under Apartheid, the prevalent and violent abuse of black citizens by some peace officers in the U.S., etc. This condition implies that political violence is justified as a means of self-defense, or in defense of others who suffer from the pains of injustice.

However, additional conditions must be satisfied for the use of political violence to be morally justified. The violence must be a reasoned response directed against those who are primarily guilty of (most responsible for) creating and sustaining the conditions of injustice in question. This means that political violence must be employed only by those who are conscientious moral agents. Political violence is not justified when it targets innocents or those guilty in merely secondary ways. Such a harsh response to injustice must be directed only at those who are guilty of the wrongdoing to which political violence is a justified response. It requires a certain degree of reasonableness on the part of those who employ political violence, for they must be capable and willing to distinguish legitimate from illegitimate targets of their retaliation to significant forms of injustice. This condition requires a degree of planning concerning the use of political violence. Such planning includes the targeting of those primarily guilty of creating and sustaining the significant form of injustice in question, as well as making reasonably sure that the means employed in the use of political violence are designed to achieve the positive social change desired. Political violence is not morally justified as an end in itself, but only as a means to the end of positive social change.

Third, morally justified political violence must be generalizable. This means that if it is justified as a response to injustice in situation X, then it is also justified in contexts of injustice relevantly similar to X. This implies that double standards do not exist within justice. If one group is morally justified in employing violence for positive aims of social justice, so is any other group that finds itself in relevantly similar circumstances.

Fourth, political violence is morally justified to the extent that those who employ it have tried in good faith other legitimate means of non-violence political change, yet have failed. This does not mean that all other means of democratic change have been attempted, but that some have been tried in good faith but have failed with no reasonable prospect of significant future success. The reason for this is that, as Rawls argues, some circumstances of injustice are so extreme that militancy is required, and there is insufficient time to exhaust all the nonviolent means of political change.[144]

Finally, whatever violence is employed must be done in proportion to the harm to which the violence is a legitimate response. This implies that harsh forms of political violence ought not to be used in response to minor cases of injustice. The use of political violence is morally justified to the extent that these conditions are satisfied, though context must help determine for the conscientious moral agent precisely which forms of violence are justified in a given case.[145]

Thus we have a set of conditions which, to the extent that they are satisfied, would morally justify the use of political violence. It is this analysis of justified political violence, I believe, which is logically consistent with Malcolm's view on social change, not to mention the basics of just war theories. The first and second conditions are held by Malcolm, while the remainder of them are not inconsistent with his stated view. We have, then, a sketch of a theory of political violence, one which finds problematic Martin's absolute moral and principled prohibition against its use, and one which finds support from Malcolm. What is needed is a full-blown analysis of morally justified political violence.[146]

The disagreement between Martin and Malcolm on the use of violence as a means of social change serves as an excellent propaedeutic for the discussion of an important problem in political philosophy: When, if ever, is the use of violence morally justified, if at all? With Martin and Malcolm, however, this problem is linked to the issue of whether or not social integration is a good thing, morally speaking. More precisely, it seems that Martin's argument against the employment of political violence requires that integration is morally good, i.e., good for U.S. blacks as well as for others in the U.S.. But this latter claim itself is in need of argumentative support. Is black integration morally good? If so, good for *whom*? If not, bad for *whom*? Whatever we do, we must never presuppose that the moral justification of violence against oppression pertains to the concerns of the oppressors. Instead, it ought to concern itself with what is best for the oppressed.

It is important, then, to consider the plausibility of the arguments which might be marshaled for ethnic integration as being a morally good thing.

---

[144] Rawls, *A Theory of Justice*, p. 367.

[145] Compare these conditions to the ones found in Corlett, *Terrorism: A Philosophical Analysis*, Chapter 5.

[146] On this score, see Corlett, *Terrorism: A Philosophical Analysis*; Ted Honderich, *Political Violence* (Ithaca: Cornell University Press, 1976); Walzer, *Just and Unjust Wars*.

In so doing, the overall plausibility of Malcolm's position on the morally justified use of violence as a means of social change can be determined. After all, there is *prima facie* reason to think that ethnic integration is not always a good thing, at least, in light of the black and Indian experiences in the U.S.. Attempts to "integrate" in the spheres of education, for example, have often led to disappointment and sometimes violence against Indians and blacks. And the evils of Indian boarding schools in the U.S. are too obvious to repeat.

Coerced integration is a bad thing, and remains bad until it is rectified as *unrectified evil is evil still*. It neither diminishes with the passage of time, nor with the self-serving, narcissistically selective memories of oppressors and many of their offspring. The only way in which it can be adequately addressed is through rectification and all that it entails. Thus liberation of oppressed peoples involves not a mere rescue mission, but the overseeing of rectification to victims of oppression by their harmful wrongdoers. God is good and just, those who are not good or just are not of God, and deserve the punishments commensurate with their culpability for harmful wrong-doings to others. Once again, retributive justice as well as distributive justice is required for authentic peace. On my liberationist account, it is God's will.

Furthermore, prevalent in the U.S. is the racist belief that blacks are, on average or generally, less qualified than whites to do a number of tasks. This is often based on the stereotypes of blacks as being "naturally" endowed to perform athletic sorts of things, but not, say, intellectual tasks. Why, then, with these and other sorts of stumbling blocks to black progress in the U.S., would one be justified in thinking that forced[147] integration is a good thing? Would not blacks in the U.S. be better-off with the option to live in a separate country, state, or otherwise apart from those who intentionally or unintentionally make their lives miserable? Moreover, do not blacks deserve to live as a solitary people (relative to their oppressors) should they (or some subset of them) desire to do so? And is not this their natural or moral right? Is this not what the individual moral right to autonomy and the group moral right to sovereignty entail? Do not blacks have a moral right to live apart from those who threaten them? Does this not suggest that integration is in need of a special moral justification in the context of U.S. oppression of blacks? Of course, a similar point can be

---

[147] That black integration in the U.S. is coerced is evidenced by the fact that most such blacks do not have viable alternatives than to remain citizens of the country that has oppressed their ancestors so badly. The lack of viable alternatives as a sufficient condition for coercion is discussed in Feinberg, *Harm to Self*.

made concerning American Indians in "U.S. territory" and under U.S. dominion and rule.

What are the arguments against ethnic integration for blacks? One such argument might be referred to as the "cultural preservation argument." This argument states that each ethnic group, *qua* ethnic group, has a particular cultural heritage which helps to identify itself over against other ethnic groups. This is especially evident in the case of ethnic groups such as U.S. blacks.

A cultural identity is not a static element of an ethnic group's identity, though it is established over time and identifiable by most, if not all, members of the group. Ethnic culture is important for at least two reasons: personal identity of in-group members and group identity. Such ethnic identity serves, among other things, to deepen one's appreciation for one's own cultural heritage. The cultural preservation argument holds that each ethnic group has a moral right to separate itself from other ethnic groups, especially from those groups and cultures which pose some significant threat to that ethnic group's existence and flourishing. Whenever an ethnic group, acting within its moral rights and liberties, is threatened by the presence of another group, that ethnic group has the moral right to separate itself from the imposing group. A paradigm case of this sort of thing would be the black person in the U.S., some of whose ancestors have been forced into slavery and all the horrors that slavery entailed, yet who sometimes faces strong and unimpeded racism even today. As long as the blacks are living under the rule of anti-black racism, blacks can never flourish as a group. Perhaps a relative few blacks can flourish, a wonderful testament to skill and determination, and some moral luck[148] (as with others who succeed). But the bulk of them will be held back by the social and political forces of racist oppression. In order to preserve that cultural heritage which is essentially black American (not necessarily African), it is essential that blacks' choice to separate themselves from those who they perceive, justifiably, as threats to black culture be respected.

A second argument against forced black integration might be referred to as the "political self-determination argument." This argument holds that it is crucial for ethnic groups such as blacks to exist and flourish as self-determining selves, choosing their own ends and legitimate means to those

---

[148] The concept of moral luck is found in Joel Feinberg, *Doing and Deserving* (Princeton: Princeton University Press, 1970), Chapter 2. It is also found in some of the influential writings of Thomas Nagel, John Rawls, and Bernard Williams.

ends without the interference of outside and threatening human forces. Unlike the cultural preservation argument the focus of which is to preserve the particular cultural identity of the ethnic group and its members, the political self-determination argument values the ability of the ethnic group and its membership to decide for itself the sort of future it wants, as well as how it will choose to attain its ends. For example, an ethnic group will (presumably) want a certain form of government. It ought to have the moral right to choose whatever form it desires, and absent external interference. This implies that it ought to be at liberty to decide for itself the contents of both its foreign and domestic policies should it have them. In any case, the political self-determination argument provides for the separation of ethnic groups on the basis of their needs for independent political power. In light of these considerations, it might be argued that blacks have a moral right to political self-determination, a right which grounds a moral claim to their not being integrated with those whom they justifiably perceive as threats to their political self-determination. To think otherwise, namely, that coerced integration is a good thing, seems to constitute a form of hard paternalism.[149]

Third, there is the justice or reparations[150] argument against coerced black integration. In some situations, an ethnic group will be victimized by aggression and violence. In the U.S., the institutionalization of slavery served to create a social condition in which a number of those whose ancestors were enslaved desire to separate themselves from others in the hopes of attaining some justice for the wrongful acts inflicted on their ancestors. This argument might also be conjoined to the cultural preservation argument in that those who employ it might hope to preserve whatever is left of their cultural heritage. But the justice or reparations argument states that, as part of a plan of compensatory justice, those blacks who desire to do so ought to be allotted resources within the country that their own ancestors were coerced to build (for no remuneration) and for the purpose of living as an independent people. A similar argument is often

---

[149] See note 135, above.

[150] For philosophical analyses of the issue of reparations to U.S. blacks, see Corlett, *Race, Racism, and Reparations*, Chapter 9; *The Journal of Ethics* 7 (2003), pp. 1–160. Also see Bernard Boxill, "The Morality of Reparation," *Social Theory & Practice* 2 (1972), pp. 113–123; "The Morality of Reparations II," in Tommie Lott and John P. Pittman, Editors, *A Companion to African-American Philosophy* (London: Blackwell Publishers, 2003), pp. 134–147; Howard McGary, *Blacks and Social Justice* (London: Blackwell Publishers, 1999).

used by certain members of indigenous groups in the U.S. in favor of their moral right to reparations and justice.[151]

Thus there are at least three arguments against forced black integration in the U.S. and in favor of black separation for those blacks who desire it: the cultural preservation argument, the political self-determination argument, and the justice or reparations argument. Although these arguments are related, they are set forth as independent arguments for the moral justification of ethnic separation, at least in some cases.

In light of the arguments against coerced black integration, that is, against the view that some such blacks are justified in not integrating with others and/or that the U.S. government ought to provide such means for their not integrating, it is incumbent on integrationists such as Martin to provide moral reasons in favor of integration in order to support his absolute moral prohibition against the use of violence. And it is clear that such reasons must defeat the claim that even some such blacks are morally justified in separating, and the arguments given above. In this way, Martin can preserve his argument against the employment of violence as a means of social change.

What arguments might be adduced by Martin to support the claims that separatism is morally unjustified for blacks? Moreover, which arguments at the same time support the claim that political violence is absolutely morally unjustified? First, it might be argued that integration is pragmatically favorable over separatism for blacks and that black separatism is based on the utopian idea that it is possible or likely that blacks can achieve it, either in the U.S. or elsewhere. But the unlikelihood of such separation counts against it as a serious moral consideration. I shall refer to this as the "pragmatic argument for black integration."

Second, it might be argued that integration is preferable to separation for blacks in that ethnicity is a morally arbitrary category on which to base the preservation of a culture, political self-determination, or justice. After all, it might be argued, all human beings derive from the same race: the human race. And this fact makes attempts to separate ourselves one from another futile in that it is technically a form of racial self-hatred. Surely, the argument continues, self-hatred is neither desirable nor justified. Thus, integration is justified as a way to recognize, socially and politically, that humans belong to the same race. I shall call this the "theoretical argument for black integration."

---

[151] Corlett, *Race, Racism, and Reparations*, Chapter 8.

However, both the pragmatic and theoretical arguments for black integration face the following difficulties. The pragmatic argument suffers from the following malady. Although it is true that "'ought' implies 'can'," it is by no means logically or practically impossible for some blacks (i.e., those who truly desire to) to achieve separation, and for the reasons cited above. From the supposition that neither the U.S. government nor U.S. society has to this point taken this matter seriously, it does not logically follow, nor does it follow morally, that effectively forced integration is morally justified. This holds because an appeal to the way things are cannot serve as a moral justification of the normative question of integration's moral justification. To argue in such a way would commit a version of the "is-ought fallacy." After all, the fact that separation of the kind discussed herein has not occurred in no wise serves as evidence for the claim that it ought not to do so. Thus the pragmatic argument for black integration does not seem to be supported by the balance of human reason.

But the theoretical argument for black integration also fails. From the plausible supposition that all humans originate from and belong to the same race, it does not logically follow that there is no good reason to, on occasion, separate ourselves on the basis of ethnicity. This is especially true in special circumstances where ethnic oppression is realized, and where it is plausible to think that ethnic separation can help to preserve an oppressed ethnic group's cultural identity, its self-determination, or its goals of attaining justice for itself. The theoretical argument for integration seems to assume that ethnic separation entails, necessarily, the denial that humans are all part of one race. But it need not, and should not do so. All the ethnic separatist needs is one or more of the above arguments offered in favor of separatism, while still holding to the view that other ethnic groups are to be respected as essentially human. There is nothing, then, about the notion of ethnic separation which entails the denial of the fact that there is only one race to which all humans belong. Furthermore, it is not morally arbitrary to separate according to ethnic groups, at least under circumstances where to do so provides an oppressed ethnic group with an opportunity to flourish absent its oppressor group. It follows from this that the theoretical argument for integration fails to justify essentially forced integration.

Of what relevance is the preceding discussion of social integration and political violence to liberation theism? In light of the arguments assessed herein, it is unclear that ethnic integration is morally required, at least in cases where ethnic oppression exists. There is little reason, then, to think that Martin's argument against political violence is plausible to the extent that it rests upon the flimsy foundation of integrationism as a moral requirement. It follows that we have more reason than not to believe that

Malcolm's position on political violence as a means of social change is more plausible than Martin's position. And this is relevant to the matter of both distributive and retributive justice in the U.S. vis-à-vis blacks. When justice for blacks is an issue, it ought not to be presumed that social integration and policies and programs that assume it bring justice to blacks.

Martin and Malcolm were two liberation thinkers who were religious in their orientations and who with all their similarities held some different views about how the spirit of God might lead the oppressed to freedom. For Martin, it was always nonviolent direct action, and never violence of any kind. For Malcolm, however, nonviolence was a desired method of liberation, but sometimes violence was necessary to combat violence, that is, in self-defense. In either case, God was the driving motivational force behind all positive social change, whether the name of that God was "*Yahweh*" or "*Allah*."

A more explicitly Christian black theology of liberation developed in the U.S. is found in Cone. For Cone, black Christian theology falls in line with Christian neo-orthodoxy, which calls for a clarification of why I refer to it as a species of radical Christian theology. I refer to Cone's theology thusly because of its revolutionary flavor, which is typically not found in Christian orthodoxy or neo-orthodoxy. But Cone does not seek to demythologize the message of Christian scripture. Nor does he attempt to provide a philosophical account of the divine as we see in Tillich. Nor does he seek to meld it with the findings of science, as we find in process theologies. In these ways, then, Cone's black Christian theology is not radical. But because the circumstance of suffering is taken as the starting point of Christian theology for Cone,[152] and because Cone emphasizes the plight of the black experience in the U.S., I believe Cone's black Christian theology is radical.

Absent from Cone's neo-orthodox black Christian liberation theology is the understanding of God's suffering, not just with us, but Her experiencing the very pains of oppression supranaturally.[153] Among other things, this implies that to harm living beings is to harm God, as implied by some American Indian religious practitioners cited in the previous chapter. This ought to underline the importance of our doing justice to those who wrongfully harm others oppressively. For they not only oppress humans, they oppress God Herself!

---

[152] James H. Cone, *God of the Oppressed* (New York: The Seabury Press, 1975), p. 163.

[153] Christopher Knight, *The God of Nature* (Minneapolis: Fortress Press, 2007), p. 130.

Furthermore, it is important to note how much of the content of Cone's theology of black liberation explicates the bases of what Martin and Malcolm expressed. I believe that it is no accident that Cone has written *Martin & Malcolm & America*, as I believe that Martin and Malcolm have had and continue to have an indelible impression on most blacks in the U.S.[154] (and elsewhere!), including Cone himself.

What is also of vital importance here is to see not only that liberation themes most important to Latin American and black Christian liberation theologies can be combined effectively with the immanentism of process theology in order to construct a more viable theism to replace orthodox and neo-orthodox Christian theism, but also that in placing liberatory themes as part of the center of such a theism, we can "slay the dragon of theological racism"[155] by recognizing the treatment of racism as a central component of any plausible theism. Not only that, but liberation theology can be made congruent with process theology on another central matter: ecological ethics. For process theology's concern for environmental preservation is shared by Cone's words that "The fight for justice cannot be segregated but must be integrated with the fight for life in all its forms,"[156] so long as we bear in mind that "If it is important to save the habitats of birds and other species, then it is at least equally important to save black lives in the ghettos and prisons of America."[157] Indeed, there is no contradiction between process theological claims and American Indian religious claims to treat the world itself as if it were God (because God is in the world) and liberationist statements that "The oppressed are called to fight against suffering by becoming God's suffering servants in the world" and ". . . when suffering is inflicted upon the oppressed, it is evil and we must struggle against it."[158] Moreover, "Humanity's meaning is found in the oppressed people's fight for freedom, for in the fight for liberation God joins them and grants them the vision to see beyond the present to the future."[159]

Of course, liberation theism must base its primary claims on a plausible political theology and philosophy, part of which must devise a meaningful

---

[154] James H. Cone makes a similar point in the Conclusion of Cone, *Martin & Malcolm & America*.

[155] Cone, *Risks of Faith*, p. 135.

[156] Cone, *Risks of Faith*, p. 138.

[157] Cone, *Risks of Faith*, p. 145.

[158] Cone, *God of the Oppressed*, p. 177. Again, Cone writes: "For it is only in the fight for justice that God is encountered; . . ." (p. 182).

[159] Cone, *God of the Oppressed*, pp. 193–194.

conception of freedom. For the main aim of liberation is to free oppressed peoples from oppression in its various forms. But we ought not to assume that the concept of freedom is transparently obvious in its content. For there can be confusions and illusions of freedom, as Solly and Eli, in Wilson's *Gem of the Ocean*, articulate about recently freed slaves in the U.S.:

> SOLLY: The people think they in freedom. That's all my daddy talked about. He died and never did have it. I say I got it but what is it? I'm still trying to find out. It ain't never been nothing but trouble.
> ELI: Freedom is what you make it.
> SOLLY: That's what I'm saying. You got to fight to make it mean something. All it mean is you got a long row and ain't got no plow. Ain't got no seed. Ain't got no mule. What good is freedom if you can't do nothing with it? I seen many a man die for freedom but he didn't know what he was getting. If he had known he might have thought twice about it.[160]

Thus liberation theisms require an adequate notion of freedom and the material means by which to realize it to accompany the content of the liberatory theme which forms the basis of their theism. Liberation theism must succeed where orthodox Christian theism fails.

As Kurt Baier argues, traditional Christian doctrine sees humans as "a creature, a divine artifact, something halfway between a robot (manufactured) and an animal (alive), a homunculus, or perhaps Frankenstein, made in God's laboratory, with a purpose or task assigned by his Maker."[161] While orthodox Christian theism "may affirm that God gives us freedom, it so severely restricts the legitimate function of that freedom as to make it a trivial possession."[162] Clearly, the melding of aspects of liberation and process theisms can do much better to resolve this problem than orthodoxy can. By declaring divine foreknowledge implausible as process theism suggests in positing a delimiting of the knowledge of God, human freedom can become meaningful. And it is precisely at this point where secular and naturalistic ideas may come into dynamic play in order to deepen theological insights.

It would seem that one moral fact that is assumed in the idea of human freedom is human voluntariness. Aristotle famously argued that the freedom to do otherwise is necessary for moral responsibility, an idea that

---

[160] Wilson, *Gem of the Ocean*, p. 28.
[161] Kurt Baier, "The Meaning of Life," in M. Weitz, Editor, *Twentieth Century Philosophy: The Analytical Tradition* (New York: The Free Press, 1966), p. 367.
[162] Delwin Brown, *To Set at Liberty* (Maryknoll: Orbis Books, 1981), p. 45.

captures the equally well-known (in philosophical circles) principle of alternative possibilities: If one can do otherwise, or possesses, at a given time, reasonably acceptable possibilities, one can be said to be morally responsible (liable) for what they do, fail to do, or attempt to do, as the case may be. And while many have argued that divine foreknowledge is incompatible with human freedom to do otherwise,[163] it is hard to see how divine foreknowledge would restrict human freedom. For if Harry G. Frankfurt[164] and John Martin Fischer[165] are correct, then it is, among other things, one's ability to have a higher-order volition (Frankfurt) or regulative control (Fischer) to do something that is sufficient for moral responsibility. On Frankfurt's analysis, one's having a higher-order volition is one's really wanting to do something, regardless of whether or not one has the ability to do otherwise. Thus even if for some reason divine foreknowledge were comprehensive as process theism denies, it need not vitiate human freedom under conditions in which humans have higher-order volitions to act, fail to act, or attempt to act, as the case may be. If this is true, then divine foreknowledge of even everything we do fails to not only vitiate human moral responsibility, but also human freedom. So voluntariness, understood in higher-order compatibilist terms, is entailed by human freedom, both metaphysically and politically. And this is especially the case on a process theistic account.

But what might that conception of freedom be in political terms? Without resorting to presuppositions that are quite philosophically indefensible (such as the special authority of Christian scripture and divine foreknowledge),[166] some fruitful things can be said here. Briefly, freedom from oppression ought to mean liberation from what and who prohibits morally innocent persons from individually autonomous and collectively sovereign lives, including the freedom of expression (I have in mind here

---

[163] For discussions of this claim, see the essays in John Martin Fischer, Editor, *God, Foreknowledge, and Freedom* (Stanford: Stanford University Press, 1989). It should be borne in mind, however, that the conception of God under discussion therein is that of an orthodox Christian one. No efforts are made by the discussants to consider process theistic ideas of the nature and function of God.

[164] Harry G. Frankfurt, *The Importance of What We Care About* (Cambridge: Cambridge University Press, 1988).

[165] John Martin Fischer, *My Way* (Oxford: Oxford University Press, 2004); John Martin Fischer and Mark Ravizza, *Responsibility and Control* (Cambridge: Cambridge University Press, 1998).

[166] For a distinctly Christian, though unorthodox, approach to this problem of divine knowledge and human freedom, see Brown, *To Set at Liberty*, pp. 56–59.

a proper interpretation of the First Amendment to the United States Constitution[167]), the freedom to choose the direction of their lives,[168] to reap a reasonable amount of the value from their labor power,[169] and the like.

If human rights amount to valid moral claims or interests that all humans have *qua* humans, then these and certain other rights are what they ought to have the freedom to exercise under certain specified conditions. Although these might not include the unqualified and vague "equality" rights of cosmopolitan "justice,"[170] it might well include certain other rights to not be exploited, to not be tortured, to due process, etc.[171] It seems, then, that a viable liberation theism is conceptually contingent on a plausible notion of human rights, which is in turn dependent on a plausible conception of freedom, among other things. Thus political theology must listen to political philosophy in this case.

And these factors ought to be read into the philosophical problem of evil if that problem is to have any normative depth. The best of theology, then, ought to inform philosophy of religion. However, one ought always to heed the caution of Kai Nielsen: "We need not be forced into religion, against our reason—against what we reasonably believe about the world—to make sense of our lives."[172]

Process Theism and Liberation Theism

While it is true that "there is no single mode of 'Liberation Theology,' and there is no single method of 'Process Theology,'"[173] it is important that we understand some of the key similarities and differences between process and liberation theisms, taken generally. And while this is not the first time in which such a comparison and contrast has been made, what I have to offer here differs importantly from certain theological attempts to

---

[167] Joel Feinberg, *Freedom and Fulfillment*, Chapter 5.

[168] Feinberg, *Harm to Self*, pp. 27f.

[169] Of course, Karl Marx made much of this point throughout many of his writings.

[170] For a critique of cosmopolitan justice, see Corlett, *Race, Rights, and Justice*, Chapter 4.

[171] Corlett, *Race, Rights, and Justice*, Chapters 5–6; Corlett, "Analyzing Human Rights."

[172] Kai Nielsen, *Naturalism and Religion* (Buffalo: Prometheus Books, 2001), p. 13.

[173] W. W. Schroeder, "Liberation Theology: A Critique from a Process Perspective," in John Cobb, Jr. and W. W. Schroeder, Editors, *Process Philosophy and Social Thought* (Chicago: Center for the Scientific Study of Religion, 1981), p. 210.

do so.[174] But prior to engaging in this exercise, it is important to understand that there has already been some thoughtful and respectful dialogue between some process and liberation theists.

While process thinkers such as John Cobb Jr. and David Ray Griffin have come to political theology somewhat late rather than in the formation of their process thinking, Schubert Ogden, Metz, and David Tracy have, along with Moltmann, addressed liberation concerns rather early on in the development of their respective theologies. My approach to these two ways of doing theology is somewhat akin to a certain other theological articulation of process theology that grounds liberation theology,[175] though my analysis is philosophical and has the much broader goal of challenging atheism and re-opening the debate about the problem of God for atheists, theists, and agnostics alike. Nonetheless, I shall focus on some of the criticisms of liberation thought since my analysis depends in part on its general viability.

Ogden argues that it is because of divine redemption that we are free to liberate others. But this includes not only humans, but the wider spectrum of living beings. He levels a criticism against liberationists, namely, that it is anthropocentric and ignores the need and theological duty to express concern for more than just humans. In distinguishing between theology and witness, Ogden points to what he sees as a limitation, not a fault, of liberation theologies, namely, that they tend not to engage in critical reflection on redemption and not just emancipation.[176]

In response to Ogden's insights, a rejoinder can be marshaled on behalf of the liberationist. While Ogden does well to make the distinction between theology and witness and to remind liberationists that there is more to a comprehensive and adequate theology than the liberation of the oppressed, it also bears noting that redemption is contingent on emancipation. Without freedom and justice, there can be no redemption, that is, insofar as redemption requires reconciliation between those alienated by oppression. It is not that redemption is not a goal, and an important one, for those who

---

[174] See John Cobb, Jr. and W. W. Schroeder, Editors, *Process Philosophy and Social Thought* (Chicago: Center for the Scientific Study of Religion, 1981), Part 3. Also see George V. Pixley, "Justice and Class Struggle: A Challenge for Process Theology," *Process Studies*, 3 (1973), pp. 159–175; Clark M. Williamson, "Whitehead as Counterrevolutionary? Toward Christian-Marxist Dialogue," *Process Studies*, 4 (1974), pp. 176–186.

[175] Brown, *To Set at Liberty*.

[176] Ogden, *Faith and Freedom*.

follow God. But if it is true that to know God is to do justice, then it would appear that, conceptually speaking, redemption is predicated on the idea of liberation from oppression. Without the latter, the former cannot possibly obtain. Not even God can effect the impossible.

One commonality between process and liberation theisms is that each one emphasizes the element of the divine being in the world. While process theism states that the spirit of God seeks to persuade people to do the right things, liberation theism tends to stress the actual doing of the right things by people. This difference in expression might well be explained in terms of their different aims and audiences. Process theists are often interested in addressing philosophical concerns about whether or not God exists, hence they address matters of God from that standpoint. On the other hand, liberation theists tend to be praxis oriented and not as concerned about addressing abstract philosophical matters. They are interested in the problems of human oppression in the here and now. And it is this issue that perhaps begins to explain the difference between process and liberation theisms when it pertains to discussions of politics. In fact, each of these theisms can embrace the idea that God wills the liberation of the oppressed, and that God is the ultimate power in the universe. Furthermore, each position can embrace the notion that God suffers with us (Patripassianism or "Matripassianism," depending on whether or not God is Father or Mother of all things good). But if liberation theism is on track, then God can and often does liberate oppression and is constantly active in the world in doing so through persuading, not coercing, us. However, She cannot do so unilaterally, but indirectly through human events and actions. God cannot do so because God lacks the power to act unilaterally given Her relations with the world—including us.[177] Thus divine responsibility for evil is diminished, and human responsibility for nonnatural evil is deepened and widened ("Diminished" because to the extent that God is responsible for nonnatural evils, the problem of evil still seems to count against the existence of God's benevolence, which is part of God's basic nature). To trim the notion of deity from omniscience and omnipotence to the most knowing and powerful being is one thing. But to then argue that God is not even omnibenevolent might well spell

---

[177] David Ray Griffin, "Values, Evil, and Liberation Theology," in John Cobb, Jr. and W. Widick Schroeder, Editors, *Process Theology and Social Thought* (Chicago: Center for the Scientific Study of Religion, 1981), pp. 193f.

doom for any idea of the nature of God that can stand as a conceptual force against atheism.

It is a grand mistake indeed to think that liberation theisms concern themselves primarily with political justice, while process theisms do not. For decades now Cobb, Jr. has devoted substantial energy to developing ideas of how process thought might shape politics, and for the sake of global justice.[178] So this is yet another feature that process and liberation theisms share in common. In fact, they each share a strong passion for global justice. However, whereas leading process thinkers tend to devote themselves to matters of global justice against the U.S. empire and in favor of resolving environmental problems, liberationists tend strongly to devote their attention to specific matters related to liberating persons from poverty and oppression.

While it is now clear how liberation theologies argue for their position, an example of the attention process theologies have for global justice is exemplified in quite recent work on politics.[179] While Griffin and Cobb Jr. address the politics, economics, and religious aspects of the U.S.'s road to empire and why this is a bad thing (even "demonic" according to Griffin) for the world and against the will and spirit of God,[180] very little is said of the problems of race and racism.[181] In fact, the solution of process theism to problems of global justice, while they do call for a "community of communities of communities"[182] and a "global democratic government"[183] which at times somewhat resembles Rawls' Law of Peoples[184] but at other

---

[178] John Cobb, Jr., *Process Theology as Political Theology* (Philadelphia: The Westminster Press, 1982); *Postmodernism and Public Policy* (Albany: SUNY Press, 2002).

[179] David Ray Griffin, John Cobb, Jr., Richard Falk, and Catherine Keller, *The American Empire and the Commonwealth of God* (Louisville: John Knox Press, 2006).

[180] Griffin, et al., *The American Empire and the Commonwealth of God*, pp. 146f. Also see p. 154.

[181] Gayraud S. Wilmore, "The New Context of Black Theology in the United States," in G. H. Anderson and T. F. Stransky, Editors, *Mission Trends No. 4: Liberation Theologies* (New York: Paulist Press, 1979), p. 120.

[182] Griffin, et al., *The American Empire and the Commonwealth of God*, pp. 101–102.

[183] Griffin, et al., *The American Empire and the Commonwealth of God*, pp. 103f.

[184] Rawls, *The Law of Peoples*. Cobb, Jr.'s view appears to seem a bit like Rawls' at some points: Griffin, et al., *The American Empire and the Commonwealth of God*, pp. 101–102. Also see Griffin's remarks on p. 117.

times aligns itself with a kind of cosmopolitan liberalism,[185] they never involve rectification of injustice by way of compensatory justice or reparations. And this is true even of Cobb, Jr. who devotes part of a chapter of a recent book to the problem of racism.

Yet despite Cobb, Jr.'s mention of repentance being important for whites in the U.S. because of their harms to blacks and Indians, and despite his insight that "Until whites recognize how deep is their self-identification as whites, they will not understand the problems they create both for themselves and for those whom they define as not white,"[186] nothing specific is articulated by him as to what form the repentance is to take:

> Is there not an argument for the alternative strategy of accepting the reality of the community constituted by the social construction of whiteness and, as a member of that community, undertaking to move it to repentance? Such repentance is not a matter of feeling guilty but of changing direction. . . .
> . . . This means acknowledging the ugly history of whiteness and repenting.[187]

This is especially disconcerting in light of Cobb, Jr.'s incisive claim that in the U.S., "The crimes of whites against blacks are too numerous and too obvious to deny, although they are often ignored."[188] For those of us greatly concerned with unrectified racist evils of the magnitudes experienced by blacks and Indians in the U.S., it would seem that repentance requires, among other things, the providing of compensatory damages to the victims or their surviving heirs. Again, unrectified evil is evil still. Without compensation, there can be no genuine repentance, and without genuine repentance there can be no genuine forgiveness. This element is absent from process accounts of political theology, regardless of how otherwise rich and informative such accounts are. But this is consistent with and more amenable to liberationist accounts such as Cone's. So while it may be true that liberation theists tend to be rather focused on the elimination of human oppression to the exclusion of more abstract matters of theology, it is also true that process theologians tend to communicate on such an abstract level that they neglect specifically what is crucial to any just and fair society, and to the will of God should God exist. No viable theology

---

[185] Griffin, et al., *The American Empire and the Commonwealth of God*, Chapter 6.

[186] Cobb, Jr., *Postmodernism and Public Policy* (Albany: SUNY Press, 2002), p. 155.

[187] Cobb, Jr., *Postmodernism and Public Policy*, p. 162.

[188] Cobb, Jr., *Postmodernism and Public Policy*, p. 159.

can ignore the central problem of God, but neither can it ignore what is fundamental to rectificatory justice.

Perhaps what partially explains this failure on the part of extremely well-meaning process theists is what Ralph Barton Perry called the "egocentric predicament." This is the difficulty in which one finds oneself such that one is unable to escape the perspective from which one functions. Of course, prejudice is a matter of degree, and process theists like Cobb, Jr. and Griffin have taken process thought a long way toward addressing racism and appreciating what liberationist theists have to offer.[189]

Even though process theists such as Cobb, Jr. and Griffin are astute about and somewhat sympathetic to some liberationist concerns, they function at such a general level of abstraction that they seem unable to address quite common implications of the U.S. racist evils of genocide, massive land theft, slavery, and Jim Crow. The political, economic, socio-psychological and other ramifications of these evils wrought on Indians and blacks in and by the U.S. require nothing short of holistic and comprehensive reparations if white appeals for social justice are to be taken seriously.

Griffin's and Cobb, Jr.'s respective pleas for global democratization ring hollow in the ears of several Indians, blacks, and those of us who stand with them. It is as if the process thinkers in the U.S. do not understand that they are advocating social justice for the world without having even addressed the unrectified evils committed at home! Jesus' words about judging the wrongs of others come to mind here: ". . . how can you say to your brother, 'Brother, let me take out the speck that is in your eye, when you yourself do not see the log that is in your own eye? You hypocrite, first take the log out of your own eye, and then you will see clearly to take out the speck that is in your brother's eye" (*Luke*, 6:41–42).

On the other hand, the ego-centric predicament works the other way insofar as liberationists often tend to ignore matters of global concern, such as the environment, in favor of freedom from oppressed peoples. As I stated earlier, what good does it do to gain freedom from human oppression if there is no longer a viable world in which to live in freedom? Hence the significance of the aim of my hybrid minimalist process-liberation theism: melding some of the basics of process and liberation theisms into a creative

---

[189] Cobb, Jr., *Process Theology as Political Theology; Postmodernism and Public Policy*, pp. 152f. Indeed, the importance of ". . . being and acting creatively and responsively to other people and our environment" is but an afterthought comprising some of the final words in Peacocke, *Creation and the World of Science*, p. 358.

but basic amalgam as a challenge to atheists and orthodox Christian theists truly interested in a plausible resolution to the problem of God.

I just stated that liberationists tend to ignore matters of environmentalism. But one notable exception to this is Cone's critique of white environmentalism wherein he charges that environmentalist ethics tend to focus more on nonhuman animal welfare than the welfare of blacks, and one way in which this manifests itself is the utter paucity of environmentalist attention paid to the fact of what Charles Mills refers to as "black trash."[190] As Cone writes:

> White ethicists and theologians sometimes refer to the disproportionate impact of hazardous waste on blacks and other people of color in the United States and Third World, and even cite an author or two, here and there throughout the development of their discourse on ecology. They often include a token black or Indian in anthologies on ecotheology, ecojustice, and ecofeminism. It is "politically correct" to demonstrate a knowledge of and concern for people of color in progressive theological circles. But people of color are not treated *seriously*, that is, as if they have something *essential* to contribute to the conversation. Environmental justice concerns of poor people of color hardly ever merit serious attention, not to mention organized resistance. How can we create a genuinely mutual ecological dialogue between whites and people of color if one party acts as if they have all the power and knowledge?[191]

Cone's words ring loudly in the ears of those who are deeply serious about theologically ecumenical discourse about politics and freedom. One careful look at the theological studies produced by leading figures on politics and society, and one sees that rarely, if ever, are Cone and other leading liberationists cited, much less discussed at length, or even given credit for their original points. In essence, environmental movements, along with their theological and philosophical thinkers, are indeed predominantly white. And it is this essential whiteness that leads many black thinkers to refer to these perspectives as being "white supremacist" in nature and function. It is not that it is thought that white thinkers intentionally develop their views in alienation from blacks. It is, rather, that white thinkers tend to ignore, out of a sort of benign neglect, the ideas of black thinkers. It is part of the "racist politics of scholarship" throughout the Academy.

---

[190] Charles Mills, "Black Trash," in L. Wuestra and Bill E. Lawson, *Faces of Environmental Racism* (Lanham: Rowman and Littlefield Publishers, 2001), pp. 73–91.

[191] Cone, *Risks of Faith*, pp. 142–143.

The racist politics of scholarship is one of the dirty little secrets of the Academy, hidden from public view by those in positions of white supremacy who have little respect for scholars of color even on matters that pertain directly to us folk of color! So it is no surprise that white theologians addressing environmental concerns fail to pay proper respect to research authored by black theologians and other black scholars. Nonetheless, the predictability of the racist politics of scholarship does nothing to excuse it. Rather, it condemns it as somewhat unscrupulous.

To the extent that the foregoing is true, then it appears that my hybrid minimalist process-liberationist theism is liberationist in at least the following respects. First, it seeks to provide the theological underpinning for real-world liberation movements of oppressed folk everywhere. But it also seeks to liberate liberation theology itself from the confines of orthodox Christian theism, neo-orthodox Christian theism, or even more progressive theisms. More deeply, black Christian liberation theism such as Cone's seeks to liberate genuine discourse about liberation from the racist confines of what he refers to as "white" theisms. This is not to say that white theists are "out to get" black ones. Rather, it is the full-scale recognition of the unintentionally racist ideologies of those who ignore or pay grossly insufficient attention to the black perspectives on various theistic concerns.

We must remember that racism is not always intentional. Indeed, responsibility for unintentional racism can at times measure quite greater than intended racism, especially where the racist folk in question refuse to admit that they are racists.[192]

Moreover, liberation theologies are criticized for supporting revolutionary ethics that simply seek to replace one form of oppression with another.[193] Yet as I argue elsewhere,[194] reparations are essential to black liberation. And it is not that liberationists have nothing to say about global justice. Indeed, the point about black reparations can not only be extended to the liberation of American Indians, but to indigenous peoples globally.[195] It is, rather, that what they have to say about it is not limited to matters that never indict morally progressive theists for their shared responsibility for racist harms. For process theism, the priority of religion and politics is on global redistributive justice and often on the globalization of democracy,

---

[192] Corlett, *Race, Racism, and Reparations*, Chapter 4.
[193] Griffin, et al., *The American Empire and the Commonwealth of God*, p. 148. This point is made by Cobb, Jr.
[194] Corlett, *Heirs of Oppression*.
[195] Corlett, *Race, Racism, and Reparations*, Chapter 8; Corlett *Heirs of Oppression*.

while for liberationists like me the emphasis is on both distributive justice and the rectification of racial injustice throughout the world. While there need not and ought not be a conflict between these approaches, process theists seem not to have fully appreciated certain of the liberationist themes. And it is vital to understand that the goal of liberation of the oppressed can surely be accomplished without the realization of the goal of global democratization. In fact, many would caution that the former requires, or at least is more likely to be achieved, without the latter goal being realized.

One fundamental reason for the differences between process and liberationist theisms along the lines enumerated lies in the fact that process theists implicitly rely on a utilitarian religious ethic which places the priority on the preservation of the global environment for the sake of humanity as a whole and on addressing issues of global hunger in order to assist the least well-off. While there is no explicit denial of the importance of these problems by liberationists, there is an implicit reliance on a rights-based religious morality, one that states that there are certain rights that have been violated and that the harmful wrongdoings must be rectified for the sake of justice and peace. Thus the rights of truly oppressed persons everywhere must be respected by way of rectificatory justice. And attention must be paid to the fact that women of oppressed groups generally suffer more than their male counterparts. Thus schemes of rectificatory justice must bear this in mind.[196] No amount of ignoring of these evils will reduce them or make them disappear into the thin air of redistribution of wealth and failure to compensate for evils of the past and present. For instance, one fact that cosmopolitan liberals tend not to see is that if oppressing peoples paid what they owe to the oppressed, many of the demands of "global justice," cosmopolitanly construed, would become otiose.

But we need not, in constructing a plausible theism, choose between these two formidable standpoints. As I have been stating throughout this book, some essential features of each position can be wedded together into a stronger position that seeks both liberation and justice for the oppressed

---

[196] Corlett, *Race, Racism, and Reparations*, p. 137f.; "Race, Racism, and Reparations," pp. 568–585; "Race, Ethnicity, and Public Policy," in Jorge Gracia, Editor, *Race or Ethnicity?*, pp. 225–247. For the general point that black liberation theologies ought to incorporate black feminist insights, see Rosemary Ruether, "Crisis in Sex and Race: Black Theology and Feminist Theology," in G. H. Anderson and T. F. Stransky, Editors, *Mission Trends No. 4: Liberation Theologies* (New York: Paulist Press, 1979), p. 187. For an actual incorporation of black feminism to analyze oppression of blacks in the U.S. and how to rectify it by way of reparations, see Corlett.

and global justice more generally. Global justice without serious attention to liberation of human oppression and racism is shallow in that it fails to respect basic human rights including those to compensation,[197] while focus on human oppression and racism, while vital, is short-sighted if there is no viable environment in which humans can live.

Moreover, process and liberation theisms concur on some further points. One is that the *Basileia tou Theou* is not, as many would have us believe, completely future-oriented. Indeed, at *Luke* 17, 20-21 Jesus reportedly states: "The kingdom of God is not coming with signs to be observed; nor will they say, 'Lo, here it is!' or 'There!' for behold, the kingdom of God is in the midst of you." Now this central point of the *kerygma* is quite amenable to process and liberation theisms in their emphases on the here and now. In the case of process theism, God is omnipresently among us, attempting to persuade us to do the right things and to avoid evil. When we do the right things, we follow God's will, and the *Basileia tou Theou* is among us, "in the midst of you," working for goodness and rightness. For liberationists, the *kerygma* is that we ought not to look away here or there for God's leadership or guidance. When we see the poor and oppressed, we see opportunities to do justice, in our midst. Interestingly, *The Gospel of Thomas* makes the same point, perhaps even more interestingly: "His disciples said to him, 'When will the kingdom come?'" Jesus said, "It will not come by looking for it. It will not be a matter of saying, 'here it is,' or 'there it is.'" Rather, the kingdom of the Father is spread out upon the earth, and people do not see it" (113). Furthermore, the *Basileia tou Theou* happens to the extent that followers of Jesus gain a certain kind of self-understanding: ". . . the kingdom is inside of you, and it is outside of you. When you come to know yourselves, then you will be known, and you will realize that it is you who are the sons of the living Father. But if you will not know yourselves, you dwell in poverty and it is you who are that poverty" (3).

Like the poor, the *Basileia tou Theou* is easily missed by those who do not understand that to know God is to do justice to the "least of these," as Jesus is reported to have said. This is surely a radical message. But so is liberation theology a shocking message to those in orthodox Christian ranks who think they know God, but in many cases have little idea as to what God is and what God is attempting to inspire us to do here in this life.

So we can see that process and liberation theologies converge on various points, hence my merging aspects of them into a unified whole in order to

---

[197] Corlett, *Heirs of Oppression.*

challenge atheism, theism, and agnosticism to either address and truly refute them in the form of my hybrid minimalist theism, or admit that atheism is a smokescreen for those who do not *want*, for whatever excuse, to believe in God, but who really have no good reason to deny the existence of God insofar as the concept of God is plausibly construed. Indeed, they stand as challenges to orthodox Christian theism to either refute them with independent argument unbiased by the conceptual whims of orthodoxy itself, or to accept the real possibility that traditional Christian theism has engaged in ideological idolatry for centuries and has not worshipped the true God. For one cannot worship who or what one does not know. And if the latter is true of orthodox Christian theism, then it too is exposed as a kind of atheism. For instead of outright denying the existence of God, orthodox Christian theism ends up worshipping a false God, which is no God at all. And if "there is no moral reason why massive blind corruption should be saved,"[198] then orthodox Christian theism must be abandoned in favor of a plausibly undogmatic search for the truth about God. It is precisely such a search that I have begun herein.

---

[198] Irwin Edman, "Religion and the Philosophical Imagination," *The Journal of Philosophy*, 25 (1928), p. 678.

CHAPTER 7

IS HYBRID MINIMALIST THEISM PLAUSIBLE?

Test all things—and firmly hold on to that which is good.

—Paul[1]

Having articulated a hybrid minimalist version of theism that is not shackled by the secondary and tertiary dogmas of orthodox Christian theism, it is time to put this process-liberation theism to the test of philosophical scrutiny. In doing so, we must recognize that objections will stem from numerous quarters. While some will criticize this hybrid brand of theism for being insufficiently "Christian" or unorthodox, others will charge that it either still falls prey to some of the objections to traditional Christian theism, creates its own problems that render it implausible, or is simply insufficiently theistic to render atheism problematic. I shall treat my hybrid minimalist process-liberation theism as a single philosophical theology, even though each element of the view has its own content and history of development, accompanied by nuances that I have not dealt with in the preceding chapters. Moreover, I shall consider various concerns that have been or may be raised of process theology, on the one hand, or liberation theology, on the other.

Orthodox Christian Theistic Objections to Hybrid Minimalist Theism

A variety of objections to the process element of my hybrid theism might be raised by orthodox Christian theists. First, it might be argued that my hybrid theism does not attach adequate importance to the authority of Christian scripture. But this objection both presupposes that Christian scripture has special authority beyond any other religious writ, and also violates the desideratum of testimony for an adequate answer to the problem of God discussed in Chapter 4.

Other Christian theists will have additional concerns with the liberatory feature of my hybrid theism. Some of these are stated rather carefully by Schubert Ogden. First, as was noted in the previous chapter, it is argued that

---

[1] *I Thesalonians*, 5:21.

liberation theologies that I employ in my minimalist theism tend to constitute more witness than theology.[2] However, this point is irrelevant to my
version of theism in that whether or not the liberation theisms of which I
make use are theologies makes no difference to the overall plausibility of
my argument. I should point out, however, that it ought to make no difference whatsoever whether or not liberation thinkers put forth a theology or
a witness. To paraphrase Socrates: what matters is not what a statement's
origin is insofar as who makes it, but whether or not it is true. This reduces
Ogden's first concern with liberation thought to a red herring.

Second, Ogden argues that liberation thinkers tend to eschew the finer
points of theology in favor of a focus on the existential meaning of God for
us in the world.[3] While I believe that this point has merit with regard to
some liberationist accounts, I see no reason why it must count against all. In
the previous chapter, I employed liberation theisms because of their emphasis on justice in the world from God through us. Yet my project is devoted
to articulating some of the finer points of philosophical theology in answer
to the atheistic challenge to the existence of God. This demonstrates how
with even minimal charity liberationist thinkers can be understood to focus
on a certain set of vital aspects of the *kerygma*, ones that the orthodox and
neo-orthodox Christian thinkers have by and large neglected for centuries.
Rather than ignore finer points of theology, liberation thought actually holds
orthodox Christian theology in particular accountable for the latter's neglect
of some of the liberatory themes it has largely ignored for centuries.

Third, Ogden charges liberationists with conflating the concepts of
redemption with emancipation as two forms of liberation.[4] It turns out
that Ogden casts this objection from within the Christian paradigm. Since
I reject that paradigm, it is easy to see that I will reject this objection to
liberation thought. Why ought we to think that redemption has anything
whatsoever to do with liberation? As mentioned in the previous chapter
with regard to Dorothee Soelle's misconception of liberation and forgiveness, redemption is not at issue here. And the more rapidly orthodox or
neo-orthodox Christian theologians understand that liberation is about
justice, the more expeditious and comprehensive understanding they will
have of the nature and function of God in the world, and of the true depth
of liberation theisms and what they can and are attempting to contribute
to a liberation theology: one that stresses the liberation of the oppressed

---

[2] Schubert Ogden, *Faith and Freedom* (Nashville: Abingdon Press, 1989), p. 31.
[3] Ogden, *Faith and Freedom*, p. 32.
[4] Ogden, *Faith and Freedom*, p. 33.

from the tyranny of oppression, and one also that attempts to liberate Christian theology itself from its closed attitude about what counts and what ought not to count as acceptable doctrine. Thus where Ogden and some other critics of liberation theologies accuse the latter of not accounting adequately for the doctrine of redemption, I counter-accuse these critics of liberation theology with failing to develop a sense of justice sufficiently sensitive to the concerns of the world and of the fact that God is just (retributively as well as distributively). And no amount of special pleading by Christian theists to the effect that God is also merciful and forgiving or such can provide sufficient reason to discount God's justice. The Christian world must come to terms with this understanding and fact about God. And simply because God is not human hardly entitles the Christian theologian to somehow make the *ad hoc* pronouncement that God's justice includes mercy and is different from ours in that it is not retributive and compensatory.

Finally, Ogden charges liberationists with having an overly restrictive view of what constitutes oppression (often focused on a particular ethnic or gender group's experience of oppression).[5] But this is hardly a serious objection, as any liberationist can easily incorporate this point into their theology. Oppression, like moral responsibility, admits of degrees. It is obvious to the charitable reader that liberationist thinkers focus on some of the most egregious forms of oppression, and some of the most longstanding and unrectified ones at that. In fact, Christian theologians ought to understand that James H. Cone, for example, emphasizes that he wants to bear theological witness to the oppression of black folk in the U.S., a group that has experienced at the hands of millions of Christian whites one of the most horrendously evil episodes in world history! Is it somehow wrong for Cone to write about that experience as a paradigmatic instance of oppression? What white theologians must understand is that these sorts of criticisms fall short of being telling, and tend to reflect an unintentional bias that self-servingly seeks to guard white Christian theology from black criticism.

However, none of the criticisms of Ogden make any difference to the assessment of the plausibility of my hybrid minimalist theism as a challenge to atheism. Perhaps some other objections are more telling.

David Tracy offers a concern for liberation theologies that differs from those articulated by Ogden. It is an objection to the neo-orthodox grounding of such views that rely heavily on a conception of the nature of God that is problematic in light of the theological implications of the problem

---

[5] Ogden, *Faith and Freedom*, p. 34.

of evil, and the failures of the ontological, cosmological, and teleological "proofs." He states:

> One cannot but ask with Marxist critics how a Christian commitment to a corporate *praxis* is finally intelligible if, even after demythologizing the "super-natural" world as not some world other than the world we actually live in, Christians continue to believe in the omnipotent, all-knowing, and unrelated God of classical theism and, at the same time, in an exclusivist understanding of revelation and Christology which threatens the ultimate value and meaning of that basic secular faith shared by all those committed to the contemporary struggle for liberation. It seems entirely appropriate to insist that if God is real, *we* as finite cannot fully understand his reality. Yet it continues to seem entirely inappropriate to employ this truism to bolster concepts of God and of Christian revelation which are neither internally coherent, nor able to illuminate our own ineluctable commitment to the ultimate meaningfulness of every struggle against oppression and for social justice and agapic love.
>
> Such largely conceptual difficulties seem to worry the eschatological theologians of *praxis* as little as they worried their neo-orthodox existentialist predecessors. For that reason, one must interpret their model for theology as an essentially neo-orthodox one. Yet how they can continue to retain that model, given their own prior commitment to the full implications of *praxis*, remains a puzzle. Why cannot that critical commitment, so admirably articulated in the critical interpretations of the social and political realities of our common experience, also be employed to interpret critically the possible conceptual incoherencies of traditional Christian symbols? Unless and until that task is attempted, it seems unlikely that the eschatological theologians can provide an adequate understanding of contemporary Christian *praxis*.[6]

Unlike Ogden, Tracy admits that liberation thinkers of *praxis* are doing theology. However, Tracy's criticism that such liberation theologies are inadequate is a bit ambiguous. For while it is true that such theologies are incomplete, lacking precisely the element he notes, they can nonetheless be adequate for their intended task(s).

Tracy is correct in implying that to the extent that liberation theologies simply adopt without much question their neo-orthodox roots concerning the authority of Christian scripture as well as uncritically accepting the orthodox Christian conception of God, such theologians end up facing some of the very same conceptual difficulties that orthodoxy faces. So it seems to do little good to argue for a liberationist way of thinking about

---

[6] David Tracy, *Blessed Rage for Order* (New York: The Seabury Press, 1975), pp. 245–246.

God and the world if the very concept of God with which liberationists are working is fundamentally flawed.

Although Tracy's concern is a good one, it does not count against my appropriation of liberation theisms insofar as my hybrid theism couples Third World liberation theism with process theism which is designed specifically to address the objections to the orthodox conception of God. Contrary to orthodox Christian theism, my hybrid theism follows process theologies in denying that, if God exists, She is omnipotent and omniscient in the strict senses of these categories, thus evading the various objections to the theistic proofs based on these and other alleged attributes of God. I see no reason to think it is conceptually absurd for liberation theologies to adopt much of what is central to process theologies, as I do. In so doing, liberationists would be able to ward-off some of the objections to their positions by representatives of the various theological quarters.

Orthodox or neo-orthodox Christian theists will also object to my hybrid minimalist theism's failure to embrace the *parousia*, the resurrection of Jesus, various reported miracles of Jesus, and the like. Of course, mine would fail to qualify as minimalist theism should it embrace the cornucopia of theistic beliefs that are found in orthodox and neo-orthodox circles of Christian faith. My attitude concerning such peripheral beliefs is that they are not central to what makes a view theistic, as I have argued. My goal is to challenge atheism by positing a theism that is unburdened by the heavy weight of inessential and highly contested dogmas. Should this hybrid minimalist theism stand up to atheological attacks, then perhaps the next philosophical move is to test one by one each of the peripheral (including many Christian) theistic beliefs for plausibility. In the meantime, it is a strong gesture toward Ockham's Razor that I keep matters as simple as possible for the time being. After all, if my hybrid minimalist theism fails, then surely the hyperbolic orthodox Christian conception of God is a *non sequitur* as the latter entails far more controversial beliefs. This holds even if it is true that each position may fail for different reasons.

Atheistic Objections to Hybrid Minimalist Theism

While atheists are unlikely to be worried about the above concerns of the orthodox or neo-orthodox Christian theist, they are more likely to register queries about whether or not my hybrid minimalist theism can provide answers to the objections to the traditional theistic properties of God, provide a cosmology that is not offensive to scientific sensibilities, as well as genuinely qualify as theistic in the requisite sense.

That the process aspect of my hybrid theory addresses scientific cosmogonological and cosmological concerns is obvious, as pointed out in Chapter 5. The process-liberationist theism I offer as a challenge to atheism embraces the best of science as a response to Rudolf Bultmann's charge to demythologize the informational content of the Christian scriptures in order to discover the *kerygma for us*. It translates the language of religious myth into a scientifically sensitive discourse that is existentially meaningful to us today. Moreover, evolutionism is embraced as a way to explain, if not the origin of the universe, its development over millennia.

However, there is the concern with my repeated claim that God is just. Insofar as this idea entails the punishment of harmful wrongdoers by God through the righteous in this world, it might be asked if in punishing such persons God is not passing judgment on Herself, as Albert Einstein asks: ". . . if this being is omnipotent then every occurrence, including every human feeling and aspiration, is also his work. How is it possible to think of holding men responsible for their deeds and thoughts before such an almighty Being? In giving out punishments and rewards he would be . . . passing judgement on himself."[7] To this thought Antony Flew adds: "For a Creator to punish creatures for what by the hypothesis he necessarily and as such (ultimately) causes them to do would be the most monstrous, perverse, and sadistic of performances."[8] These two challenges to the idea that God is just (ones that, unlike Marilyn McCord Adams' orthodox Christian challenge to the retributive justice of God considered in Chapter 5 meant to preserve, among other things, an anti-punishment theological agenda) challenge the concepts of divine omnipotence and omnibenevolence.

In reply to these two concerns, it might be argued that both Einstein's and Flew's objections presuppose an orthodox Christian conception of God as the omnipotent ("almighty," as Einstein states) creator of all things and who controls all things such that She is ultimately responsible for them. But this is precisely what my hybrid theism denies in its appropriation of process theism's conception of the nature and function of God in the world. God is not properly understood as omnipotent, though divine omnibenevolence would appear to imply divine justice. On this understanding of God, God is not ultimately responsible for what humans do badly as divine persuasion is not the same thing as omnipotence, and hence God cannot be rightly held accountable for it. And this reply serves as the basis for a

---

[7] Albert Einstein, *Out of My Later Years* (London: Thames and Hudson, 1950), pp. 26–27.

[8] Antony Flew, *Atheistic Humanism* (Buffalo: Prometheus Books, 1993), p. 28.

response to Einstein's concern about God passing negative judgment on Herself. For if the bad deeds of humans are the responsibility of those humans committing them, then God is exonerated from responsibility for them and hence does not condemn Herself in punishing them.

Conversely, God is not responsible for what humans do that is praiseworthy for the same reason that She is not responsible for what they do badly. After all, it seems arbitrary to hold that God is not responsible for blameworthy outcomes but is responsible for praiseworthy ones. Admittedly, this seems to pose a problem of a nonresponsible deity, which seems counterintuitive. However, if a plausible distinction can be made between what God does "on Her own" versus what She does by way of divine persuasion through humans, perhaps this quandary can be resolved. Nonetheless, the problem appears to be resolvable in terms of a recognition of God's limited power. Given that God is not omnipotent, one would expect that God's responsibility for outcomes is also limited, making God nonresponsible for various outcomes in the world. So there is no conceptual absurdity regarding God's limited responsibility for outcomes in the world in light of limited divine power. But it might well be that God can be rightly held responsible in the praiseworthy sense for Her positive means of persuasion in the world that fail to issue in human action that is praiseworthy. Of course, there is shared responsibility between God and humans in the world, a notion that may make God partially responsible for bad outcomes in the world to some extent, depending on the facts of each case. But even if this is true, God's limited power mitigates blameworthiness that may accrue to God, as it is humans who fail to do the right things even when persuaded by God. One question here is the extent to which divine shared responsibility with humans is not just mitigated, but excused.

Unlike either Einstein or Flew, I believe that moral responsibility (human voluntariness, knowledge, intentionality, guilt and fault) admits of degrees and that one ought to be held accountable and punished only to the extent that she wrongfully harms others.[9] Thus the alleged puzzle about divine self-punishment need not overly concern us, unless, of course, we are unduly wedded to orthodox Christian theism and its hyperbolic notions of the nature and function of God.

Generally, whatever problems traditional Christian theism faces because of its misattributions to God of such properties as omniscience and omnipotence are not faced by my hybrid minimalist theism nearly as much as

---

[9] J. Angelo Corlett, *Responsibility and Punishment*, 3rd Edition (Dordrecht: Springer, 2006), Library of Ethics and Applied Philosophy, Volume 9, Chapter 1.

they face orthodox Christian theism, making my theism a better candidate to challenge atheism's claim to victory regarding the problem of God. Its ability to embrace the best of scientific knowledge allows it to adopt whichever scientific cosmology turns out to be right, without forfeiting the reality of God in the process. God is naturalized, to be sure; God is "grounded." But God is still conceived to be essentially spirit, the most powerful, the most just, the most knowing, etc. being. And it is this set of divine properties that makes God worthy of our ultimate concern, and the object of our prayers in that God is that spirit which seeks to persuade us toward the good at all times. And it is by way of the process of prayer that we can connect with that spirit in order to do the right things, e.g., to focus ourselves on that which is good, right, and just in every respect.

If it remains a concern that the God of hybrid minimalist theism is insufficiently powerful to grant answers to prayers in extraordinary contexts, perhaps it is because most theists and atheists alike prefer to construe God as that genie who grants wishes to those who ask, and ask in earnest and with persistence. But if God exists, God is no genie, nor has She ever been one. God is that ultimate spiritual reality extant in the universe seeking to bring everything into a harmonious whole amidst the human frailties of greed, avarice, egoism, and all manner of wrongdoing motivated by them.

And if the atheist insists that my hybrid minimalist theism, for all its virtues, fails to prove the existence of such a being, the following might be offered as replies. First, if that is so, then I concur with Bertrand Russell in pointing out that it is also the case that we nonetheless stand in the same position of this conception of God's not being disproven. Second, my hybrid minimalist theism has taken us some distance away from the highly problematic orthodox Christian conception of God, a philosophical move that should receive a chorus of expressions of gratitude even from the staunchest atheist. A new conceptual vista has been opened, even if it admittedly draws from two traditions in Christian theology heretofore largely ignored by both atheists and most orthodox Christian theists. Moreover, if hybrid minimalist theism is in the end implausible, then we have good reason to believe that any theism that is maximalist is less likely to be true to the extent that maximal theisms entail the content of my minimalist theism.

While the atheist can take considerable comfort in the possibility that my hybrid minimalist process-liberationist theism is in some ways underdeveloped, it hardly serves as solace for orthodox Christian theists who are honest enough to grant reason and science their proper status in philosophy of religion. However, since the plausibility of even hybrid minimalist theism is not yet disproven, I offer the New Agnosticism as the position that is best to adopt, all relevant things considered, until arguments can be adduced to disprove the most plausible forms of theism and adequately support atheism, properly construed.

However, an atheist might argue that I have depicted atheism in a way that is problematic such that no reasonable person would become an atheist, or in such a way that it cannot be justified. In Part I, I defined "theism" as the view that claims that God exists, and "atheism" as its logical contradictory: It is not the case that God exists. But, it might be argued, belief in and acceptance of propositions comes in degrees of strength of conviction, allowing for the probability of belief or disbelief in God. Thus statements such as "It is probably the case that God exists" may count as theistic, and claims such as "It is probably not the case that God exists" might count as atheistic. So my construal of atheism and theism in the strict senses is too narrow.

In reply to this concern, it might be argued that even if probabilistic senses of atheism and theism were legitimate, the objection fails to recall the crucial distinction between the questions of definition and justification regarding atheism and theism. Thus even if probabilistic versions of these positions were legitimate and meaningful, *ceterus paribus*, it hardly follows from this that atheism or theism is plausible.

Second, as noted in Part I, to define "atheism" or "theism" in probabilistic terms requires a non-question-begging and non-self-serving construal of these categories in light of the fact that agnosticism is typically couched probabilistically. So how can atheism and theism be distinguished from agnosticism probabilistically, nonarbitrarily, and without conceptual confusion?

If the atheistic reply is that a probabilistic construal of atheism is essential to capture the fallibilistic nature of some of its adherents, then perhaps the atheist should understand that she is not an atheist at all, but really an agnostic. How ironic that so many staunch atheists attempt to hide behind the veil of a position that so many of them ridicule as being "fence-sitting" (Richard Dawkins) or otherwise inferior to atheism!

Furthermore, if atheism can rightly enjoy the conceptual freedom of embracing without conceptual absurdity probabilistic notions regarding the existence of God, then by parity of reasoning so can theism. But this is where the attempt of atheists to co-opt agnosticism goes awry. Few, if any, theists consider themselves to be agnostics. In fact, even atheists quite often refer to theists as "believers." It just is part of theism to be wedded to the view that God exists. In fact, it would make little or no sense at all to the typical theist to deny this claim, or to couch it in probabilistic terms. So by parity of reasoning, given the strident atheism that we witness in Kai Nielsen,

Dawkins, and so many others, it appears to be little more than an attempt to escape the pains of refutation for the atheist to then attempt to adopt agnosticism as a form of atheism. This is especially suspicious when there is no independent argument provided for the distinction between the two positions.

But again, my arguments against atheism count even against the probabilistic varieties, as there has been no atheistic refutation or even serious consideration of the plausibility of particular varieties of theism. Thus as argued in Part I, the sample size of tested theisms by atheists is so small that it becomes insulting for atheists to employ the rhetorical "ploy" (Nielsen's word for some theists) of shifting to a kind of probabilism regarding God's possible existence. What makes any atheist sensitive to inductive reasoning and the scientific method they so greatly admire think that the refutation of a sample size of one popular theism counts as an adequate defense of the claim that it is not the case that God exists or that it is probably not the case that God exists?

Thus major concerns from orthodox Christian theism and atheism have been addressed. Perhaps there are yet other concerns with my hybrid minimalist theism. What are they? And can they be answered plausibly? Perhaps there are queries from a radical wing of religious thought.

Further Objections

One must be ever mindful of an even more radical critique of my hybrid minimalist theism. It is that which originates from the indigenous experience and focuses on the liberationist aspect of my proposal. Of liberation theisms, Vine Deloria, Jr. states that "Liberation theology, then, was an absolute necessity if the establishment was going to continue to control the minds of minorities. If a person of a minority group had not invented it, the liberal establishment most certainly would have created it."[10] These are strong words, accusing liberationists of unwittingly participating in "the latest gimmick to keep minority groups circling the wagons with the vain hope that they can eliminate the oppression that surrounds them. It does not seek to destroy the roots of oppression, but merely to change the manner in which oppression manifests itself."[11]

---

[10] Vine Deloria, Jr., "A Native American Perspective on Liberation," in G. H. Anderson and T. F. Stransky, Editors, *Mission Trends No. 4: Liberation Theologies* (New York: Paulist Press, 1979), p. 262.

[11] Deloria, Jr., "A Native American Perspective on Liberation," p. 262.

Deloria, Jr. seems to interpret liberation theologies as more reformist than revolutionary, contrary to Cobb, Jr.'s interpretation of liberation theisms. For Deloria, Jr. goes on to define "liberation" as that which "requires a rejection of everything we have been taught and its replacement by only those things we have experienced as having values."[12] And he seems to understand liberation theisms as those which suggest "that people can be made to change their oppressive activity by intellectual reorientation alone."[13]

But Deloria, Jr. misunderstands liberation theisms on this matter. The praxis element so central to liberation theisms, whether Latin American or black, places social, political, economic, and religious change by way of doing the will of God at the forefront of its quest to know God and to do justice. Furthermore, Deloria, Jr.'s other criticism is hyperbolic in that liberation need not require the "rejection of everything" taught us. The basics of reason ought not to be rejected, for instance. Nor should the teachings of love, peace, justice, and fairness, among others. Yet this is not mere reformation, but such principles can be used in revolutionary movements. These are not merely Western concepts, but human ones. And it need not prohibit us from agreeing with Deloria, Jr. that "religious, political, economic, and historical analyses of human activities that have been derived from the Western tradition do not have an absolute claim upon us. We are free to seek a new synthesis that draws information from every culture, . . ."[14]

It seems, then, that both process and liberation theisms evade Deloria, Jr.'s radical critique. My hybrid minimalist theism, in its explicit rejection of Christian orthodoxy, is certainly quite in line with Deloria, Jr.'s concern about not allowing such an influence to determine the terms of a plausible theism. That process and liberation theologies originate from the Christian tradition is hardly a sufficiently good reason to reject them as Deloria, Jr. argues we should. And this is especially true given that my hybrid minimalist theism refuses to buy into anything that is less than revolutionary. Perhaps what Deloria, Jr. espouses is the fallacy of condemning liberation theologies because of their origin in the Christian faith. But while Christianity has a most evil history—especially in the Americas—this is insufficient reason to condemn theological movements seeking to revolutionize it.

Perhaps it is true that "liberation theology must once again rebel; this time, however, it must rebel against itself . . . by refusing to become a

---

[12]   Deloria, Jr., "A Native American Perspective on Liberation," p. 263.
[13]   Deloria, Jr., "A Native American Perspective on Liberation," p. 263.
[14]   Deloria, Jr., "A Native American Perspective on Liberation," p. 268.

theology for the middle class"[15] and by refusing to be co-opted into mainstream theological discourse.[16] Perhaps, moreover, liberation theologies "suffer from debilitating conditions which cause them to ignore the primary oppression that comes from a person's class standing" due to liberationist myopic focuses on certain particularities of this or that ethnicity or gender, as the case may be.[17]

Whatever ways in which particular liberationist theists might[18] or might not focus too much on the oppression of this or that ethnic or gender group, it is clear that my hybrid minimalist theism does not commit this error. It appropriates insights from liberationists like Cone and Gustavo Gutiérrez, among others, to highlight the importance of placing justice at the core of a plausible theism. Yet it is not committed to the idea that American Indians and blacks are the only oppressed groups in the world, or that ethnicity or gender are the only factors that anchor oppression. Socioeconomic class often, if not always, also plays a critical role in oppression. And considerations of justice (both distributive and retributive) must be brought to bear on the problems of oppression.

Another radical critique of my hybrid minimalist theism might originate from leftist social, political, legal, and moral philosophy and theology. It states that the hybrid minimalist conception of God as just is far too retributivist and vengeful, reflective of the "Old Testament" manner in which *Yahweh* sometimes metes out punishment. It hardly reflects the "New Testament" God of love brought to us in the person and teachings of Jesus of Nazareth: "Judge not, unless you will be judged" (*Luke* 6:37). The argument that

---

[15] Ivan Petrella, *Beyond Liberation Theology* (London: SCM Press, 2008), p. 122.

[16] Petrella, *Beyond Liberation Theology*, p. 116.

[17] Petrella, *Beyond Liberation Theology*, p. 84f.

[18] If the goal is to provide a comprehensive theistic analysis of oppression and justice, then it is surely a mistake to think that the focus on the liberation from oppression of this or that particular group is adequate. However, it is equally problematic for one to assume that the mere focus on such instances of oppression themselves are problematic if they in fact do not claim to provide such a comprehensive account. Thus the charge of "monochromaticism" against liberationists in general or of several in particular (see Petrella, *Beyond Liberation Theology*, pp. 84f.) must answer to the rebuttal that the aims of such theisms are not comprehensive at all, but rather constitute a variety of foci on particular problems of group oppressions and why and how they deserve serious consideration, theologically and otherwise. Furthermore, the additional charge of identity essentialism (Petrella, *Beyond Liberation Theology*, pp. 140–141) is contingent on the legitimacy of the overarching theistic aim of overcoming identity considerations when pursuing justice, a charge that is mostly assumed rather than supported by rational argument.

reconciliation between humans (oppressors and oppressed) requires forgiveness, and that forgiveness requires apology, and that apology requires
compensation by oppressors of those whom they oppress does not make
room for divine "love of God through Christ the Lord." As such, an important element of God's dealing with us is omitted from the account, it might
be argued. At best, then, it is a partial but misleading or one-sided picture
of God's nature and function in the world.

In reply to this line of criticism, it should be pointed out that retributive
punishment and vengeance are quite dissimilar notions. First, while retribution requires that a punished person deserves it because she is guilty of
a harmful wrongdoing, vengeance makes no such commitment to its way
of doing "justice." Second, while retribution seeks to ground its response to
harmful wrongdoing in proportionality, however, approximate, vengeance
knows no such limitations. Third, while vengeance is typically emotive in
form and substance, retribution need not be. Fourth, while retribution
works within the legal system to effect its primary aims, vengeance need
not and typically does not do so. The widespread lynching of thousands of
blacks throughout U.S. history is a stark example of each of these features
of vengeance, as is, of course, the lynching of Jesus himself. Retribution
would surely out of principle never condone such injustices. While there
are yet other ways in which retribution differs from vengeance,[19] it must
not be forgotten that even should there in the end be no significant difference between the two (surely retribution can take on the form of vengeance in some cases), it is an error of presumption to think that vengeance
is necessarily or always morally unvirtuous.[20] An Aristotelian way to think
about this is the simple point that, other considerations aside, moral virtue
consists in the mean between two extremes of excessiveness. Thus between
the excesses of being always and absolutely forgiving and merciful, on the
one hand, and never being forgiving and merciful (vengeance) on the other,
lies that moral virtue of retribution. Perhaps ignorance of this fact has

---

[19] Corlett, *Responsibility and Punishment*, p. 33; Joel Feinberg, Editor, *Reason
     and Responsibility* (Belmont: Dickenson Publishing Company, Inc., 1965),
     pp. 296–299; Robert Nozick, *Philosophical Explanations* (Cambridge: Harvard
     University Press, 1981), pp. 366–368. The more general point that punishment
     is not revenge is made in Ted Honderich, *Punishment*, Revised Edition
     (London: Penguin, 1976), p. 14.

[20] Peter A. French, *The Virtues of Vengeance* (Lawrence: University Press of
     Kansas, 2001); Jeffrie G. Murphy, *Retribution Reconsidered* (Dordrecht:
     Kluwer Academic Publishers, 1992), pp. 61–85.

misled so many leftists to think that divine or human goodness excludes divine retribution.

To be sure, many philosophers and theologians are concerned about unfairness shot through and through legal systems. This unacceptable fact makes them reluctant to endorse retributivism in that no matter how well-meaning and intentioned it is, it becomes corrupt and unfairness results in a system of punishment and compensation. But while it is true that criminal and tort systems of justice are corrupted, it is far from obvious that they cannot at least sometimes find justice in a case and mete it out fairly. While every system of justice requires constant and diligent efforts at reform or revolutionary change, this must never cease efforts at meting out genuine justice when it can be achieved. And this is especially true in the case of reparative justice to existing and identifiable indigenous and other groups that have been shown by way of clear evidence to have experienced tremendous rights violations at the hands of still identifiable oppressors. The abuse of the justice system hardly implies that we ought to give up on justice, especially in those that are not hard cases.

But the objection to retribution is also concerned with the apparent lack of divine love in my hybrid minimalist account of God's nature and function. The charge that divine love is being replaced by divine retributive justice, even vengeance, neglects to consider the strong possibility that the very idea of divine love cannot be cashed out in reasonably acceptable terms without the notion of divine retribution. God's love is not universal in the sense that God's love is always expressed to all persons at all times absolutely. If some persons oppress others, they are not deserving of God's love, and shall not (cannot?) receive or experience it without rectification. To deny this is to misunderstand God's justice! It is to problematically describe God such that no matter what one does, no matter how evil one is, they still stand to experience God's love. But God's grace only comes to those who truly repent and hence qualify for it. It is not unconditional. It is, rather, that divine reconciliation does require forgiveness and apology, which in turn requires rectificatory justice. After all, a sure sign that one has changed her ways is that she has in fact done so—hence the compensatory justice aspect of apology. Why anyone would then think that those who fail to make true apology are entitled to forgiveness and mercy is beyond reason and reasonableness.

Love is not a feeling of gratification one experiences as the result of the self-granting of excuses by those who commit harmful wrongdoings. It is, rather, what reason requires of those who wrongfully harm others. Divine love is earned by what harmful wrongdoers do to make themselves worthy of God's grace. And if it be replied by the theologian that this is a "theology" based on works and not divine grace, my reply is that it is an ethic based on reason and reasonableness, which trumps any idea of apologizing for the sake of avoiding compensation or punishment. All too often what results in "God's" grace and forgiveness and mercy ends up serving the interests of those who proclaim most loudly that "sinners" ought to be forgiven and shown mercy, such that unrectified evils do not inconveniently come back to haunt the pocketbooks of those who stand most to lose by the rectification of injustices. Witness orthodox and neo-orthodox Christianity in the U.S. and its attitude against compensatory justice for Indians and blacks. Thus it appears that this concern with the hybrid minimalist theism is unfounded, as it is based on the question-begging assumptions that the very notions I am attacking are themselves true.

What needs to be supported is the age-old tradition in many Christian theological circles of presumptuously thinking that sins can be "washed away by the blood of the lamb" by a simple confession of the sin (apologizing), without devoting sufficient attention to the rectification of the harmful wrongdoing.[21] This surely is a poisonous theology as it mocks the lynching of Jesus by making it out to be some quasi-spiritual phenomenon that mysteriously erases sin by divine grace.

Retributive justice is not about vengeance, but about effecting genuine apologies and rectification so that some at least general sort of societal reconciliation between criminals and others can possibly occur as a privilege granted by victims and society to genuinely repentant harmful wrongdoers. In this sense, divine love can be realized on earth, through the actions of those who do justice and know and love God, whether or not they are Christians, Jews, or Muslims.

What hybrid minimalist theism achieves, then, is the "grounding of God" in the world by way of the demythologization of theism in terms of some of the basics of process and liberation theisms. Instead of positing some otherworldly deity that intervenes periodically in the affairs of the world as "He" pleases, as orthodox and neo-orthodox Christian theism postulates, hybrid minimalist theism makes no commitment to

---

21 For those who doubt that a theistic notion of rights and rectification can be brought together, consider that even 12-step programs of substance abuse both recognize the importance of a "higher power" and of compensatory justice toward those whom the addicts have wronged. Nothing in principle rules out this joining of God and justice, though it requires for many a excising of certain long-cherished doctrines from what is truly essential to a viable theistic standpoint.

the Christian conception of God. Moreover, it concurs with process theology's agreement with naturalism that nothing beyond the natural order exists, except insofar as nonphysical things do such as spirit, thoughts, feelings, and the like. What is meant here is that there is no separate realm where God exists quite apart from the world, created and/or evolved, where God alone exists. Rather, God is grounded in the world with us, and this ought to provide us eternal hope and strength to approach life's difficulties most of which we have created ourselves. We can, however, resolve them by seeking truth, justice, and righteousness by way of reason that we are so very fortunate to possess as perhaps the greatest testimony to God's presence in the world. That the world is in such poor condition is mostly due to the fact that so many do not use their reason, or misuse it out of greed, or for other egoistic purposes. But this hardly speaks against the existence of God, who "stands" waiting to persuade and influence us to do the right things here and there throughout our lives—if we would just listen, and diligently obey the voice of reason.

While many philosophers and theologians seem to think that making everyone somehow equal will resolve many of the world's problems, such utopian ideology ignores the real world justice that stands in need of realization. Why not devote sufficient attention to the paying of reparations to the many groups to whom the U.S. owes them? Is it because so many U.S. leftists would lose so much and that members of the reparated groups would then be economically and politically superior to them? Whatever the case, justice is one of God's ways of being in the world. Those who seek to realize true justice in the world know and love God.

And no amount of seeking justice for nonhuman animals more than justice for human ones will suffice here. Peter Singer is a case in point. While his work on the rights of nonhuman animals is quite important, even though derivative of historical utilitarian attitudes on nonhuman animals, his unabashed utilitarianism makes no room for compensatory moral rights for humans![22] This is precisely the kind of thinking that needs to be exposed for the morally hypocritical ideology that it is, as it often seeks rights for nonhuman animals but embraces, knowingly or not, a utilitarian ideology that cannot even in principle make room for compensatory moral rights for humans. As we know, the ethics of utilitarianism—act or rule—is

---

[22] Peter Singer, *Animal Liberation* (New York: Avon, 1972); *One World* (New Haven: Yale University Press, 2002).

faulted for not allowing for rights and justice considerations, as each is subsumed under considerations of overall social utility maximization.[23] Perhaps this is a reason why so many philosophers and theologians seem clearly more concerned with environmental matters than they are about matters of race and social justice, why they are more concerned about distributive justice than they are about retributive and compensatory justice.[24] Whatever the case, if God exists, to know Her is to do justice both retributively and distributively, both regarding humans and non-humans alike.

---

[23] John Rawls, *A Theory of Justice* (Cambridge: Harvard University Press, 1971), pp. 3–5.

[24] See, for examples, Allen Buchanan, *Justice, Legitimacy, and Self-Determination* (Oxford: Oxford University Press, 2004); Thomas Pogge, *Poverty and Human Rights* (London: Polity, 2002); Janna Thompson, *Taking Responsibility for the Past* (London: Polity, 2002). For a critique of such a view, see J. Angelo Corlett, *Race, Rights and Justice* (Dordrecht: Springer, 2009), Law and Philosophy Series, Volume 85, Chapter 4.

CONCLUSION

The argument of this book has been that, if orthodox Christian theism suffers from severe implausibility in light of the many problems that it cannot seem to resolve after centuries of defense by some of the most brilliant minds in history, it is a mistake to infer from this supposition that atheism, properly construed, is epistemically justified in a robust sense. For even its most respected proponents commit the errors of atheism. First, they commit the straw person fallacy of thinking that theism is best understood in terms of the hyperbolic orthodox Christian conception of God's nature (e.g., omnipotent, omniscient, transcendent, etc.) and function. Second, atheists tend also to commit the bifurcation fallacy in thinking that either orthodox Christian theism is sound, or atheism must be the result, when in fact there are more plausible conceptions of theism than the orthodox Christian one. Third, they often tend to commit a fallacy of equivocation between atheism and agnosticism in attempting to stipulatively define "atheism" in probabilistic terms, and arbitrarily, when in fact agnosticism just is the view that construes the existence of God (among other things) probabilistically. Finally, they tend also to commit the fallacy of hasty conclusion insofar as atheists reason that the orthodox Christian theistic view of the nature of God is representative, with its numerous attendant problems, of what a viable theism must be vis-à-vis the nature of God.

Thus even if orthodox Christian theism is highly problematic, atheism is not at this time a justified inferential position to adopt for the serious thinker. Atheism cannot justify itself unless and until it is the case that significant and unresolved problems arise for theisms of the most plausible varieties—especially ones that can evade many or all of the difficulties posed by atheism to orthodox Christian theism. Contrary to both orthodox Christian theism and atheism, then, neither of such views is plausible in light of the current state of the evidence, and the New Agnosticism is the most justified position for the time being.

What partly underlies the errors of atheism is the thoroughgoing "double-duping" by orthodox Christian theism of unsuspecting parishioners, on the one hand, and atheists, on the other, into thinking that the Christian brand of theism is worthy of the amount of attention it has received. Moreover, part of this double-duping has succeeded in persuading atheists to think that the orthodox conception of the nature of God is the only one worthy of our serious philosophical attention. This idea plays into the atheist's agenda of easily refuting the idea of God without delving more deeply into the problem of God.

One might infer, then, that orthodox Christian theists and atheists in a sense deserve one another as interlocutors. Neither one seems to be interested in deeper discussion about the problem of God, at least, a depth that requires honesty, sincerity and open-mindedness sufficiently strong to actually change one's view should the arguments justify it. Rather, each side in its philosophical and theological presumptuousness is thoroughly convinced that it is right about the matter of God, regardless of how carefully some atheists flesh out their view in terms of probabilities, and in light of the fact that increasing numbers of respected (even many Christian) theists adopt theistic positions that do not fall as easy prey to various atheistic objections.

What is needed, instead of theistic or atheistic ideological dogmatism, is a New Agnosticism replete with a fresh attitude toward the problem of God. It touts open-mindedness, sincerity, and truth-seeking. Furthermore, it is unafraid to mine the radical theologies for truths that can advance the discussion in fruitful dialogue. On this score, the New Agnosticism is gratefully indebted to the theologies of Rudolf Bultmann, John Cobb, Jr., James H. Cone, David Ray Griffin, Gustavo Gutiérrez, Charles Hartshorne, Jürgen Moltmann, Paul Tillich, among others from the radical and secular theological spectrum for their tremendous and significant influence on my thinking so that I could attempt to push this vital discussion into new depths vis-à-vis the theism-atheism debate.

Why agnosticism? And why the *New* Agnosticism? Because for all the ways in which the hybrid minimalist theism I have traced as a synthesis of process and liberation theologies improves the lot of theism quite substantially in terms of the nature and function of God, there are some significant questions that remain: Can a plausible theism incorporate the most plausible theory of mind? Must the most plausible and theoretically adequate theism include an element of nonmaterialism? And must theism worthy of the name employ a doctrine of immortality of the soul? Can theism survive without such controversial views?

Furthermore, my hybrid minimalist theism might well be challenged for being overly minimalist. What, it might be asked, is the real difference between it and a rationalistic and humanistic ethic that has nothing to do with God? What real difference, in other words, does God make in the hybrid minimalistic scheme of things?

These are important questions, and they require answers. And it is sincerely hoped that the arguments contained herein spark fruitful philosophical and theological discussion to resolve these and related queries. But for the moment, at least, the errors of atheism make atheism unjustified in anything but a rather weak sense, at best.

BIBLIOGRAPHY

Ackerman, H. C. "The Differentiating Principle of Religion," *The Journal of Philosophy*, 19 (1922), pp. 317–325.

Adams, Marilyn McCord. *Horrendous Evils and the Goodness of God* (Ithaca: Cornell University Press, 1999).

—. The Problem of Hell: A Problem of Evil for Christians," in E. Stump, Editor, *Reasoned Faith* (Ithaca: Cornell University Press, 1993), pp. 301–327.

Adams, Robert. "Middle Knowledge and the Problem of Evil," *American Philosophical Quarterly*, 14 (1977), pp. 109–117.

Aguilar, Mario. *The History and Politics of Latin American Theology*, Volumes 1–2 (London: SCM Press, 2007–2008).

Ahern, Dennis. "Foreknowledge: Nelson Pike and Newcombe's Problem," *Religious Studies*, 15 (1979), pp. 475–490.

Allen, Diogenes. "The Witness of Nature to God's Existence and Goodness," *Faith and Philosophy*, 1 (1984), pp. 27–48.

Almeder, Robert F. *Beyond Death* (Springfield: Thomas, 1987).

Altizer, Thomas J. J. *The Gospel of Christian Atheism* (Philadelphia: The Westminster Press, 1966).

—. and William Hamilton. *Radical Theology and the Death of God* (Indianapolis: The Bobbs-Merrill Company, Inc., 1966).

—. and William A. Beardsley and J. Harvey Young, Editors, *Truth, Myth and Symbol* (Englewood Cliffs: Prentice-Hall, Inc. 1962).

Alves, Rubem. *A Theology of Human Hope* (Washington, D.C.: Corpus Books, 1969).

Anselm. *Basic Writings*, S. N. Deane (trans.) (LaSalle: Open Court, 1962).

Assman, Hugo. *Opresión-Liberación Desafío a los Christianos* (Montevideo: Editorial Tierra Nueva, 1972).

Audi, Robert. "Belief, Faith, and Acceptance," *International Journal for Philosophy of Religion*, 63 (2008), pp. 87–102.

—. *Religious Commitment and Secular Reason* (Cambridge: Cambridge University Press, 2000).

Augustine. *Confessions*, J. K. Ryan (trans.) (New York: Image Books, 1960).

Ayer, A. J. *Language, Truth, and Logic* (London: Victor Gollancz LTD, 1948).

—. *The Problem of Knowledge* (Harmondsworth: Penguin Books Ltd, 1980).

—. "The Vienna Circle," in A. J. Ayer, W. C. Kneale, G. A. Paul, D. F. Pears, P. F. Strawson, G. J. Warnock, and Richard Wollheim, Editors, *The Revolution in Philosophy* (London: Macmillan & CO LTD, 1963), pp. 70–87.

Baier, Kurt. "The Meaning of Life," in M. Weitz, Editor, *Twentieth Century Philosophy: The Analytical Tradition* (New York: The Free Press, 1966), pp. 361–379.

Baldwin, James. *The Fire Next Time* (New York: The Dial Press, 1963).

Barbour, Ian G. *Issues in Science and Religion* (New York: Harper Torchbooks, 1966).

—. *Religion in an Age of Science* (New York: Harper & Row Publishers, 1990).

—. *When Science Meets Religion* (New York: Harper & Row Publishers, 2000).

Barth, Karl. *Anselm* (New York: The World Publishing Company, 1960).

—. *Church Dogmatics*, Volume 2, G. T. Thomson (trans.) (New York: Charles Scribner's Sons, 1955).

—. *Evangelical Theology*, G. Foley (trans.) (Grand Rapids: W. B. Eerdmans Publishing Company, 1963).

Basinger, David. "Divine Omniscience and Human Freedom: A 'Middle Knowledge' Perspective," *Faith and Philosophy*, 1 (1984), pp. 291–302.

—. "Hick's Religious Pluralism and 'Reformed Epistemology'," *Faith and Philosophy*, 5 (1988), pp. 421–432.

—. "Plantinga, Pluralism, and Justified Religious Belief," *Faith and Philosophy*, 8 (1991), pp. 67–80.

—. "Pluralism and Justified Religious Belief," *Faith and Philosophy*, 13 (1996), pp. 260–265.

Beattie, Tina. *The New Atheists* (Maryknoll: Orbis Books, 2007).

Behe, Michael. *Darwin's Black Box* (New York: Simon & Schuster, 1996).

Benn, Piers. "Some Uncertainties about Agnosticism," *International Journal for Philosophy of Religion*, 46 (1999), pp. 171–188.

Berkhof, L. *Systematic Theology* (Grand Rapids: W. B. Eerdmans Publishing Co, 1939).

Black, Max, Editor, *The Importance of Language* (Englewood Cliffs: Prentice-Hall, 1962).

Blackburn, Simon. *Ruling Passions* (Oxford: Oxford University Press, 1998).

Blassingame, John W. *The Frederick Douglass Papers*, Volume 2, 1847–1854 (New Haven: Yale University Press, 1979–1985).

Bloch, Ernst. *Atheism in Christianity*, J. T. Swan (trans.) (New York: Herder & Herder, 1972).

Boethius. *The Consolation of Philosophy*, R. Green (trans.) (Indianapolis: The Bobbs-Merrill Company, Inc., 1962).

Bonhoeffer, Dietrich. *Letters and Papers from Prison*, E. Bethge, Editor (New York: The Macmillan Company, 1971).

Bonino, José Miguez. *Doing Theology in a Revolutionary Situation* (Philadelphia: Fortress Press, 1975).

Bonting, S. L. *Creation and Double Chaos* (Minneapolis: Fortress Press, 2007).

Boxill, Bernard. "Morality of Reparations," *Social Theory & Practice* 2 (1972), pp. 113–123.

—. "The Morality of Reparations II," in T. Lott and J. P. Pittman, Editors, *A Companion to African-American Philosophy* (London: Blackwell Publishers, 2003), pp. 134–147.

Braaten, Carl. *The Future of God* (New York: Harper & Row Publishers, 1969).

Brightman, E. G. *An Introduction to Philosophy* (New York: Henry Holt and Company, 1925).

Brown, Delwin. *To Set at Liberty* (Maryknoll: Orbis Books, 1981).

Brown, Robert McAfee. *Religion and Violence* (Philadelphia: The Westminster Press, 1973).

—. *Spirituality and Liberation* (Philadelphia: The Westminster Press, 1988).

—. *Theology in a New Key* (Philadelphia: The Westminster Press, 1978).

Bruce, F. F. *The New Testament Documents: Are They Reliable?* (Downers Grove: InterVarsity Press, 1975).

Brunner, Emil. *Dogmatics*, Volume 2 (Philadelphia: The Westminster Press, 1952).

Buchanan, Allen. *Justice, Legitimacy, and Self-Determination* (Oxford: Oxford University Press, 2004).

Bultmann, Rudolf. *Jesus Christ and Mythology* (New York: Scribners, 1958).

—. *Theology of the New Testament* (New York: Scribners, 1951–1955).

Burke, Michael B. "Theodicy with a God of Limited Power: A Reply to McGrath," *Analysis,* 47 (1987), pp. 57–58.

Burrows, Millar. *The Dead Sea Scrolls* (New York: Viking, 1955).

Carter, B. "Large Number Coincidences and the Anthropic Principle in Cosmology," in M. S. Longair, Editor, *Confrontation and Cosmological Theories with Observational Data* (Dordrecht: D. Reidel Publishing Company, 1974), pp. 291–298.

Chafer, L. S. *Systematic Theology,* Volume 1 (Dallas: Dallas Seminary Press, 1947).

Chandler, Hugh S. "Divine Intervention and the Origin of Life," *Faith and Philosophy,* 10 (1993), pp. 170–180.

Chardin, Teilhard de. *The Future of Man,* N. Denny (trans.) (New York: Harper & Row Publishers, 1964).

—. *The Hymn of Universe* (New York: Harper & Row Publishers, 1961).

—. *The Phenomenon of Man,* B. Wall, Translator (New York: Harper & Row Publishers, 1965).

Clark, Steve, Editor, *Malcolm X Talks to Young People: Speeches in the US, Britain, Africa* (New York: Pathfinder Press, 1991).

Clayton, Philip. *God and Contemporary Science* (Grand Rapids: W. B. Eerdmans Publishing Company, 1997).

—. *God and Contemporary Thought* (Edinburgh: Edinburgh University Press, 1997).

—. *Mind and Emergence* (Oxford: Oxford University Press, 2004).

—, Editor, *The Oxford Handbook of Religion and Science* (Oxford: Oxford University Press, 2006).

—. and J. Schloss, Editors, *Evolution and Ethics* (Grand Rapids: Eerdmans, 2004).

—. and Jim Schall, Editors, *Practicing Science, Living Faith* (New York: Columbia University Press, 2007).

—. and Paul Davies, Editors, *The Re-Emergence of Emergence* (Oxford: Oxford University Press, 2006).

—. and M. Richardson, Editors, *Science and the Spiritual Quest* (London: Routledge, 2002).

Cobb, John, Jr. *A Christian Natural Theology* (Philadelphia: The Westminster Press, 1965).

—. *God and the World* (Philadelphia: The Westminster Press, 1969).

—. *Postmodernism and Public Policy* (Albany: SUNY Press, 2002).

—. *The Process Perspective* (St. Louis: Chalice Press, 2003).

—. *Process Theology as Political Theology* (Philadelphia: The Westminster Press, 1982).

—. and David Ray Griffin. *Process Theology* (Philadelphia: The Westminster Press, 1976).

—. and Clark H. Pinnock, Editors, *Searching for an Adequate God* (Grand Rapids: W. B. Eerdmans Publishing Company, 2000).

—. and W. W. Schroeder, Editors, *Process Philosophy and Social Thought* (Chicago: Center for the Scientific Study of Religion, 1981).

—. *The Process Perspective,* J. B. Slettom, Editor (Atlanta: Chalice Press, 2008).

Coburn, Robert C. "God, Revelation, and Religious Truth: Some Themes and Problems in the Theology of Paul Tillich," *Faith and Philosophy*, 13 (1996), pp. 3–33.

Commonweal (1973), pp. 314–316.

Cone, James H. *A Black Theology of Liberation* (Maryknoll: Orbis Books, 1990).

—. *God of the Oppressed* (New York: The Seabury Press, 1975).

—. *Martin & Malcolm & America: A Dream or a Nightmare?* (Maryknoll: Orbis Books, 1991).

—. *Risks of Faith* (Boston: Beacon Press, 1999).

—. *Speaking the Truth* (Grand Rapids: W. B. Eerdmans Publishing Co., 1986).

—. *The Spirituals and the Blues* (New York: Seabury Press, 1991).

Cooper, John M. and D. S. Hutchinson, Editors, *Plato: Complete Works* (Indianapolis: Hackett Publishing Company, 1997).

Cooper, John W. *Panentheism: The Other God of the Philosophers* (Grand Rapids: Baker Academic, 2006).

Corlett, J. Angelo, "Analyzing Human Rights," in *Human Rights After 9/11* (Philadelphia: University of Pennsylvania Press, in press).

—. *Analyzing Social Knowledge* (Totowa: Rowman & Littlefield Publishers, 1996).

—. "Epistemic Responsibility," *The International Journal of Philosophical Studies*, 16 (2008), pp. 179–200.

—. "Evil," *Analysis*, 64 (2004), pp. 81–84.

—. "Forgiveness, Apology, and Retributive Punishment," *American Philosophical Quarterly*, 43 (2006), pp. 25–42.

—. *Heirs of Oppression* (forthcoming).

—. *Interpreting Plato's Dialogues* (Las Vegas: Parmenides Publishing, 2005).

—. "Is the *Passion of the Christ* Racist? Due Process, Responsibility, and Punishment," in J. Gracia, Editor, *Mel Gibson's Passion and Philosophy* (LaSalle: Open Court, 2004), pp. 101–110.

—. "Political Integration, Political Separation, and the African-American Experience: Martin Luther King, Jr. and Malcolm X on Social Change," *Humboldt Journal of Social Relations*, 21 (1995), pp. 191–208.

—. "Race, Ethnicity, and Public Policy," in Jorge Gracia, Editor, *Race or Ethnicity?* (Ithaca: Cornell University Press, 2007), pp. 225–247.

—. *Race, Racism and Reparations* (Ithaca: Cornell University Press, 2003).

—. "Race, Racism, and Reparations," *Journal of Social Philosophy*, XXXVI (2005), pp. 568–585.

—. *Race, Rights, and Justice* (Dordrecht: Springer, 2009). Law and Philosophy Series, Volume 85.

—. *Responsibility and Punishment* (Dordrecht: Kluwer Academic Publishers, 2001). Library of Ethics and Applied Philosophy, Volume 9.

—. *Responsibility and Punishment*, 3rd Edition (Dordrecht: Springer, 2006). Library of Ethics and Applied Philosophy, Volume 9.

—. "The Right to Civil Disobedience and the Right to Secede," *The Southern Journal of Philosophy*, 30 (1992), pp. 20–21.

—. *Terrorism: A Philosophical Analysis* (Dordrecht: Kluwer Academic Publishers, 2003). Philosophical Studies Series, Volume 101.

Cornwell, John. *Darwin's Angel* (London: Profile Books, 2007).

Cousineau, Phil, Editor, *A Seat at the Table* (Berkeley: University of California Press, 2006).

Cox, Harvey. *The Feast of Fools* (New York: Harper & Row Publishers, 1969).

—. *The Secular City* (New York: The Macmillan Company, 1965).

Crisp, Roger. "The Avoidance of the Problem of Evil: A Reply to McGrath," *Analysis*, 46 (1986), p. 160.

Critic (1973), p. 84.

Crosby, Michael H. *They Will be Done; Praying the Our Father as Subversive Activity* (Maryknoll: Orbis Books, 1977).

Cupitt, Don. *Taking Leave of God* (New York: Crossroad, 1981).

Darwin, Charles. *The Descent of Man* (New York: D. Appleton, 1883).

—. *Genetics and the Origin of Species* (New York: Columbia University Press, 1937).

—. *Heredity and the Nature of Man* (New York: Harcourt, Brace & World, 1964).

—. *On the Origin of Species* (London: J. Murray, 1859).

Davis, Reginald F. *Frederick Douglass: A Precursor of Liberation Theology* (Macon: Mercer University Press, 2005).

Davis, Stephen T. "Is it Possible to Know that Jesus Was Raised from the Dead?" *Faith and Philosophy* 1 (1984), pp. 147–159.

—."Doubting the Resurrection: A Reply to James A. Keller," *Faith and Philosophy,* 7 (1990), pp. 99–111.

Dawkins, Richard. *The God Delusion* (New York: Houghton Mifflin Company, 2006).

—. *The Blind Watchmaker* (Harlow: Longman, 1986).

De La Torre, Miguel A., Editor, *Handbook of U.S. Theologies of Liberation* (Atlanta: Chalice Press, 2008).

— and Edwin David Aponte, Editors, *Handbook of Latina/o Theologies* (Atlanta: Chalice Press, 2006).

Deloria, Vine, Jr. *God is Red* (Golden: Fulcrum Publishing, 1994).

—. "A Native American Perspective on Liberation," in G. H. Anderson and T. F. Stransky, Editors, *Mission Trends No. 4: Liberation Theologies* (New York: Paulist Press, 1979), pp. 277–282.

Deltete, Robert J. and Reed A. Guy, "Hartle-Hawking Cosmology and Unconditional Probabilities," *Analysis,* 57 (1997), pp. 304–315.

Dembski, William. *No Free Lunch* (Lanham: Rowman & Littlefield Publishers, 2001).

—. *The Design Inference* (Cambridge: Cambridge University Press, 1998).

Dennett, Daniel. *Darwin's Dangerous Idea* (New York: Simon & Schuster, 1995).

Denton, Michael. *Evolution* (London: Burnett Books, 1991).

Dilley, Frank. "A Finite God Reconsidered," *International Journal for Philosophy of Religion,* 47 (2000), pp. 29–41.

Dobzhansky, T. *Genetics and the Evolutionary Process* (New York: Columbia University Press, 1971).

—. *Mankind Evolving* (New York: Bantam Books, 1970).

Donovan, Peter. *Religious Language* (New York: Hawthorne Books, Inc., 1976).

Dubois, W. E. B. *An ABC of Color* (New York: International Publishers, 1963).

Dupré, Louis. "On the Intellectual Sources of Modern Atheism," *International Journal for Philosophy of Religion,* 45 (1999), pp. 1–11.

Durkeim, Emile. *The Elementary Forms of the Religious Life* (New York: The Free Press, 1915).

Dworkin, Gerald. "Paternalism," in Joel Feinberg and Hyman Gross, Editors, *Philosophy of Law,* 5th Edition (Belmont: Wadsworth Publishing Company, 1995), pp. 209–218.

—. "Paternalism: Some Second Thoughts," in Joel Feinberg and Hyman Gross, Editors, *Philosophy of Law,* 5th Edition (Belmont: Wadsworth Publishing Company, 1995), pp. 219–223.

Eberle, Christopher J. *Religious Conviction in Liberal Politics* (Cambridge: Cambridge University Press, 2002).

Eco, Umberto and Carlo Maria Martini. *Belief or Nonbelief?* M. Proctor (trans.) (New York: Arcade Publishing, 1997).

Edman, Irwin. "Religion and the Philosophical Imagination," *The Journal of Philosophy,* 25 (1928), pp. 673–685.

Edwards, D. L., Editor, *The Honest to God Debate* (Philadelphia: The Westminster Press, 1963).

Edwards, Paul. "Atheism," in Paul Edwards, Editor-in-Chief, *The Encyclopedia of Philosophy,* Volume 1, Reprint Edition (New York: Macmillan Publishing Co. & The Free Press, 1972).

Einstein, Albert. *Out of My Later Years* (London: Thames and Hudson, 1950).

Everitt, Nicholas. *The Non-Existence of God* (London: Routledge, 2004).

Feinberg, Joel. *Doing and Deserving* (Princeton: Princeton University Press, 1970).

—. *Freedom and Fulfillment* (Princeton: Princeton University Press, 1992).

—. *Harm to Self* (Oxford: Oxford University Press, 1986).

—. *Problems at the Roots of Law* (Oxford: Oxford University Press, 2003).

—, Editor, *Reason and Responsibility* (Belmont: Dickenson Publishing Company, Inc., 1965).

Fenn, Richard. *Beyond Idols* (Oxford: Oxford University Press, 2001).

—. *Time Exposure* (Oxford: Oxford University Press, 2001).

Fergusson, David. *Community, Liberalism, & Christian Ethics* (Cambridge: Cambridge University Press, 1998).

Ferré, Frederick. *Philosophy of Technology* (Englewood Cliffs: Prentice-Hall, 1988).

—. *Shaping the Future* (New York: Harper & Row, 1976).

Fierro, Alfredo. *The Militant Gospel* (Maryknoll: Orbis Books, 1977).

Fischer, John Martin. "Epicureanism about Death and Immortality," *The Journal of Ethics,* 10 (2006), pp. 355–381.

—, Editor, *God, Foreknowledge, and Freedom* (Stanford: Stanford University Press, 1989).

—. *My Way* (Oxford: Oxford University Press, 2004).

—. and Mark Ravizza. *Responsibility and Control* (Cambridge: Cambridge University Press, 1998).

Fisher, Fred L. *Jesus and His Teachings* (Nashville: Broadview, 1972).

Flew, Antony. *Atheistic Humanism* (Buffalo: Prometheus Books, 1993).

—. *Atheism and Humanism* (Buffalo: Prometheus Books, 1993).

—. *God and Philosophy* (New York: Harcourt, Brace and World, 1966).

—. *The Presumption of Atheism* (London: Elek for Pemberton, 1976). Also (Buffalo: Prometheus Books, 1976) and (New York: Barnes & Noble, 1976).

—. and A. MacIntyre, Editors, *New Essays in Philosophical Theology* (London: SCM Press, 1955).

—. *Philosophy and Atheism* (Buffalo: Prometheus Books, 1985).

—. "Theology and Falsification," in Antony Flew and A. MacIntyre, Editors, *New Essays in Philosophical Theology* (London: SCM Press, 1955), pp. 96–98.

Frankfurt, Harry G. *On Bullshit* (Princeton: Princeton University Press, 2006).

—. *The Importance of What We Care About* (Cambridge: Cambridge University Press, 1988).

Freire, Paulo. *Pedagogy of the Oppressed,* M. B. Ramos (trans.) (New York: The Seabury Press, 1968).

—. *Education for Critical Consciousness* (New York: Continuum, 1980).

French, Peter A. *The Virtues of Vengeance* (Lawrence: University Press of Kansas, 2001).

Fuller, Steve. *Science vs. Religion* (Cambridge: Polity, 2007).

Fulmer, G. "The Concept of the Supernatural," *Analysis,* 37 (1977), pp. 113–116.

Gaillie, W. B. "Essentially Contested Concepts," in M. Black, Editor, *The Importance of Language* (Englewood Cliffs: Prentice-Hall, 1962), pp. 121–146.

Gamow, George. *The Creation of the Universe* (New York: The Viking Press, 1952).

Gellman, Jerome J. "Religious Diversity and the Epistemic Justification of Religious Belief," *Faith and Philosophy,* 10 (1993), pp. 345–364.

—. "Epistemic Peer Conflict and Religious Belief: A Reply to Basinger," *Faith and Philosophy,* 15 (1998), pp. 229–235.

Gilkey, Langdon. *Maker of Heaven and Earth* (New York: Doubleday and Company, 1959).

Gilson, E. *God and Philosophy* (New Haven: Yale University Press, 1941).

Goldman, A. I. *Knowledge in a Social World* (Oxford: Oxford University Press, 1999).

Gracia, Jorge. "History and the Historiography of Philosophy," in D. M. Borchert, Editor, *Encyclopedia of Philosophy,* 2nd Edition (London: Macmillan Publishing Company, 2006).

—, Editor, *Race or Ethnicity* (Ithaca: Cornell University Press, 2007), pp. 225–247.

Grayling, A. C. "Dawkins and the Virus of Faith," in A. Grafen and M. Ridley, Editors, *Richard Dawkins* (Oxford: Oxford University Press, 2006), pp. 243–247.

Griffin, David Ray. *Evil Revisited* (Albany: SUNY Press, 1991).

—. *God, Power, and Evil: A Process Theodicy* (Philadelphia: The Westminster Press, 1976).

—. "Process Philosophy of Religion," *International Journal for Philosophy of Religion,* 50 (2001), pp. 131–151.

—. "Process Theology and the Christian Good News: A Response to Classical Free Will Theism," in J. Cobb Jr. and C. H. Pinnock, Editors, *Searching for and Adequate God* (Grand Rapids: W. B. Eerdmans Publishing Company, 2000), pp. 1–38.

—. "The Rationality of Belief in God: A Response to Hans Küng," *Faith and Philosophy,* 1 (1984), pp. 16–26.

—. *Reenchantment without Supernaturalism* (Ithaca: Cornell University Press, 2001).

—. *Religion and Scientific Naturalism* (Albany: SUNY Press, 2000).

—. In Response to William Haskar," in J. Cobb, Jr. and C. H. Pinnock, Editors, *Searching for an Adequate God* (Grand Rapids, W. B. Eerdmans Publishing Company, 2000), pp. 246–262.

—. "Theism and the Crisis in Moral Theory: Rethinking Modern Autonomy," in George Allan and Merle Allshouse, Editors, *Nature, Truth, and Value: Exploring the Thought of Frederick Ferré* (Lanham: Lexington Books, 2005), pp. 199–220.

—. "Values, Evil, and Liberation Theology," in J. Cobb, Jr. and W. W. Schroeder, Editors, *Process Philosophy and Social Thought* (Chicago: Center for the Scientific Study of Religion, 1981), pp. 183–196.

Griffin, David Ray, John Cobb Jr., Richard Falk, and Catherine Keller. *The American Empire and the Commonwealth of God* (Louisville: John Knox Press, 2006).

Grigg, Richard. *Beyond the God Delusion* (Minneapolis: Fortress Press, 2008).

Gutiérrez, Gustavo. *Essential Writings* (Maryknoll: Orbis Books, 1996).

—. "Freedom and Salvation: A Political Problem," in R. H. Stone, Editor, *Liberation and Change* (Atlanta: John Knox Press, 1977), pp. 3–94.

—. *A Theology of Liberation,* Caridad Inda and John Eagleson (trans.) (Maryknoll: Orbis Books, 1973).

Habermas, Jürgen. *Between Naturalism and Religion,* C. Cronin (trans.) (Cambridge: Polity, 2008).

Harris, Sam, *Letter to a Christian Nation* (New York: Alfred A. Knopf, 2006).

Hartshorne, Charles. *Anselm's Discovery* (LaSalle: Open Court, 1965).

—. *The Divine Relativity* (New Haven: Yale University Press, 1948).

—. *The Logic of Perfection* (LaSalle: Open Court Publishing Company, 1962).

—. *Man's Vision of God* (Hamden: Archon Books, 1964).

—. *Natural Theology for Our Times* (La Salle: Open Court, 1950).

Hasker, William. "The Foundation of Theism: Scoring the Quinn-Plantinga Debate," *Faith and Philosophy,* 15 (1998), pp. 52–67.

—. "Can Philosophy Defend Theology? A Response to James Keller," *Faith and Philosophy,* 11 (1994), pp. 272–278.

Haught, John F. *God and the New Atheism* (Louisville: Westminster John Knox Press, 2008).

Hawking, S. W. *A Brief History of Time* (New York: Bantam, 1988).

Hepburn, R. "Demythologizing and the Problem of Validity," in A. Flew and A. MacIntyre, Editors, *New Essays in Philosophical Theology* (London: SCM Press, 1955), pp. 227–242.

Herrmann, Eberhard. "On the Distinction Between the Concept of God and Conceptions of God," *International Journal for Philosophy of Religion,* 63 (2008).

Herzog, Frederick. *Liberation Theology* (New York: The Seabury Press, 1972).

Hick, John. "The Epistemological Challenge of Religious Pluralism," *Faith and Philosophy,* 14 (1997), pp. 277–286.

—. *Evil and the God of Love,* Revised Edition (New York: Harper & Row Publishers, 1978).

—, Editor, *The Existence of God* (New York: The Macmillan Company, 1964).

—. *Philosophy of Religion* (Englewood Cliffs: Prentice-Hall, 1963).

—. *Philosophy of Religion,* 4th Edition (Englewood Cliffs: Prentice-Hall, 1990).

—. "Religious Pluralism and the Rationality of Religious Belief," *Faith and Philosophy,* 10 (1993), pp. 242–249.

—. "Religious Pluralism and Salvation," *Faith and Philosophy*, 5 (1988), pp. 365–377.

—. *Who or What is God?* (London: SCM Press, 2008).

Hodge, Charles. *Systematic Theology*, Volume 1 (Grand Rapids: Wm. B. Eerdmans Company, 1977).

Holyoake, G. J. *The Origin and Nature of Secularism* (London: Watts, 1896).

Honderich, Ted. *After the Terror* (Edinburgh: University of Edinburgh Press, 2002).

—. *Political Violence* (Ithaca: Cornell University Press, 1976).

—. *Punishment*, Revised Edition (London: Penguin, 1976).

Hopfe, Lewis M. *Religions of the World* (Beverly Hills: Glencoe Press, 1976).

Hoyle, Frederick. *The Nature of the Universe* (New York: Harper and Brothers, 1950).

Hume, David. *Dialogues Concerning Natural Religion*, N. K. Smith, Editor (Indianapolis: Bobbs-Merrill, 1976).

Hume, Robert E. *The World's Living Religions* (New York: Charles Scribner's Sons, 1959).

Hunt, David P. "Evil and Theistic Minimalism," *International Journal for Philosophy of Religion*, 49 (2001), pp. 133–154.

Huxley, Aldous. "Words and Their Meanings," in M. Black, Editor, *The Importance of Language* (Englewood Cliffs: Prentice-Hall, 1962), pp. 1–12.

Ice, J. L. and J. J. Carey, Editors, *The Death of God Debate* (Philadelphia: The Westminster Press, 1967).

Jackson, Timothy P. *The Priority of Love* (Princeton: Princeton University Press, 2003).

James, William. *Varieties of Religious Experience* (New York: New American Library, 1958).

Jansen, J. F. *The Resurrection of Jesus Christ in New Testament Theology* (Philadelphia: The Westminster Press, 1980).

Jonas, Hans. *Philosophical Essays* (Englewood Cliffs: Prentice-Hall, 1974).

Jones, Kathleen. *Challenging Richard Dawkins* (Norwich: Canterbury Press, 2007).

Jones, William R. *Is God a White Racist?* (New York: Doubleday, 1973).

The Journal of Ethics, 7 (2003), pp. 1–160.

The Journal of Ethics, 10 (2006), pp. 1–204.

The Journal of Religion (1973), pp. 108–110.

Kant, Immanuel. *Religion and Rational Theology*, Allen Wood, Editor and Translator (Cambridge: Cambridge University Press, 1996).

—. *Religion within the Bounds of Mere Reason and Other Writings*, George Di Giovanni and Allen Wood (Translators) (Cambridge: Cambridge University Press, 1998).

Kaufmann, Walter, Editor. *The Portable Nietzsche* (New York: The Viking Press, 1954).

Keller, C., M. Nauser and M. Rivera, Editors, *Postcolonial Theologies* (St. Louis: Chalice Press, 2004).

Keller, James. "Accepting the Authority of the Bible: Is it Rationally Justified?" *Faith and Philosophy*, 6 (1989), pp. 378–397.

—. "Is it Possible to Know that Jesus was Raised from the Dead?" *Faith and Philosophy*, 2 (1985), pp. 147–159.

—. "On the Issues Dividing Contemporary Christian Philosophers and Theologians," *Faith and Philosophy*, 10 (1993), pp. 68–78.

—. "Method in Christian Philosophy: Further Reflections; Response to Plantinga," *Faith and Philosophy*, 5 (1988), pp. 165–167.

—. "Response to Davis," *Faith and Philosophy*, 7 (1990), pp. 112–116.

—. "Should Christian Theologians Become Christian Philosophers?" *Faith and Philosophy*, 12 (1995), pp. 260–280.

Kemp, Kenneth W. "The Virtue of Faith in Theology, Natural Science and Philosophy," *Faith and Philosophy*, 15 (1998), pp. 462–477.

Kenny, Anthony. *The Five Ways* (Notre Dame: University of Notre Dame Press, 1969).

—. *The God of the Philosophers* (Oxford: Oxford University Press, 1979).

—. *The Unknown God* (London: Continuum, 2004).

—. *What I Believe* (London: Continuum, 2006).

Kierkegaard, Søren. *Fear and Trembling* and *The Sickness Unto Death* (Princeton: Princeton University Press, 1954).

King, Martin Luther, Jr. "An Address Before the National Press Club," in James M. Washington, Editor, *A Testament of Hope: The Essential Writings of Martin Luther King Jr.* (New York: Harper & Row, 1986), pp. 99–105.

—. "The Current Crisis in Race Relations," in James M. Washington, Editor, *A Testament of Hope: The Essential Writings of Martin Luther King Jr.* (New York: Harper & Row, 1986), pp. 85–90.

—. "An Experiment in Love," in James M. Washington, Editor, *A Testament of Hope: The Essential Writings of Martin Luther King Jr.* (New York: Harper & Row, 1986), pp. 16–20.

—. "The Most Durable Power," in James M. Washington, Editor, A Testament of Hope: The Essential Writings of Martin Luther King Jr. (New York: Harper & Row, 1986), pp. 10–11.

—. "Next Stop: The North," in James M. Washington, Editor, *A Testament of Hope: The Essential Writings of Martin Luther King Jr.* (New York: Harper & Row, 1986), pp. 189–194.

—. "Nonviolence: The Only Road to Freedom," in James M. Washington, Editor, *A Testament of Hope: The Essential Writings of Martin Luther King Jr.* (New York: Harper & Row, 1986), pp. 54–61.

—. "Nonviolence and Racial Justice," in James M. Washington, Editor, *A Testament of Hope: The Essential Writings of Martin Luther King Jr.* (New York: Harper & Row, 1986), pp. 5–9.

—. "The Rising Tide of Racial Consciousness," in James M. Washington, Editor, *A Testament of Hope: The Essential Writings of Martin Luther King Jr.* (New York: Harper & Row, 1986), pp. 145–151.

—. "Showdown for Nonviolence," in James M. Washington, Editor, *A Testament of Hope: The Essential Writings of Martin Luther King Jr.* (New York: Harper & Row, 1986), pp. 64–72.

—. "Walk for Freedom," in James M. Washington, Editor, *A Testament of Hope: The Essential Writings of Martin Luther King Jr.* (New York: Harper & Row, 1986), pp. 82–84.

Klein, Charles J. "On the Necessary Existence of an Object with Creative Power," *Faith and Philosophy* 17 (2000), pp. 369–381.

Knight, Christopher. *The God of Nature* (Minneapolis: Fortress Press, 2007).

—. *Wrestling With the Divine* (Minneapolis: Fortress Press, 2001).

Küng, Hans. *Does God Exist?* E. Quinn (trans.) (New York: Doubleday and Company, 1980).

—. *Why I am Still a Christian* (New York: Houghton Mifflin, 2006).

Lack, David. *Evolutionary Theory and Christian Belief* (London: Methuen, 1957).

Lactantius. "On the Anger of God," in W. Fletcher, Translator, *The Writings of the Ante-Nicean Fathers* (Grand Rapids: W. B. Eerdmans, 1951), Volume 7.

Lehrer, Keith. *Theory of Knowledge,* 2nd Edition (Boulder: Westview Press, 2000).

—. Thomas Reid (London: Routledge & Kegan Paul, 1989).

Leslie, John. *Value and Existence* (Oxford: Basil Blackwell, 1979).

Levine, Michael P. "Contemporary Christian Analytic Philosophy of Religion: Biblical Fundamentalism, Terrible Solutions to a Horrible Problem, and Hearing God," *International Journal for Philosophy of Religion,* 48 (2000), pp. 89–119.

Lloyd, A. H. "The Passing of the Supernatural," *The Journal of Philosophy, Psychology, and Scientific Methods,* 7 (1910), pp. 533–553.

Mackie, J. L. *The Miracle of Theism* (Oxford: Oxford University Press, 1982).

Maimonides, Moses. *Guide to the Perplexed*, Volume 1, S. Pines (trans.) (Chicago: The University of Chicago Press, 1963).

Malcolm X. "Twenty Million Black People in a Political, Economic, and Mental Prison" in Bruce Perry, Editor, *Malcolm X: The Last Speeches* (New York: Pathfinder Press, 1989).

Markosian, N. "On the Argument from Quantum Cosmology Against Theism," *Analysis,* 55 (1995), pp. 247–251.

Martin, Michael. *Atheism, Morality, and Meaning* (Amherst: Prometheus Books, 2002).

—, Editor, *The Cambridge Companion to Atheism* (Cambridge: Cambridge University Press, 2006).

Marxsen, W. *The Resurrection of Jesus of Nazareth* (Philadelphia: Fortress Press, 1970).

McDaniel, Jay and Donna Bowman, Editors, *Handbook of Process Theology* (Atlanta: Chalice Press, 2006).

McGary, Howard. *Blacks and Social Justice* (London: Blackwell Publishers, 1999).

McGrath, A. and J. McGrath. *The Dawkins Delusion?* (Downers Grove: IVP Press, 2007).

McGrath, P. J. "Atheism or Agnosticism," *Analysis,* 47 (1987), pp. 54–57.

—. "Evil and the Existence of a Finite God," *Analysis,* 46 (1986), pp. 63–64.

McLaughlin, R. "Necessary Agnosticism?" *Analysis,* 44 (1984), pp. 198–202.

Mesle, Robert C. *Process Theology* (Atlanta: Chalice Press, 2008).

Metz, Johann Baptist. *Faith in History and Society* (New York: Seabury Press, 1980).

—. *Theology of the World,* W. Glen-Doepel (trans.) (New York: Herder and Herder, 1969).

Miethe, T. L., Editor, *The Resurrection Debate* (New York: Harper & Row Publishers, 1987).

Mills, Charles. "Black Trash," in L. Wuestra and B. E. Lawson, *Faces of Environmental Racism* (Lanham: Rowman and Littlefield Publishers, 2001), pp. 73–91.

Mitcham, Carl and Jim Grote, Editors, *Theology and Technology* (Lanham: University Press of America, 1984).

Mitchell, Basil. *The Justification of Religious Belief* (Oxford: Oxford University Press, 1973).

Moltmann, Jürgen. *Religion, Revolution and the Future*, M. D. Meeks (trans.) (New York: Charles Scribner's Sons, 1969).

—. *Theology of Hope*, J. W. Leitch, Translator (New York: Harper & Row Publishers, 1967).

Morris, T. V. "Agnosticism," *Analysis*, 45 (1985), pp. 219–224.

Murphy, Jeffrie G. *Retribution Reconsidered* (Dodrecht: Kluwer Academic Publishers, 1992).

Nagel, Thomas. *Mortal Questions* (Cambridge: Cambridge University Press, 1979).

Nielson, Kai. *Naturalism and Religion* (Buffalo: Prometheus Books, 2001).

—. *Philosophy & Atheism* (Buffalo: Prometheus Books, 1985).

Noss, John B. *Man's Religions*, 5th Edition (New York: Macmillan Publishing Co. Inc., 1974).

Nozick, Robert. *Philosophical Explanations* (Cambridge: Harvard University Press, 1981).

O'Connor, David. *God and Inscrutable Evil* (Lanham: Rowman & Littlefield Publishers, Inc., 1998).

Ogden, Schubert. *Faith and Freedom* (Nashville: Abingdon Press, 1989).

Oppy, Graham. "Arguments from Moral Evil," *International Journal for Philosophy of Religion,* 56 (2004), pp. 59–87.

Otte, Richard. "Evidential Arguments from Evil," *International Journal for Philosophy of Religion,* 48 (2000), pp. 1–10.

Otto, Rudolf. *The Idea of the Holy*, J. W. Harley (trans.) (Oxford: Oxford University Press, 1950).

Pannenberg, Wolfhart. *Jesus – God and Man* (Philadelphia: The Westminster Press, 1968).

Peacocke, Arthur. *All That Is* (Minneapolis: Fortress Press, 2007).

—. *Creation and the World of Science* (Oxford: Oxford University Press, 2004).

—. *God and the New Biology* (London: Dent & Sons, 1986).

—. *Theology for a Scientific Age* (London: SCM, 1993).

Perry, Bruce, Editor, *Malcolm X: The Last Speeches* (New York: Pathfinder Press, 1989).

Petrella, Ivan. *Beyond Liberation Theology* (London: SCM Press, 2008).

—. *The Future of Liberation Theology* (Burlington: Ashgate, 2004).

Phillips, D. Z. "Religion, Philosophy, and the Academy," *International Journal for Philosophy of Religion,* 44 (1998), pp. 129–144.

Phillips, J. B. *Your God is Too Small* (New York: The Macmillan Company, 1961).

Pike, Nelson. "Divine Foreknowledge, Human Freedom and Possible Worlds," *The Philosophical Review,* 86, No. 2 (1977), pp. 209–216.

—. *God and Timelessness* (London: Routledge, 1970).

Pixley, George V. "Justice and Class Struggle: A Challenge for Process Theology," *Process Studies*, 3 (1973), pp. 159–175.

Plantinga, Alvin. "Advice to Christian Philosophers," *Faith and Philosophy*, 1 (1984), pp. 253–271.

—. *God and Other Minds* (Ithaca: Cornell University Press, 1967).

—. *The Nature of Necessity* (Oxford: The Clarendon Press, 1974).

—. *Warranted Christian Belief* (Oxford: Oxford University Press, 2000).

Pogge, Thomas. *Poverty and Human Rights* (Cambridge: Polity, 2002).

Polanyi, Michael. *The Tacit Dimension* (London: Routledge & Kegan Paul, 1967).

Polkinghorne, John. *Belief in God in an Age of Science* (New Haven: Yale University Press, 1998).

Pollock, John. *Contemporary Theories of Knowledge* (Totowa: Rowman & Littlefield Publishers, 1986).

Putnam, Hilary. "On Negative Theology," *Faith and Philosophy*, 14 (1997), pp. 407–422.

Quine, W. V. O. *The Web of Belief* (New York: Random House, 1978).

Ramsey, Ian. *Christian Discourse: Some Logical Explorations* (Oxford: Oxford University Press, 1965).

—. *Religious Language* (London: SCM Press, 1957).

Rauschenbusch, Walter. *A Theory for the Social Gospel* (New York: Abingdon Press, 1917).

Rawls, John. *A Theory of Justice* (Cambridge: Harvard University Press, 1971).

—. *Collected Papers*, S. Freeman, Editor (Cambridge: Harvard University Press, 1999).

—. "The Justification of Civil Disobedience," in J. P. White, Editor, *Assent/Dissent* (Dubuque: Kendall/Hunt Publishers, 1984), pp. 225–236.

—. *The Law of Peoples* (Cambridge: Harvard University Press, 1999).

—. *Political Liberalism* (New York: Columbia University Press, 1993).

Reid, Thomas. *The Works of Thomas Reid, D. D.*, W. Hamilton, Editor (Edinburgh: James Thin, 1895).

Rice, Hugh. *God and Goodness* (Oxford: Oxford University Press, 2000).

Robinson, John A. T. *Exploration into God* (Stanford: Stanford University Press, 1967).

—. *Honest to God* (Philadelphia: The Westminster Press, 1963).

—. *In the End God* (New York: Harper & Row Publishers, 1968).

—. *The Human Face of God* (Philadelphia: The Westminster Press, 1973).

Rodríguez, Rubén R. *Racism and God-Talk* (New York: New York University Press, 2008).

Rowe, William. "Does Panentheism Reduce to Pantheism? A Response to Craig," *International Journal for Philosophy of Religion*, 61 (2007), pp. 65–67.

—. "The Problem of Divine Sovereignty and Human Freedom," *Faith and Philosophy*, 16 (1999), pp. 98–101.

Ruether, Rosemary. "Crisis in Sex and Race: Black Theology and Feminist Theology," in G. H. Anderson and T. F. Stransky, Editors, *Mission Trends No. 4: Liberation Theologies* (New York: Paulist Press, 1979), pp. 175–187.

Russell, Bertrand. *Atheism: Collected Essays: 1943–1949* (New York: Arno Press, 1972).

—. *Why I am Not a Christian*, Paul Edwards, Editor (New York: Simon and Schuster, 1957).

Santayana, George. "Philosophical Heresy," *The Journal of Philosophy, Psychology, and Scientific Methods,* 12 (1915), pp. 561–568.

Schilpp, P. A. "A Rational Basis Demanded for Faith," *The Journal of Philosophy,* 21 (1924), pp. 209–212.

Schroeder, W. W. "Liberation Theology: A Critique from a Process Perspective," in J. Cobb, Jr. and W. W. Schroeder, Editors, *Process Philosophy and Social Thought* (Chicago: Center for the Scientific Study of Religion), pp. 210–241.

Seckel, Al, Editor, *Bertrand Russell on God and Religion* (New York: Prometheus Books, 1986).

Sessions, William Ladd. *The Concept of Faith* (Ithaca: Cornell University Press, 1994).

Sheldon, W. H. "The Rôle of Dogma in Philosophy," *The Journal of Philosophy,* 24 (1927), pp. 393–404.

Singer, Peter. *Animal Liberation* (New York: Avon, 1972).

—. *One World* (New Haven: Yale University Press, 2002).

Smart, Ninian. *In Search of Christianity* (New York: Harper & Row Publishers, 1979).

—. *The Religious Experience of Mankind,* 2nd Edition (New York: Charles Scribner's Sons, 1976).

—. *Worldviews* (New York: Charles Scribner's Sons, 1983).

Smith, Huston. *The Religions of Man* (New York: Harper & Row Publishers, 1958).

Smith, Michael. *The Moral Problem* (Oxford: Oxford University Press, 1995)

Smith, Quentin. "Stephen Hawking's 'Cosmology and Theism'," *Analysis,* 54 (1994), pp. 236–243.

Sober, Elliot. "Intelligent Design and Probability Reasoning," *International Journal for Philosophy of Religion,* 52 (2002), pp. 65–80.

Soelle, Dorothee. *Political Theology,* J. Shelley (trans.) (Philadelphia: Fortress Press, 1974).

Stout, Jeffrey. *Democracy & Tradition* (Princeton: Princeton University Press, 2004).

—. *Ethics after Babel* (Princeton: Princeton University Press, 1988).

Stubenberg, L. "The Principle of Disbelief," *Analysis,* 48 (1988), pp. 184–190.

Swinburne, Richard. *The Coherence of Theism* (Oxford: Clarendon Press, 1977).

—. *The Concept of Miracle* (London: London University Press, 1981).

—. *The Existence of God* (Oxford: Oxford University Press, 1979).

—. *Faith and Reason* (Oxford: Oxford University Press, 1981).

—. *Is There a God?* (Oxford: Oxford University Press, 1996).

Temple, William. *Christianity & the Social Order* (New York: The Seabury Press, 1977).

Thielicke, Helmut. *The Silence of God,* G. W. Bromily (trans.) (Grand Rapids: W. B. Eerdmans Publishing Company, 1962).

Thompson, Janna. *Taking Responsibility for the Past* (Cambridge: Polity, 2002).

Tillich, Paul. *Systematic Theology,* Volumes 1–3 (Chicago: The University of Chicago Press, 1951).

—. *The Shaking of the Foundations* (New York: Charles Scribner's Sons, 1948).

Tracy, David. *Blessed Rage for Order* (New York: The Seabury Press, 1975).

Vahanian, Gabriel. *The Death of God* (New York: George Braziller, 1957).

van Buren, Paul M. *The Secular Meaning of the Gospel* (New York: The Macmillan Company, 1963).

van Inwagen, Peter. "Some Remarks on Plantinga's Advice," *Faith and Philosophy*, 16 (1999), pp. 164–172.

Walzer, Michael. *Just and Unjust Wars*, 2nd Edition (New York: Basic Books, 2000).

Ward, Keith. *Is Religion Dangerous?* (Oxford: Lion Hudson, 2006).

Weber, Stephen L. *Proofs for the Existence of God*: *A Meta-Investigation* (Ann Arbor: University Microfilms Inc, 1970).

Wells, W. R. "Is Supernaturalistic Belief Essential in a Definition of Religion?" *The Journal of Philosophy*, 18 (1921), pp. 269–275.

Whitehead, Alfred North. *Process and Reality* (New York: The Humanities Press, 1929).

—. *Religion in the Making* (New York: The Macmillan Company, 1957).

Will, James E. "Dialectical Panentheism: Towards Relating Liberation and Process Theologies," in J. Cobb and W. W. Schroeder, Editors, *Process Philosophy and Social Thought* (Chicago: Center for the Scientific Study of Religion, 1981), pp. 242–259.

Williamson, Clark M. "Whitehead as Counterrevolutionary? Toward Christian-Marxist Dialogue," *Process Studies*, 4 (1974), pp. 176–186.

Wilmore, Gayraud S. *Black Religion and Black Radicalism*, 2nd Edition (Maryknoll: Orbis Books, 1983).

—. "The New Context of Black Theology in the United States," in G. H. Anderson and T. F. Stransky, Editors, *Mission Trends No. 4: Liberation Theologies* (New York: Paulist Press, 1979), pp. 211–231.

Wilson, August. *Gem of the Ocean* (New York: Theatre Communications Group, 2006).

Wood, Allen. "The Duty to Believe According to the Evidence," *International Journal for Philosophy of Religion*, 63 (2008), pp. 7–24.

Woolman, John. *The Journal of John Woolman* and *A Plea for the Poor* (Gloucester: Peter Smith, 1971).

Index